To Stewart,
('mon the Jays)
Tom Hosie

PARTICK THISTLE LEGENDS

By Niall Kennedy & Tom Hosie

Published by:
Yore Publications
12 The Furrows, Harefield,
Middx. UB9 6AT.

© Niall Kennedy & Tom Hosie 2007

....

All rights reserved.
No part of this publication may be reproduced
or copied in any manner without the prior permission
in writing of the copyright holders.

British Library Cataloguing-in-Publication Data.
A catalogue record for this book
is available from the British Library.

ISBN 978 0 9552949 9 0

Printed and bound by:
The Cromwell Press, Trowbridge

Introduction:

Players are what makes us want to go to watch football. Sure, it's becoming more and more difficult for football supporters to identify with players nowadays. Club loyalty is, more often than not, a thing of the past – players move from club to club and it's very rare for a player to be identified with one club any more. No longer do players sign for a club as a youngster and end their careers at that same club.

Most of the players in this book could be regarded as one-club men. For long periods of Partick Thistle's history, often determined by club finances, the club's managers have looked to develop and retain young talent and build teams instead of buying established players through the transfer market. And all too often these young talents would remain at the club, although many were forced to leave as large transfer fee offers from buying clubs were too appealing to decline.

Whether the players have given long periods of dedicated service or lit up the Partick Thistle team with prestigious talent for lesser periods, they are the players who have made Partick Thistle. Players who have made great saves and important tackles, scored famous goals and won big matches. Players who have contributed immensely to the history of Partick Thistle and made Partick Thistle the club that we know and love today.

It was difficult to choose the players that should be included in this book. We started with loose criteria. We wanted to honour the players who have won trophies for Thistle in 1921 and 1971 – legendary players in legendary line-ups that were known off by heart by fans young and old, from different eras. We wanted to credit players who had represented Thistle on the international stage with distinction. We also wanted to pay tribute to the one-club men who had represented Thistle throughout their careers. And we had space to include a few wild-cards – players who have contributed something intangible but still deserved to be included in this roll of Partick Thistle honour. We'd like to think that this book would help you remember your own memories of these Thistle Greats.

Inevitably we will have missed some players that you may think we should have included. Hopefully you will remember them with as much affection as we have remembered those who are included. If we could have, we would have included more.

(Continued)

(INTRODUCTION CONTD.)

There was also an argument that we should have expanded the book to include non-players who have contributed hugely to the history of Partick Thistle. People like Molly Stallon and Robert Reid, managers George Easton, Donald Turner, Bertie Auld and John Lambie, or directors such as Jimmy Aitken, the Reid family, or Richie Robertson. In the end we decided it should concentrate on players only, but that's not to disregard the huge contribution these people made to the club.

Writing the biographies was a huge job. Many of the players had been forgotten by all but a few people, and existing information about them was in very short supply. We revisited contemporary newspapers – the Daily Record, Evening Times and Sunday Mail gave up gems of information that allowed us to build up fascinating pictures of long-past players who have never had their careers documented.

We hope you will enjoy reading and remembering these players as much as we have enjoyed writing and remembering them.

Niall Kennedy and Tom Hosie

Statistical Notes:
Due to ongoing research the appearances and goals credited to players may differ with the figures previously published in The Official History, in 2002. The figures in this book should be regarded as being accurate.

Dates and places of birth and death have been noted where available, and all references are complete up to the end of the 2006-07 season.

Acknowledgements:
Robert Reid, Stuart Deans, Stephen McEwan, Tommy Taylor, Steve Emms, Colin Jose, John Lerwill, Iain Manson, Mel ap Ior Thomas, the members of scottishleague.net, Malcolm and Davie at the Mitchell, Dave Twydell, Maureen Sprott, Sandra McGuire.

Copyright:
In the majority of cases the copyright holder was not identified on the item, and/or not traced, although doubtless many originated from the newspapers referred to and others. Therefore our apologies to any newspapers, and others, should copyright have inadvertently been infringed.

Front Cover Design by 'kasule.co.uk'. Players: From top left, clockwise:
Alex Raisbeck, Alan Rough, Peter McKennan & Kenny Arthur.
Rear Cover Design by Dave Twydell. Players: From left to right, top to bottom:
Willie Bulloch, Eddie McLeod, Jimmy McGowan, Donnie McKinnon, Denis McQuade, Chic Charnley.

Muirhead and Lambie shake hands before the Rangers v. Partick Thistle match at Ibrox Park, Glasgow on Saturday. ("Daily Record.")

An exciting moment in the Rangers v. Partick Thistle game in the Charity Cup-tie at Ibrox Park on Saturday—Jackson (Thistle) clears from Marshall. Rangers won 2-1.—"Daily Record" photograph.

AT FIRHILL PARK.—O'Hare and Alan Morton in action during the Rangers versus Partick Thistle match on Saturday, when Rangers won 6-0.

THE LEGENDS

Tom	Adams	David	Johnstone
Alan	Archibald	Sam	Kennedy
Kenny	Arthur	Andy	Kerr
John	Ballantyne	James	Kinloch
John	Blair	Alex	Lambie
Jimmy	Bone	Bobby	Law
Walter	Borthwick	Bobby	Lawrie
John	Bowie	Tommy	Ledgerwood
Frank	Branscombe	Johnny	MacKenzie
Hugh	Brown	Ian	McDonald
Willie	Bulloch	Jimmy	McGowan
Stewart	Calderwood	Peter	McKennan
Jackie	Campbell	Archie	McKenzie
Kenny	Campbell	Donnie	McKinnon
Harry	Chatton	Eddie	McLeod
James	Charnley	Jimmy	McMenemy
Frank	Coulston	Jamie	McMullan
Tom	Crichton	Davie	McParland
George	Cummings	Denis	McQuade
Peter	Curran	Alex	McSpadyen
Jimmy	Davidson	Davie	Mathers
Jamie	Doyle	David	Ness
Alex	Elliot	George	Niven
Tommy	Ewing	Alex	O'Hara
Alex	Forsyth	Denis	O'Hare
Bobby	Gibb	Donald	Park
James	Gibson	Willie	Paul
Johnny	Gibson	Alex	Rae
Neil	Gibson	Alex	Raisbeck
Ronnie	Glavin	Alan	Rough
Robert	Gray	Willie	Salisbury
Bobby	Grove	Willie	Sharp
Alex	Hair	George	Smith
William	Hamilton	Dougie	Somner
John	Hansen	Hugh	Strachan
Joe	Harris	George	Sutherland
John	Harvey	John	Torbet
Bobby	Henderson	Jimmy	Walker
Joe	Hogan	Kenny	Watson
Bobby	Houston	Brian	Whittaker
Willie	Howden	Andrew	Wilson
Jackie	Husband	Matt	Wilson
Johnny	Jackson	Alex	Wright
Bobby	Johnstone		

Tom Adams

1912 - 1920

When Tommy Adams was signed from Queen's Park in May 1912 it had been a quick promotion, from the junior ranks to professional football. Adams had been playing for Rutherglen Glencairn in early 1912 before signing for the amateurs and then making the quick transition to pro footballer in just a few months. Tommy was highly admired by those in the know, and regarded as *"one of the most promising defenders in the country"* by the newspapers.

A versatile full-back, comfortable on the right or left, Tommy was brought to Firhill as cover for the veteran captain and right-back Archie McKenzie, who was increasingly prone to injury. However, his home debut was at left-back, and Tom made such a good impression that several commentators wondered what should be done with Willie Bulloch, the regular left-back. Tom remained at left-back for a number of games before spending the rest of the season between left and right.

Season 1912-13 was a poor season for a young player to be making his first steps in. Thistle finished second bottom of the division, but the position was largely caused by injuries to key players such as McKenzie, Willie Hamilton, and John Marshall. However, the experience of playing behind the legendary Alex Raisbeck, and alongside Bulloch and McKenzie meant that Tom was well placed to step into a regular game when McKenzie called it a day midway through the 1913-14 season.

The full-back partnership of Adams and Bulloch clicked immediately. *"Powerful, brainy and understanding each other thoroughly, Bulloch and Adams are as safe as houses,"* said the Daily Record. They were to form a strong partnership for six years.

Tom made headlines in December 1913, and not for his play on the field, as he accused linesman Pettigrew of being corrupt after a 0-1 defeat by Morton. Tom accused the official of betting on the result of the game. Pettigrew was cleared and Adams fined £5, and the Scottish League banned all officials and players from betting on games that they were involved in.

1914-15 was a further improvement, triggered in part by Tom's blossoming relationship with his half-back partner Jimmy McMullan, and in the following seasons Tom helped Thistle to a number of failed attempts to bring silverware back to Firhill. There was disappointment in Charity Cup finals (1916, 1918) and Glasgow Cup finals (1914, 1917, 1919). However, the near cup success was matched by improved League performances, too. Some creditable top five positions were achieved at the end of a number of seasons.

While Tom was credited with being able to clear his lines and keep the opposition forwards away from his goal, he preferred to do this not just by kicking, but also by reading the game. This anticipation meant his job was far easier than it might have been, had he not been such a clever defender.

Tom was playing some of the best football of his career at the end of the 1917-18 season. He had been established as Thistle's first choice right-back for three years, with Bulloch the left-back for the same amount of time. Both players must have been looking forward to the following season, when Tommy contracted rheumatic fever. He missed much of the 1918-19 season.

He returned for the last few games of the season, and started the next campaign in his regular right-back role, but the illness had taken its toll on his fitness.

"Not quite the reliable back he used to be" was a comment heard regularly on the terraces at Firhill, and this was a blow to a proud man.

Tom was unable to end the season in the first team – new signing Walter Borthwick had replaced him. Tom accepted that his career was over, and retired from football during the close season of 1920.

Appearances 230, goals 0.

ALAN ARCHIBALD
1997 - 2003 AND 2007 - DATE

Born 13 December 1977 in Glasgow.

Season 1996-97 was in the main a miserable one for Partick Thistle. Relegated in heartbreaking circumstances from the Premier Division the season before, Thistle, under Murdo MacLeod, were unable to sustain any kind of promotion challenge. With dark clouds starting to circulate overhead only the Thistle under 18 team offered any kind of optimism for the future. Not for many years had Thistle had cause to harbour high hopes for a number of talented young players. Producing some excellent performances along the way the Thistle under 18 side reached the final of the Glasgow Cup. They may well have lost the final heavily to Celtic but before the season's end many of that team were given their first taste of first team football.

The first to do so was Alan Archibald. As debuts go it was a low key affair. Less than 1,000 were at East Fife's Bayview Park home on 5 April 1997 to witness Thistle record an easy win against a poor home side. Few Thistle fans present that afternoon could have imagined that the second half substitute for Thistle would have two spells as a Thistle player clocking up a total of over 250 appearances in the process. Following his debut Archibald made a further four appearances, including two starts, before the season's completion.

It took him a little time to establish himself in the Thistle side the following season but once he had done so he became a feature in the Thistle defence.

From the end of October to the very end of the season he failed to start just one game and his emergence as a player of some potential was a rare bright point of a miserable season that culminated in relegation to the Second Division.

Playing his football at a lower level didn't seem to hamper Archibald's development at all even though it soon became clear that Thistle wouldn't be making a rapid return to the First Division. He became a regular in the Scotland Under 21 squad and was twice capped at that level.

Whilst Archibald's career was on the up, Thistle's fortunes remained very much on a down slope and for a while Archibald found himself dragged down by that. As Thistle finished the 1999-00 season in miserable fashion some Thistle fans even began to wonder whether he should be retained.

Fortunately manager John Lambie continued to show faith in Archibald and he was more than rewarded for that faith. Thistle won the 2000-01 Second Division in a canter with Archibald missing just two games. It was a similar story the following season as well. This time Archibald missed a grand total of four games as Thistle followed up their Second Division title win by winning the First Division title 12 months later.

Against all the odds Thistle retained their SPL status at the end of the 2002-03 season with Archibald, as ever, a real stalwart in the Thistle defence. His days at Firhill, however, were soon to be at an end. A whole host of players left Firhill at the end of the season and Archibald was one of the first to leave when, with the season barely over, he joined Dundee United.

He was a great success in his first season at Tannadice. He played in every game and was voted by the United supporters as their Player of the Year. His personal success continued the following season when he, again, played in every United fixture and ended the season by featuring in the Scottish Cup Final against Celtic although he had the disappointment of finishing on the losing side. He would remain very much a regular at Tannadice for the next season and a half.

A hugely popular player during his first stint at Firhill it was always hoped that Archibald would at some stage return to Firhill. He eventually did so just before the transfer deadline in January 2007 but only after Thistle had been trying to sign him for over a year. He made his debut for Thistle second time around against Ross County and typically carried off the Man of the Match award.

As a defender Archibald has quite naturally concentrated on preventing goals rather than scoring them but he has found the net for Thistle on eight occasions. The first of those eight goals could easily have been Thistle's last ever goal. With the club's financial crisis such that closure looked imminent the home fixture with St Mirren could easily have been the last ever game. The fans rallied though and a decent crowd turned out proving that there was still life in Partick Thistle. On the field Thistle soon found themselves trailing 0-2 and it was an Archibald goal that hauled Thistle, who would go on a draw 2-2, back into the game. Other notable Archibald strikes include a double at Arbroath during Thistle's First Division winning season and another double against Hearts in the SPL in what was Archibald's 200th appearance for Partick Thistle.

Now once again playing under Ian McCall, the manager that took him to Dundee United, Archibald has an important role to play at Firhill as McCall tries to restore the club's fortunes.

Appearances 244, goals 8

Capped Scotland Under 21s v Lithuania 1998

First Division Championship winner – 2001-02
Second Division Championship winner 2000-01

Kenny Arthur

1997 - 2007

Born 7 December 1978 in Bellshill.

Few players experienced the ups and downs of life at Firhill to the degree that Kenny Arthur did. Kenny is something of a rarity at Firhill in recent history – a player that has come through the youth ranks and gone on to make a sizeable contribution to the Thistle first team. Kenny's association with Partick Thistle began while he was still at school. While still an 'S' Form signing, the club had to seek the permission of his headmaster to allow him to play in a midweek afternoon reserve game.

Despite his clear promise Kenny's Thistle career was nearly over before it had properly begun. He was thrust into first team action during arguably the Club's darkest hour. In November 1997 the very existence of Partick Thistle was called into question. Kenny's first team debut against Stirling Albion on 12 November 1997 could easily have been Thistle's last ever fixture such were the club's financial problems at the time.

Kenny could perhaps have wished for a gentler debut as well. Thistle were in next to no time 2-0 down and following red cards for Calum Milne and Billy MacDonald found themselves down to nine men. Despite that Thistle fought back to draw 2-2 and it was that kind of fighting spirit that allowed the club to survive. Not though without cost, with Thistle relegated in heartbreaking fashion on the last day of the 1997-98 season. Kenny's contribution in his debut season in the Thistle first team was to make 20 appearances keeping his first clean sheet in a 1-0 win against Falkirk at Brockville in December.

With the club still very much at a low ebb, Thistle found life hard in Division Two. Indeed in season 1998-99 they very nearly dropped down to Scotland's basement League. There was some consolation though for a still young and largely inexperienced Kenny Arthur who, after seeing off the challenge of Stevie Ross, established himself as Thistle's first choice 'keeper.

Kenny's time at Firhill though was not without its dark periods and season 1999-00, with Thistle once again under the management of John Lambie, was a miserable one for Arthur. Kevin Budinauckas was John Lambie's preferred option in goal with Kenny making just the five first team appearances. It was hardly a vintage season for the club either. Thistle finished the season in fifth spot some way behind the three promotion winning teams.

Better times though were round the corner for both Thistle and Kenny Arthur. The Jags won the 2000-01 Second Division title in a canter. Kenny initially had to fight off the challenge of Michael Brown but once he had made his place in the Thistle goal his own he went from strength to strength. Thistle conceded less than a goal a game on route to the title and on 14 separate occasions Kenny kept a clean sheet.

Twelve months later Thistle were celebrating again, this time as the First Division trophy headed to Firhill.

Although Kenny missed the promotion clinching fixture against St Mirren he played in 30 games and kept six clean sheets. In addition he became the first Thistle 'keeper since Alan Rough in 1979, to play in a Scottish Cup Semi-Final as Thistle reached the last four of Scotland's premier cup competition before losing 3-0 to Rangers.

Season 2002-03, Thistle's first in the brave new world of the SPL, was a hugely successful one for both Thistle and Kenny Arthur. Despite the predictions of so called experts of an immediate return to the First Division Thistle survived comfortably enough in the higher League. Kenny played just short of 40 times for Thistle that season and his form earned him international recognition with a call up to the Scotland squad and a place on the bench for a European Championship Qualifier in Lithuania. The season finished on a real high for Kenny when he was capped at 'B' level for Scotland in a Firhill fixture against Northern Ireland.

From the highs of being part of an SPL Thistle side and on the fringes of the Scotland squad came the lows of relegation in each of Kenny's next two seasons at Firhill. Kenny though had a pivotal role to play as Thistle began the climb back up the Leagues in season 2005-06. Thistle's route out of the Second Division was a fairly circuitous one. After finishing fourth in the League Thistle were handed a second chance of promotion via the newly introduced play-offs. The play-off final between Peterhead and Thistle went right down to the wire with Thistle emerging victorious at the end of a penalty shoot-out with Kenny, as he had done earlier in the season during a Scottish Cup replay against Inverness Caledonian Thistle, playing his role in Thistle's success.

Kenny's role in Thistle's play-off win served only to cement his already huge popularity with the Thistle fans.

Season 2006-07 was a richly deserved testimonial season for Kenny the highlight of which being a fixture with a Celtic XI at Firhill. In May 2007 Kenny left Thistle to join Accrington Stanley.

Appearances 287, goals 0.
First Division Championship winner – 2001-02
Second Division Championship winner 2000-01
Capped for Scotland 'B' v Northern Ireland 2003

JOHN BALLANTYNE

1921 - 1924 & 1928 - 1934

Born 27 October 1899 in Maryhill, Glasgow.

Johnny Ballantyne had a great career in Scottish football ahead of him in 1924. He was the darling of the Firhill forward line; cool, keen, and enterprising, he played with confidence and elegance. His decision to emigrate to the United States came as a shock to everyone at Firhill who saw Johnny as an important part of the team which was being developed after the 1921 Cup Final team had dispersed, and which Thistle fans hoped was going to take the club to further honours.

The departure left a bitter taste – Johnny had been paid his close-season wages after signing a new contract for the 1924-25 season, but Thistle were stunned when news trickled back that he had boarded a ship bound for Boston on the east coast of America. It transpired that Johnny had been persuaded by Scottish international Tommy Muirhead to join the Boston Wonder Workers team in the American Soccer League. Tempted by the promise of a new life and riches, Johnny was one of a number of Scottish and Irish players who made for the new world. In the spirit of Christopher Columbus Johnny didn't now what to expect and when he arrived he was met by the immigration authorities, tipped off by Thistle officials, concerned that he had no visa. Some fast talking, and the promise to return his summer wages, saw Johnny released from his contract by Thistle, and the US Football Association eventually allowed him to join his new club. Johnny played for four seasons in America before returning to his local team, where he was welcomed with open arms.

Johnny was Firhill born and bred, and joined Thistle as a rather lightweight, but clever, inside-forward from Ashfield in May 1921, making his debut earlier than expected after Jimmy McMenemy returned from a tour of the US, overweight and unfit. The senior player regained his place in the team and Johnny had to content himself with fleeting appearances in the first XI for a season. However, when he did appear he did enough to impress, despite the disadvantage of his physique. What he did have was a quick brain, and clever feet too. He was regarded as the brains of the front line, and Willie Salisbury in particular benefited from his intelligent passing. Johnny was also pressed into service at centre-forward, a strange choice for someone as slight and small, but what couldn't be questioned was his effort and bravery, as the Daily Record reported.

"Ballantyne, the embryo centre-forward, keen, cool, and enterprising, took his men along in rattling good style, and after Blair had slashed the ball where he shouldn't, the little fellow had the temerity to try his strength with the weighty Dens Park backs. He may not have the physique for the position, but he has a clear brain and twinkling feet; he isn't a bad shot, and he is brave."

On 3 May 1924 Johnny played what appeared to be his last game for the club, setting Hugh Collins up for a debut hat-trick in a 6-4 win over Third Lanark. A few weeks later he set sail for Boston.

Daily Mail / The Mail on Sunday
HOROSCOPE MATCH

**Match the star sign and cash amount to those published in The Mail.
See The Mail for full prize details.**

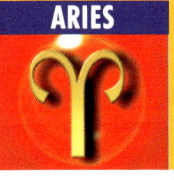

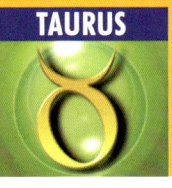

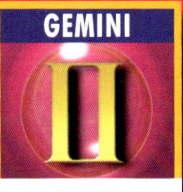

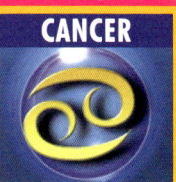

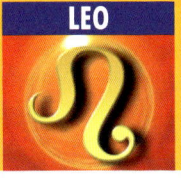

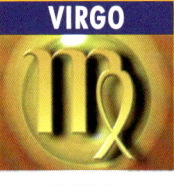

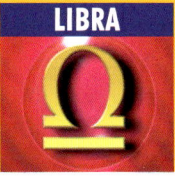

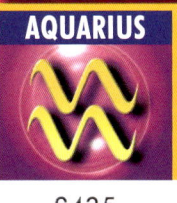

ARIES	TAURUS	GEMINI	CANCER
£5400	£160	£230	£5500

LEO	VIRGO	LIBRA	SCORPIO
£4150	£720	£910	£3450

SAGITTARIUS	CAPRICORN	AQUARIUS	PISCES
£3250	£510	£425	£1250

VALID JAN 3 - JAN 29

CODE: MC LG

PLUS EXTRA CHANCE HOROSCOPE MATCH

HOW TO PLAY
- Go to **mailbingo.com** and register a few details and your email address.
- Match the star sign and cash amount to the one displayed on screen - AND YOU COULD WIN A CASH PRIZE - UP TO £10,000!
- Come back every day for another chance to win!

WIN £10,000

Coffee Break Bingo

Get Up to £125 FREE at Coffee Break Bingo!
Sign up and deposit between £10 and £125 today and we will DOUBLE it!

Terms and conditions apply. Over 18s

Daily Mail / The Mail on Sunday

JANUARY 2009 — INSTANT CASH

VALID: JAN 3 – JAN 9
YOUR CHANCE TO WIN
SCRATCH OFF PANEL

REVEAL 3 IDENTICAL AMOUNTS TO WIN THAT AMOUNT. A BONUS CASH AMOUNT WILL APPEAR IN TODAY'S MAIL. IF YOU WIN AND REVEAL A LUCKY HORSESHOE ON THE SAME DATE YOUR PRIZE WILL BE DOUBLED.

VALID: JAN 10 – JAN 16
instant CASH
SCRATCH OFF PANEL

REVEAL 3 IDENTICAL AMOUNTS TO WIN THAT AMOUNT. A BONUS CASH AMOUNT WILL APPEAR IN TODAY'S MAIL. IF YOU WIN AND REVEAL A LUCKY HORSESHOE ON THE SAME DATE YOUR PRIZE WILL BE DOUBLED.

VALID: JAN 17 – JAN 23
OVER £12 MILLION WON ALREADY
SCRATCH OFF PANEL

REVEAL 3 IDENTICAL AMOUNTS TO WIN THAT AMOUNT. A BONUS CASH AMOUNT WILL APPEAR IN TODAY'S MAIL. IF YOU WIN AND REVEAL A LUCKY HORSESHOE ON THE SAME DATE YOUR PRIZE WILL BE DOUBLED.

VALID: JAN 24 – JAN 30
ARE YOU A LUCKY WINNER?
SCRATCH OFF PANEL

REVEAL 3 IDENTICAL AMOUNTS TO WIN THAT AMOUNT. A BONUS CASH AMOUNT WILL APPEAR IN TODAY'S MAIL. IF YOU WIN AND REVEAL A LUCKY HORSESHOE ON THE SAME DATE YOUR PRIZE WILL BE DOUBLED.

PLUS - PLAY HOROSCOPE MATCH AT mailbingo.com

HOW TO PLAY INSTANT CASH
Scratch off the panel only for the week shown. Each panel is a separate weekly game. Reveal three identical cash amounts on one panel to win that prize. If you reveal two amounts the same plus "BONUS CASH AMOUNT SEE THIS WEEK'S MAIL" on one panel check the same week's Daily Mail or Mail on Sunday to see if your two cash amounts match the one in the newspaper. Bonus cash amounts are displayed at Northcliffe House (Young Street entrance), London W8; 200 Renfield Street, Glasgow G2; and 52 Preston New Road, Blackburn (Monday Friday, 10am to 4pm) Full rules available from: Instant Cash Gamecard Rules, PO Box 2, Blackburn BB1 6AB and at www.dailymail.co.uk. Se also Daily Mail and The Mail on Sunday. No purchase necessary. See Instant Cash gamecard rules at www.dailymail.co.uk

HOW TO CLAIM INSTANT CASH AND HOROSCOPE MATCH
To claim an Instant Cash or Horoscope Match prize you must telephone the Claimline 0844 8000812 on the day of your win or the next working d Claimline open between 9.30am and 4pm Monday to Saturday (except public holidays). Calls charged at national rate.
Instant Cash or Horoscope Match can be played only if you are 18 years or over and resident in the United Kingdom, the Channel Islands and t Isle of Man. Phone 0906 651 3299 to hear previous bonus cash amounts against which you can still claim. Your call should cost no more than 6

After his four years in America Johnny wanted to settle down, back in his home country and felt obliged to offer his services to Thistle.

They were keen to find a replacement for Jimmy McDougall, who had signed for Liverpool. A deal was struck and the prodigal son returned to Maryhill. He was an instant hit. Goals in his first two games saw instant forgiveness. The Daily Record resumed their membership of his fan club too.

"His variety of moves was without limit. He could bring the ball through himself, swing it to the right or left, or sweep it through the centre. His lead was an inspiration to others".

Johnny combined well with Davie Ness, John Torbet, Sandy Hair and Harry Gibson, and all finished the season in double figures for goals – only two other clubs scored more League goals than Thistle. Johnny was news again, and there was interest from England after just a few months of his return, but this time Johnny wanted to stay put. He also rejected the chance of playing for Scotland in Paris preferring to travel with Thistle on a tour of Norway. Johnny made a huge impression with the Norwegian fans and decided to remain in Norway to recuperate from an injury and have an extended holiday at the same time.

When he returned refreshed, in August 1930, he took his place in a forward line of prodigious ability - Davie Ness, Willie 'Golden' Miller, Johnny Simpson and Johnny Torbet were all talented players - but Johnny Ballantyne was the star amongst them. He was given a roving role, collecting the ball from Eddie McLeod and placing it wide to the wingers or through the middle for Simpson to score 34 goals.

The season was a success for all the playing staff; the first to take Thistle to the top of the League for the first time ever, though it wasn't sustained. Thistle finished the season in fourth place; the best League position yet achieved. It was a particular success for Johnny, who was recognised at international level, playing for the Scottish League at Firhill against the Irish League in October 1930, then being tipped for a cap against the English League along with McLeod and Torbet. Unfortunately, none of the three played against England.

Football tactics were changing. Centre-halves were becoming a third defender, and inside forwards often dropped back to help the half-backs. As a player, who liked to drift from front to back, it was a natural tactic for Johnny to employ and the role pleased him.

He looked happiest when he was out of position, linking with George Cummings and McLeod, making it difficult for his opponents to keep him under control. However Thistle missed the best of Johnny in 1932 and 1933 as he was often injured, and he was getting to the veteran stage by the time he helped them to their first Glasgow Cup win in 1934.

Johnny's place in the team was under threat from Archie Hastie and despite scoring against Queen's Park in March 1935 it was to be his last game for Thistle.

Falkirk jumped at the chance of taking Johnny until the end of the season, but his efforts were not enough to save the Bairns from relegation in April. Johnny returned to Firhill but was placed on the transfer list, joining Queen's Park Rangers for a season in the English League Division 3 South before retiring from football.

Appearances 328, goals 82.
Glasgow Cup winner 1934
Capped for Scottish League v Irish League 1930

JOHN BLAIR

1920 - 1925

Born 26 August 1898 in Ardrossan

After 15 mins of the 1921 Scottish Cup Final Jimmy McMenemy sent John Blair off towards goal, but Rangers captain Jimmy Bowie cleared the danger. Five minutes later Bowie was off the field repairing his shorts when McMenemy passed ball left to left-half Walter Borthwick who played a deep cross to the right. Jimmy Kinloch dummied and John Blair, coming inside from the right wing, shot past Rangers goalkeeper William Robb from distance. The ball nested inside Robb's right-hand post for a goal.

In later years John Blair expressed sympathy to Robb; the Thistle scorer felt that Robb's view of his shot had been obscured by one of his defenders, but at the time John didn't care. His goal had won Thistle the Scottish Cup.

When John Blair signed for Partick Thistle from Saltcoats Victoria in February 1920 he was said to be one of the best outside-rights in the junior game. He made his debut four days later, replacing Irish internationalist Johnny Houston, in a game against Ayr United, and kept the experienced Houston out of the side for most of the remaining games that season. The following season Houston retired and John was Thistle's first choice for the right wing position.

John was a strong running winger who gave strength to his colleagues inside, and particularly liked to shoot instead of providing his teammates with the service they wanted. However, he wasn't wasteful with his shooting, finishing his first two full seasons as joint top scorer.

~ 14 ~

He combined well with Jimmy Kinloch in particular as his inside-right, and with Joe Harris, who supported him from right-half.

It was fitting that the Scottish Cup should provide John with the pinnacle of his career, because it had been in the earlier rounds of the competition that he had made an impact and secured his place in the final. The early rounds of the Cup had been a struggle for Thistle to get through. In the second round John almost scored against Hibs to take Thistle through, but he eventually made the breakthrough in the second replay of the tie, combining with McMenemy to set up Robert McFarlane with the only goal of the game.

In the quarter-final second replay against Motherwell, John was again the initiator of the winning goal, setting up Alex Lauder with the winner. In the semi-final against Hearts John came close to becoming the match winner, but goalkeeper Sandy Kane saved his team on a number of occasions.

John had to be content with waiting until the final for his Scottish Cup goal.

His crossing and scoring abilities, and his goal in the British Cup Winners Cup victory against English Cup holders Tottenham, were recognised in January 1922 when he was tipped for a Scotland cap in the game against Wales, but the selectors didn't choose him. His form dipped, around the start of the 1922-23 season and the Sunday Mail warned him that he should buck up his ideas, or face being dropped from the team. In fact he remained in the first team, but it wasn't a successful season for Thistle in general and John in particular. Indeed it was only the lack of a challenger that saw John complete the majority of the season still in the first team.

Come August 1923, a challenger had arrived at Firhill, ironically a near neighbour of John's in Saltcoats – Davie Ness. Indeed after just a handful of games, Ness made his debut in September, and had effectively taken John's right wing position for himself. A handful of games as an inside forward followed as John tried to get back in the team, but they weren't successful. The Daily Record felt that he didn't have "the craft and footwork required" to play inside.

The following season, 1924-25, John again only played a handful of games, as cover for Ness at outside-right, or Kinloch at inside-right.

While John's Thistle career came to a finish at the end of the 1924-25 season, it had effectively ended with the arrival of Davie Ness in 1923. John returned to his Ayrshire roots, playing junior football with Saltcoats Vics until 1929.

Appearances 170, goals 36.
Scottish Cup winner 1921

Jimmy Bone

1968 - 1972

Born 22 September 1949 in Bridge of Allan

Jimmy first came to Thistle's attention while playing with Airth Castle Rovers and after impressing in a series of trial matches he became a Thistle player in April 1968.

Bone wasted no time at all in establishing himself in the Thistle first team. He first wore Thistle colours in a pre-season friendly fixture away at Bury and duly scored his first Thistle goal in a 3-3 draw. His competitive debut followed in a League Cup-tie at Morton and he scored in that fixture as well as Thistle ran out 3-1 winners.

Thistle's final League position of 14th at the end of the 1968-69 season was the Club's lowest for 43 years but for the still teenage Bone it was a highly successful one. His debut goal against Morton was just one of sixteen, including a hat-trick against Hearts, which he would score in his first season and would comfortably finish the season as Thistle's leading goalscorer.

Bone would match that tally of 16 goals the following season as well and would again finish the season atop the Thistle goalscoring chart. It was though an even more miserable season for Thistle. Thistle managed to collect just a miserly 17 points and finished bottom of the League. The next season Thistle would play their football outside Scotland's top League for the first time since season 1901-02. Although it didn't feel it at the time it turned out to be blessing in disguise.

With Davie McParland now occupying the manager's office at Firhill the squad was restructured with a whole crop of young starts starting to truly blossom. Promotion and then the Second Division title were secured with Jimmy Bone having his most prolific season yet in front of goal. He would finish the season with 18 goals to his name but for the only time in his Thistle playing career he didn't finish the season as leading goalscorer. That honour went to Frank Coulston who scored 26.

Further, more high profile success, was just around the corner for Thistle. Thistle's run in the League Cup took them all the way to the final where they came up against the all conquering Celtic team of that era. Thistle though recorded a genuinely stunning win and it was Bone that famously *"walked the ball into the net"* to make the half-time score 4-0.

That success increased the prominence of a number of Thistle's younger stars and Jimmy Bone was no exception. In January 1972 he was capped for Scotland at Under 23 level for the very first time in a Pittodrie fixture against Wales. The following month he would again represent Scotland Under 23s, this time against England at the home of Derby County. On 13 February 1973 Jimmy scored for the under 23s against England at Rugby Park in a 1-2 defeat.

His, all too short Thistle career though was soon to end. On 19 February Bone played for Thistle for the very last time. He wasn't able to sign off with a goal either as Thistle and Dundee drew 0-0 at Firhill. A few days later he was off to England to join Norwich City.

Bone may have been with Norwich for a relatively short period of time but he still made a big impact while at Carrow Road. His efforts while at Norwich were acknowledged as part of the Club's Centenary Celebrations when he was inducted into the Norwich City Hall of Fame.

While at Norwich Bone was able to add to his international honours. He was again capped at Under 23 level before in June 1972 he won the first of the two caps he would earn at full international level. In the Independence Cup tournament in Brazil he replaced Denis Law during the course of a 2-2 draw with Yugoslavia in Belo Horizonte. A further cap would follow in October 1973 when he played, and scored, in a 4-1 win over Denmark in Copenhagen.

After leaving Norwich City Bone would join Sheffield United before returning to Scotland when Celtic paid a reported £30,000 for his services. His time with Celtic was relatively brief but he went on to enjoy successful spells with Arbroath, St Mirren and Hearts. In addition he spent a period playing with Hong Kong Rangers.

In 1984 he made the first steps into football management when he took up the role of player-manager at Arbroath. He left Gayfield to become Assistant Manager at St Mirren and in 1987, alongside Alex Smith, he helped steer St Mirren to a Scottish Cup triumph.

He became a manager in his own right again at Airdrieonians and led Airdrie to promotion to the Premier League. After a spell coaching in Africa he returned to Scotland to become manager of St Mirren and was also the manager of East Fife and Stenhousemuir. In addition he again teamed up with Alex Smith this time as Assistant Manager of Ross County.

In January 2005 Jimmy returned to Firhill to take up the position of Assistant Manager to Dick Campbell and together they led Thistle to promotion from the Second Division at the end of the 2005-06 season. Campbell left Firhill in March 2007 and was succeeded by Jimmy on a caretaker basis - a position he held until Ian McCall's appointment as Thistle manager in May 2007.

Appearances 160, goals 85
League Cup winner 1971
Second Division Championship winner 1970-71
Capped for Scotland Under 23s v England 1972, 1973; v Wales 1972.

Other honours (with Norwich City)
2 Scotland international appearances,
Football League Division Two winner 1972

WALTER BORTHWICK

1918 - 1923

Born 9 January 1899 in Newington.

Watty Borthwick was brought to Partick Thistle from Hibernian in a bit of a panic in the summer of 1918 as regular right-back as Tom Adams was laid low with rheumatic fever. It took Watty a few weeks to establish himself as Thistle's new full-back, partnering up with the experienced Willie Bulloch. There was a contrast in styles – Bulloch liked to play football out of defence, while his new partner hadn't grasped the sophisticated aspects of defending, preferring a no-nonsense belt up the park. His hefty kicking was put to positive use, and often opposition defences quaked as Watty ran forward to thunder a free-kick towards the goal. His only goal for Thistle came from a long-range free-kick against Hearts not long after his debut in 1918.

Watty remained as Thistle's first choice right-back for the remainder of the 1918-19 season, occasionally showing his versatility by filling in at left-back and left-half. Thistle ended the season in fourth place in the League, and with a reputation for not giving away many goals.

The following season saw Adams return and he and Watty alternated the right-back jersey, though the regular changes disrupted the previous tight defence. By the next season Watty had fallen further out of contention for a regular first-team game, but remained match fit, standing in for injured players, his dour tacking and uncomplicated style meaning he could be relied on in any situation.

It wasn't just any situation, however, when Watty was called in to replace the injured Jamie McMullan at left-half in the final of the Scottish Cup.

Thistle were forced to field a strange half-back line as Willie Hamilton was also unfit. Watty, Joe Harris and Matt Wilson were under severe pressure in the early part of the game, but unexpectedly, the enforced changes began to work. Watty's greater height, compared to the diminutive McMullan, was important in defying Rangers' attack in the air.

Watty was known as a spoiler for good reason, so it took Rangers by surprise when he stepped out of defence to take a pass from Jimmy McMenemy, beat his lauded international opponent Andy Cunningham, and play a perfect cross-field pass to John Blair on the right-wing. Blair scored a great goal – a goal that was to be the winning goal. Rangers threw everything at Thistle but the makeshift team held on to lift the trophy.

Watty received recognition for his final performance when he was selected for the Glasgow team to play Edinburgh later in the year, but the following two seasons saw him chosen for the Thistle team on only a handful of occasions.

During the summer of 1923 Thistle released Watty, and he returned to Nithsdale Wanderers, the team Hibs had signed him from.

Appearances 74, goals 1.
Scottish Cup winner 1921

JOHN (JACKY) BOWIE

1915 - 1922

Born 12 January 1895 in Govan, Glasgow.

Jacky Bowie arrived at Firhill in August 1915 as a highly-rated young outside left from St Anthony's, part of manager George Easton's policy of signing the most promising juniors from around the west of Scotland. Others to be signed around this time included Joe Harris and Jamie McMullan.

Such was Jacky's reputation that he found himself immediately promoted to the Thistle first team for the start of the season, replacing Frank Branscombe on the left wing. There he teamed up with another new player – William Leitch from Port Glasgow Juniors. It was a bold move by Easton, replacing a successful partnership with two untried youngsters and after early games questions were asked about Jacky's readiness for senior football. *"He must throw off that slackness. He must go in to win".*

"Everything doesn't come to him who waits", said one expert in the Scottish Referee. However, Easton had faith, and his gamble paid off. Between them Bowie and Leitch missed just six League games all season, and scored 21 goals, helping Thistle to fifth in the table and an, unfortunate, Glasgow Charity Cup Final defeat, at the end of the season. Jacky scored 13 of the goals, showing an eye for goal that would help the club in later years.

In his first season Jacky helped to provide the goals. He was noted for his wing play, his speed, and Neil Harris in particular benefited from his fine crossing. In his second season Jack varied his play, learned how dangerous a winger can be when cutting inside, and helped himself to 13 goals again, ending 1916-17 season as top scorer.

Fans favourite Branscombe had returned to Firhill but Jacky retained his outside left jersey showing how much he had improved since his signing.

1917-18 was another consistent season for Jacky – he was one of the first names on the teamsheet, and his play and goals took Thistle to the Glasgow Cup and Glasgow Charity Cup finals that season. Both, again, ended in defeat.

Jacky's eye for goal had been noted, and when the team had a problem at centre-forward, he volunteered himself for the position. His place at outside-left was taken by another new signing, Willie Salisbury, ironically also signed from St Anthony's. Jacky was a success in the centre, scoring 18 times in the League, although he quickly discovered that he preferred the more open spaces of the wide areas of the pitch than the congestion of the centre.

Neil Harris returned at centre-forward for the 1919-20 season and Jacky returned to the left where he remained until a serious injury against Clyde in September 1920 required a cartilage operation. Recovery wasn't as quick as was hoped for, and the gloomy news that Jacky expected never to play again was reported.

Fortunately the reports were premature, and a huge roar went up from the Thistle fans when Jacky returned to the team in 1921, helping out notably in the run to the Scottish Cup Final. However, full fitness hadn't returned and Jacky was unable to hold down a regular place in the team and missed out on the team's big day in the final against Rangers.

At the end of the season Thistle announced that they were willing to let Jacky go to another club, but the player preferred to remain at Firhill and fight for his first-team place again. Jacky started the season as third choice outside-left, but in a surprise nod to his reputation, was chosen to play for Glasgow against Edinburgh in September 1921. When Salisbury was injured a month later Jacky was asked to fill in and did so, keeping Salisbury out for a number of weeks.

A freak accident at Govan Cross Subway Station shortly before Xmas 1921 saw Jacky stumble and injure his head. Thistle retained him till the end of the season, but Jacky never played for Thistle again.

After leaving Firhill in the summer of 1922, Jacky spent some years playing in lower division football before retiring from the game.

Appearances 204, goals 66.

Frank Branscombe

1909 - 1915 and 1916 - 1917

Born 6 May 1889 in Dennistoun, Glasgow.

Partick Thistle teams have often been conspicuous by their inclusion of wingers, from John Campbell and Willie Freebairn in the 19th century, to Alex McSpadyen and Johnny McKenzie in the 40s, to Bobby Houston and Denis McQuade in the 70s; wingers have added flair to Partick Thistle. Frank Branscombe is another of the legends of the Firhill wings, so popular with the fans that he was known simply as 'Frank' – no surname was required.

Frank joined Thistle from Clydebank as a nippy young winger in 1909 and made his debut against Third Lanark in a 1-7 defeat in February 1909 – a bad result in a terrible season. Although Frank joined as a winger Thistle were trying to replace Sam Kennedy, their veteran centre forward, and Frank was played often away from his favoured wide position. His 13 performances weren't memorable for his goalscoring – two goals – but in a barren time for the team, it was reckoned by some that the only commendable aspect of the season was Frank's attempts to lead his forward teammates.

Optimism was higher at the start of the next season as Thistle moved into the new ground at Firhill, in September 1909, but the team were still rebuilding, and a number of big-name players were brought in, including Scottish internationalist captains Neil Gibson from Rangers and Alex Raisbeck from Liverpool. Frank's first full season was difficult. In a game against Hibernian Frank was involved in a collision with James Main. Although no blame was directed towards Frank, when Main died from his injuries two days later, Frank's confidence was affected. It wasn't until November that he persuaded the selectors that he was due a regular game, but that was the chance he needed, and he was a fixture for the rest of the season. Frank began the next season as first choice left winger again, and Thistle got off to a good start in the League. Partnering Willie Gardiner, the pair helped the team to touching distance of Rangers at the top of the League, and they remained there for the remainder of the season as Thistle ended the 1910-11 season unbeaten at home.

If there was a failing in Frank's play it was his erratic shooting. Often he would attempt outrageous shots from wide positions, and this frustrated his teammates.

1911-12 saw Frank lose his place to the well-regarded ex-Southampton winger George Coham, and he spent most of the season playing in the reserves, losing the Reserve Cup Final to Rangers, before pipping them to the Reserve League title at the end of the season.

Coham returned to England, and Frank returned again to the first team's left wing at the start of 1912-13 where he retained his place and started to improve his shooting, ending the season as top scorer with 19 goals from his wide position. He was becoming known for his ferocious shot – one near miss hit the post and the rebound landed at the halfway line.

Despite being with Thistle for just four and a half years Frank was rewarded with a benefit match in August 1913 – a game against Rangers at Firhill which Thistle won 1-0. The game was notable for Frank's long crossfield passes from one wing to the other.

Frank remained a regular in the team at outside left for the next two seasons before he left Firhill and joined Vale of Leven for the start of the 1915-16 season. He scored many goals for Vale and attracted Rangers, who he helped out for a number of games that season.

However, he returned again to Thistle in May 1916 as the club struggled to fill the left wing position for the Glasgow Charity Cup. Frank's three goals in two games took Thistle to the final of the competition, where unfortunately they lost to Celtic.

Those guest performances at the end of the season saw Frank rewarded with a contract for the 1916-17 season, and he fulfilled it until January 1917. With pressure on able-bodied men to join the First World War effort, Frank retired from football and took a job as a machinist in a munitions factory.

Frank returned to Firhill one more time, seven years after he had left, turning out for Dunkeld and Birnham in the Scottish Cup in 1924. Thistle won 11-0.

Appearances 216, goals 55.
Capped for Scottish League v Irish League 1914;
Southern League 1911.

Hugh Brown

1944 - 1951

Born 7 December 1921 in Carmyle, Glasgow. Died July 1994.

Hugh Brown was a versatile player, capable of playing in the half-back line or as an inside forward, and his Thistle career was littered with transfer gossip. The rumours began just a couple of years after he made his first appearance – testament to his rapid progress as a player in demand by the top English clubs. Brown himself admitted that he regularly changed his mind between leaving Firhill, and staying to play for Partick Thistle. When he had set his mind to departing, and his dream move seemed imminent, he appeared to be jinxed. Injuries and inconsistent play scuppered a number of big money moves – fees that at that time would have been the most money ever received for a transferred player from Firhill.

For a player who was on the brink of a number of lucrative transfers, and was capped for his country, his eventual move to a new club was a bit of an anti-climax.

Hugh Brown was signed after a Thistle scout saw his outstanding display at right-half for Yoker in a cup-tie against Renfrew in October 1944. He was a strapping six feet tall, almost 13 stone, and tremendously fit, as befits spells in both the navy and the army during the war. Indeed he was still serving both when he signed and when he made his debut a few months later. Service duties prevented him from appearing regularly until May 1945. At this late stage of the season the Summer Cup was beginning, and Hugh, on leave, played in every game, moving to inside-right to assist Jack Johnson.

Thistle reached the final and beat Hibs 2-0, Johnston scoring both goals. Hugh ended his first season with a winners medal.

Army commitments near London made Hugh miss a chunk of the 1945-46 season, but he returned from England, after a brief spell guesting for Chelsea, to a regular place in the team. With the war over, players stationed around the country were returning home, their periods as guesting players having ended. Bill Shankly had been playing for Thistle, and Hugh replaced the Scotland internationalist towards the end of the 1945-46 season. The Thistle fans were delighted to see the big man return.

This marked a period of consistency for Hugh – in 1946-47 he missed only one game, but the season also marked his first transfer request, following his first taste of international football. In October 1946 he turned out alongside Jackie Husband against Wales. Scotland lost 1-3 and the papers reported that Hugh was perhaps not yet ready for international football. His transfer request, days later, was turned down.

Later that season both Brown and Husband turned out for the Scottish League team who lost to England 1-3. Both players then travelled to play Belgium and Luxembourg during the close season. No doubt the international experience was adding to Hugh's desirability and there seems little doubt that some of the 'tapping-up' of Scottish players by English clubs in 1947 involved him.

Hugh was a great favourite with the Thistle fans. A burly, non-stop, player, there was nothing he liked more than to push forward from his half-back position to support his forwards. Willie Sharp and Willie O'Donnell regularly had to cover back as Hugh rampaged towards the opposition goal. He had a powerful shot but, as the Daily Record reported, *"when he hits the ball it goes, not it is true, always in the direction he has intended"*.

In 1948 a new club was reported as being interested in signing Hugh almost every week. The player himself admitted that *"a move would do me good"* but also admitted that it was his own inconsistent play that had stopped any interested clubs from making Thistle an offer. Middlesborough, in particular, were keen, and as the end of 1948 loomed, it seemed likely that the transfer would happen. However, a knee injury, suffered at Third Lanark, postponed the move. Hugh rushed back to the team and inflamed the injury. A devastated Hugh was out for the remainder of the season, and the beginning of the next.

In total Hugh was out of the team for eleven months, and when he returned, interest from English clubs had cooled. He was welcomed back to the team, however, and surprised everyone when he was asked to cover the outside-right position against Third Lanark. His big, barrelling shape wasn't the traditional wingers' build, but the Evening Times reported a display of *"talented and eruptive forward skill"*. Hugh scored a hat-trick and a new career as a winger might have beckoned. Unfortunately, a re-occurrence of his knee trouble ruled him out for the rest of the season, just as things seemed to be improving for him.

Injury blighted the following season too. Hugh played just a few matches in 1950-51 and he did turn out in the Glasgow Cup Final against Celtic in September 1951.

The game ended in a draw, and Hugh must have been keen to play in the final, and claim a winner's medal. Poor weather meant that the replay didn't happen till March, and by then Hugh had played his last game for Thistle.

It was just another example of the bad luck that had affected a career that had promised so much.

Hugh got a move in 1951, though it wasn't the one he might have dreamed of. He moved to Torquay, where he played for a season before retiring from the game.

Appearances 149, goals 18.
Summer Cup winner 1945
Capped for Scotland v Belgium 1947;
v Luxembourg 1947; v Wales 1946.
Capped for Scottish League v English League 1947.

WILLIE BULLOCH

1909 - 1923

Born 15 November 1895 in Larkhall.

Willie Bulloch had been a young journeyman half-back, playing with Port Glasgow Athletic, Tottenham Hotspur, Kilmarnock and Larkhall Royal Albert, achieving little of note, before Thistle director Willie Lindsay convinced his fellow directors that Willie had the potential to be the club's regular left-back.

Willie joined Thistle in the summer of 1909, at the age of 23, in time for the opening game at Firhill. Although Willie didn't play, he made his debut a month later against Bathgate in October. Thistle were required to play two games that day - a Qualifying Cup-tie and a League game. With the playing squad stretched, seven young members of the reserve team were asked to play in the Bathgate cup-tie, Willie included. It was to be Willie's only game of that season until a Charity Cup-tie on the last day of the season – the left-back position was held by Archie McKenzie or James Bennett.

However, come the next season, Willie was first choice and beside Archie McKenzie and with Alex Raisbeck in front of them, the Thistle defence ensured that the 1910-11 season was completed without a home defeat. Willie missed just one game throughout the season and became known generally as a reliable back, able to kick long and tackle boldly. One criticism was that he sometimes tried to beat his man before clearing with the result of lost possession. The following season was again successful for Thistle in general, and Willie in particular. Just three games were missed in 1911-12.

One of these missed first team games was at the end of April 1912. While the first team played Hearts, Willie was helping the reserve team beat Rangers to win the Scottish Reserve League. An earlier opportunity that season for Willie, and Thistle, to win a medal had come in the Glasgow Cup Final in October, when Rangers won the game 1-0.

Willie had settled down at full-back, and had become known for his consistent play and ability to interpret the opposition's attacks, but when Willie Hamilton was injured in September 1912, Bulloch was asked to move forward and fill in at half-back. This he did, but he was criticised for being "*too ladylike*" in a position that required an aggressive approach to the game. He was relieved to be moved back, where it was considered he "*should never be played anywhere but at left back*".

His cool, studied style, combined with his desire to play football out of defence and entertain the fans rather than employing a boot up the field earned Willie a growing reputation and the captaincy of the team between 1913 and 1921.

It also gained him further international recognition. Willie had already been selected for a Scottish League match in 1911 against the English Southern League. In 1914 Willie again played for the Scottish League, in a 2-1 win in Belfast over the Irish League.

Willie began to develop a great understanding with Tommy Adams, and their *"safe-as-houses"* full-back partnership, and Willie's left-sided alliance with Jimmy McMullan in front of him, helped Thistle to a League position of fifth in 1915-16, and to a Glasgow Charity Cup Final that same season; the final was lost to Celtic 0-2. In the following four seasons the duo continued to play together, and three more Cup Finals were reached. In the Glasgow Cup final in 1917 Rangers defeated Thistle 1-4, while in the 1918 Charity Cup Final Celtic again defeated Thistle 0-2. The disappointing run of lost finals continued with the 1919 Glasgow Cup – a 0-1 defeat by Celtic.

Of course manager George Easton was disappointed not to win at least one of the trophies, but he was quick to recognise the contribution of his captain. Willie was granted a benefit match. In those days the public interest in benefit matches was waning, so Willie benefited financially from the Thistle share of the gate for a League game against Kilmarnock in September 1919.

Those unfortunate cup final results only inspired Willie and in 1921 he captained the famous team that beat Rangers 1-0 in the Scottish Cup Final at Parkhead, taking the lead then defending valiantly. His mates responded to his example and Willie went on to lift the trophy.

Willie didn't have much time to enjoy the Scottish Cup winning feeling. He was invited to tour Canada with a selection of top Scottish players, including Jimmy McMenemy. The tour saw Willie play 15 games in the unofficial internationals.

The tour took it out of Willie, and he was unfit when he returned to Firhill. However, he returned to fitness, form, and the first team later in the season, leading the team to a second consecutive Scottish Cup semi-final.

The opponents were Rangers, and they took revenge for the previous season, beating Thistle 2-0.

The following season was notable for early season defensive collaborations with Tom Crichton, before Willie decided that he had had enough of playing football every week. His last game was a 0-1 defeat to Alloa Athletic in February 1923.

After 14 years of playing football at a high level Willie couldn't entirely stay away from the game, and Partick Thistle. He was contracted to coach the Thistle players from the start of the 1923-24 season, and was instrumental in bringing through players in his own position like Stewart Calderwood and developing those such as Denis O'Hare and Crichton, into top class full-backs, until 1928 when he left Firhill and retired from football.

Appearances 473, goals 8.
Scottish Cup Winner 1921
Capped for Scottish League v Irish League 1914;
v Southern League 1911.

STEWART CALDERWOOD

1926 - 1938

Born 3 December 1905 in Darleith, Dumbartonshire

Stewart Calderwood signed for Partick Thistle from Rutherglen Glencairn in the close season of 1926 as one of the most promising junior full-backs in Scotland, and made an almost immediate impact in the Thistle first team. He made his first team debut at left-back a month into the 1926-27 season in a 5-0 win over Kilmarnock, replacing Charlie McKendrick who had been part of a defence that had shipped 14 goals in the first five games of the season.

Left-back had been a problem position for Thistle since Tom Crichton had to retire due to injury the previous year. Stewart gave the back line some consistency, and began a partnership with Denis O'Hare. Both players made their debuts in that win over Kilmarnock and they remained together for three seasons. In front of Johnny Jackson, Denis and Stewart were a solid defence. Also making his debut in 1926 was Eddie McLeod, and he and Stewart were to combine well on the left side of the defence for a number of years.

Cup competitions were the main source of success in Stewart's first season. The semi-final of the Scottish Cup was reached before a defeat to East Fife ended the run. However, in the Glasgow Charity Cup, Thistle reached the final at Hampden and triumphed 6-3 over Rangers – the first time that Thistle had lifted the old trophy.

Stewart was a never say die defender, stylish in his tackling, and able to clear the ball from defence. *"Could get plenty of boot behind the heavy ball"*, one newspaper described him. However, he wouldn't just clear the ball at the first opportunity. Rather he would hold the ball, or move forward with it until the best time to pass it. The Daily Record was fulsome in its praise.

"Calderwood, in particular, thrived on the work. His tackling was done in a determined, fearless way, and, if he was beaten, he never stopped to grumble about it, but went after his man instantly."

Through the next few seasons Stewart was to find competition for the left-back jersey from Robert Paton and particularly Jimmy Rae until the latter's departure for Plymouth Argyle. By then Stewart had been asked to move across the defence to the right, replacing his old mate Denis O'Hare who had been forced to leave the club through injury. Alongside Rae, and laterally George Cumming, Stewart's performances defined reliability as he missed just three games in three seasons at right-back.

It was a good spell for Thistle and Stewart. The Scottish Cup Final was reached, but ultimately lost to Rangers, in 1930, while the following seasons saw Thistle finish fourth and then sixth, in the League.

The Glasgow Cup Final was reached, and lost, again to Rangers, in 1932, then reached again in 1934. This time Thistle beat Rangers 1-0 to won the competition for the first time.

Stewart was a member of the teams that played in the Scottish Cup Final and replay, and the Glasgow Cup Finals and also the team that beat Cowdenbeath in October 1930 to put Thistle top of the Scottish League for the first time.

Recognition was forthcoming from outwith Firhill for Stewart. He played in the SFA's international trial in January 1931, though selection didn't come about. He was also chosen as a reserve for Scotland's game against Ireland in 1934, but again wasn't selected. However, he did represent Glasgow against Sheffield in October 1932.

Recognition came from Thistle for Stewart's eight years service at Firhill when he was appointed captain for the team in August 1934, an honour which he retained for the next three seasons, leading Thistle to the local cup double of Glasgow Cup and Charity Cup in 1934-35.

Stewart's left-back partner in 1935 was Scotland cap George Cumming, and when Cumming moved to Aston Villa, Stewart quickly seized the tag of *"the best left back in Scotland"* when he moved back to his original position of left-back. He was certainly one of the most dependable penalty takers in Scotland. A five out of five record in penalty goals in 1936 gave him the title of *"the man who never misses"*.

Although Stewart started 1937-38 season as first-choice right-back he was soon under pressure from young Peter Curran. Stewart was dropped in November, and this was the trigger for a transfer request the following month. Thistle agreed, and Stewart was free to find himself another club.

After a spell at Queen's Park Rangers in the months before the outbreak of war, Stewart enlisted with the RAF, and soon found himself training the RAF select side. After the cessation of hostilities he retired from football.

Appearances 420, goals 9.
Glasgow Cup winner 1934
Glasgow Charity Cup winner 1927, 1935

Jackie Campbell

1963 - 1982

Born 27th February 1946 in Airdrie.

In Thistle's all time appearance list Jackie Campbell is bettered by just two players, Alan Rough and Davie McParland, two players whose names are written large across Thistle's history. Jackie Campbell's contribution to the Thistle cause in just under 20 years at Firhill is no less significant.

Jackie's talents as a footballer were first noticed while playing for his school team, alongside, interestingly enough, future Thistle team-mate Tommy Rae. Jackie came to Thistle's attention when he was spotted by a Thistle scout in 1963 while playing in the Airdrie and Coatbridge Under 18 Amateur League with Greengairs United. So good was the scout's assessment of the 17 year old central defender that Campbell was offered the chance to sign provisional forms at Firhill without having to play in a trial match. Thistle owe whoever that scout was a huge debt of gratitude.

The bulk of Jackie's appearances for Thistle would be as a centre-back but it was as a right-back that he made his Thistle debut in a match against Celtic at Firhill in March 1964. He played a total of six games in his first season at Firhill all as a right sided full-back – he had impressed in that position during a practice game. Indeed it wouldn't be until the 1971-72 season that the Thistle fans would see Jackie feature in the heart of the Thistle defence.

Season 1971-72, as every Thistle fan knows, was a momentous one in the history of Partick Thistle Football Club. Thistle's run in the League Cup took Thistle all the way to the final where against all the odds Celtic were defeated 4-1. Thistle's League Cup winning team, Hugh Strachan aside, was talented but young and inexperienced at that level. At the age of 25 Campbell could almost have been considered a veteran.

Injury, including a mysterious skin ailment that proved resistant to both diagnosis and treatment, had curtailed Campbell's first team involvement in the two seasons prior to 71/72. He was unable to play much part in Thistle's unsuccessful fight against relegation, and although he played four times in the Thistle side that would win the Second Division title, the League Cup victory was Jackie's first real taste of success.

Thistle would have further opportunities of cup glory in the 1970s, for they reached the League Semi-Final in 1975 and the Scottish Cup Semi-Final in 1978 and 1979. Jackie featured in all of those matches but Thistle were unable to progress beyond the last four. He did play in the Thistle side that lifted the Glasgow Cup by beating Celtic in 1981 but that was hardly comparable.

Campbell would play in close on 600 fixtures for Partick Thistle but he scored just once. His solitary goal came in an almost typically crazy Partick Thistle match.

On 16 August 1975 Thistle travelled through to Perth to face St Johnstone in a League Cup-tie. When Thistle found themselves trailing 2-0 after just 11 minutes all seemed lost. After 20 minutes though Dougie Somner hauled Thistle back into the match, and his goal was swiftly followed by an equaliser from John Craig. Enter Jackie Campbell. Playing in the right-back role that he made his Thistle debut in eleven years earlier, Campbell ventured forward, played a one-two at the edge of the box before rifling a shot into the back of the net. Thistle went on to win 4-2.

Helping to prevent goals rather than scoring them was Jackie's main job at Firhill. On one occasion he took that role to the extreme. In January 1975 Thistle were playing Motherwell at Fir Park in a Scottish Cup match when John Arrol, preferred at the time in goals to Alan Rough, broke his leg after a clash with Motherwell's Willie Pettigrew. In the days long before substitute goalkeepers, someone was going have to take over the role of Thistle's last line of defence. With three quarters of the game still to play it fell to Jackie Campbell to fill that role. He did so with no little aplomb as Thistle earned a Firhill replay after a no scoring draw. Typically, with Alan Rough restored to the side, Thistle lost the replay.

In October 1980 the Thistle fans were given the opportunity to acknowledge the contribution that Campbell had made to Partick Thistle when Firhill hosted his richly deserved testimonial match. Two teams made up of current Thistle players and guests played out an entertaining 6-6 draw.

Jackie's playing career could have had a happier ending. He last saw competitive first team action against Dundee United in March 1982. Thistle would be relegated at the end of that season and Jackie's last game, a 5-1 defeat, was one of a number of unhappy afternoon's Thistle would have. Campbell was by this time assisting manager Peter Cormack in a player-coach role but relegation ended Campbell's association with Partick Thistle. It wasn't perhaps the happiest way in which to part company with the football club that had played a big part in his life.

In a programme interview Jackie gave his definition of the term professional in the context of a footballer. He considered it to be somebody who always gave 100% whether in training or playing. It had to be someone who led by example whenever possible and contributed fully to the team effort all the time and never floated on the crest achieved by his team mates. He could easily have been describing himself.

Appearances 579, goals 1
League Cup winner 1971
First Division Championship winner 1975-76
Second Division Championship winner 1970-71
Glasgow Cup winner 1981

KENNY CAMPBELL

1920 - 1922

Born 6 September 1892 in Cambuslang, Glasgow. Died 28 April 1977.

When Liverpool's Scottish internationalist Kenny Campbell bought a house in Cardonald, close to Ibrox, the Glasgow newspapers gleefully announced his imminent signing to Rangers. However, it was Partick Thistle that stole Campbell from under the blue noses for a club record fee of £1750, and Kenny joined the legacy of great Thistle goalkeepers such as John McCorkindale and Willie Howden.

Liverpool had stolen young Campbell from under the noses of Scottish clubs when they signed him in the summer of 1911 as a Junior internationalist, after spells with Clyde Vale, Rutherglen Glencairn, Cambuslang Rovers, and he became the last line of their defence the following season, remaining first choice until the outbreak of the war, playing in the FA Cup final in 1914, and unfortunately losing to Burnley. For a number of seasons Kenny and Ireland goalkeeper Elisha Scott vied for the jersey.

Although not the regular choice for Liverpool, Kenny's form when chosen was such that he attracted the admiration of the Scottish selectors. Kenny played against England, Wales and Ireland in 1920. *"At last Scotland have found a replacement for Jimmy Brownlie,"* declared the Daily Record, happy with Kenny's form.

By the time Kenny played for Scotland he had already turned out once as a guest for Thistle, replacing Alec Stewart, who was playing for the Scottish League v English League, in 1919. Kenny's game was a 1-1 draw against Celtic and he played his part well until the late stages of the game, when an equaliser was eventually lost.

As Scott increased his hold on the goalkeeper's position at Liverpool, Kenny began to think of a move, and his Thistle and Scotland experiences led him to think of a return to Glasgow, feeding the Daily Record with a story of his desire to come home. Manager George Easton signed Scotland's international goalie with a £1,750 transfer fee – the biggest Thistle had ever paid for a player – immediately after he conceded five goals, but played brilliantly, for Scotland against England in April 1920.

Kenny replaced Rab Bernard for a few games at the end of the 1919-20 season, and was fully in place for the start of the following season. Thistle had high hopes for the forthcoming term, having added a further internationalist, Jimmy McMenemy, to the team. A number of good performances from Kenny lifted Thistle to third in the League. Come the start of 1921, Kenny's *"wonderful saves from long and close range, catlike agility, grand judgement and coolness"* being credited regularly for the team's form.

League form and luck was also transferred to the Scottish Cup, and after the quarter final against Motherwell Kenny exclaimed *"With a little bit of the good luck we have had in the ties we may just land the cup"*.

That luck and resolve did stay with the players, taking them through to a Cup Final against Rangers. A degree of luck was required as a strong Rangers side attacked incessantly, but Kenny, and his defence of Tom Crichton and Willie Bulloch, defended brilliantly to help Thistle lift the trophy.

Kenny's club form, before and after the Cup Final, had kept him in the international team, and he became the second Partick Thistle player to captain Scotland, against Wales in 1921, leading out clubmates Jamie McMullan and Joe Harris. A further four caps and a League cap was won while at Firhill. The season following the Cup win was another successful one, for the club and for Kenny. The Daily Record recognised his form after a 0-1 defeat to Rangers:

"And what a goal Campbell kept! All sorts and conditions of shots – high and low, and breast and shin high came alike to the Cambuslang custodian. Kenny was as nimble as a kitten; he held the ball as if it were in a vice; when clearing he left precious little on for the incoming forwards."

The higher reaches of the League were again achieved, while the semi-final of the cup was again reached, but this time lost. However, the season had been a turbulent one for Kenny. His wife had remained in Liverpool and was ill. Kenny had hoped to return south to tend her, seeking a new club in the summer of 1921, but was persuaded to remain at Firhill for another year. An impasse, unfortunately, was reached in the summer of 1922. Kenny again asked to be released, but Thistle didn't want to lose the player. With a transfer to an English League club impossible because of Thistle's attitude, Kenny signed for non-League New Brighton, and Thistle received no financial compensation for a player they had invested heavily in just a few seasons earlier.

Although Kenny apologised to Thistle for his actions, and hoped they might release him from his registration, there were a number of directors at Firhill who were furious and wanted Kenny kept out of football. However, after a few months Tottenham Hotspur and Stoke City expressed an interest in signing Kenny, and Thistle were happy to negotiate a deal. Stoke were the lucky team, and signed Kenny in March 1923. A spell at Leicester City followed by another at New Brighton before Kenny retired from football in 1931.

Appearances 96, goals 0.
Scottish Cup winner 1921
Capped for Scotland v England 1922; v Ireland 1921, 1922; v Wales 1921, 1922 (captain).
Capped for Scottish League v Irish League 1921.
Other honours (with Liverpool) 3 Scotland appearances

Harry Chatton

1923 - 1926

Born 23 April 1899 in Enniskillen

There are few footballers able to boast of playing for two different national teams while playing in Scotland. Harry Chatton is one of them. He is also the only such player to play full international football against Scotland.

When Thistle signed Harry from Dumbarton in 1923, as a replacement for right-half Joe Harris, he was already well regarded both in Scotland and in his native Ireland. He made his debut in the Charity Cup semi-final against Queen's Park and immediately impressed. *"Neat, nippy, accurate, he never wasted a ball,"* said the Sunday Mail. So well regarded, in fact, that after just one game Liverpool made an enquiry about his availability in the close season of 1923.

Thistle, though, weren't keen to let their man go. While signed mainly as a right-half, Harry had shown versatility at Dumbarton, and in his first few months at Firhill was asked to play across the half-back line, at inside-right, and even as a makeshift centre-forward in two games. Harry did well at centre scoring two goals. However, it was as a tigerish right-half and as a centre-half that he continued to make his name at Firhill. In one game against Airdrie he became involved in a scuffle with Hughie Gallacher. Both players were sent off, and as they left the field more fighting broke out between them. Both players were suspended. It wasn't all aggression with Harry though.

He anticipated the game well, and was highly regarded as a good passer of the ball from half-back – Jamie Kinloch and Bobby Grove especially benefiting from his well-placed passes.

In October 1924 Harry was selected to play for Ireland against England at Goodison Park in a 1-3 defeat, and was again asked to play a few months later when Ireland were to face Scotland. Harry was surprised to learn that he would play at left-half instead of his now customary centre-half position but travelled, along with five other Irish caps playing in Scotland, with the Scottish party. The Scottish press reported that Harry didn't reach the level of his club form in the game in Belfast. Scotland won 3-0. Harry returned to the international team in October 1925 to face England, again in Belfast. This time at centre-half, he kept the English forwards at bay and the game ended 0-0.

International experience and good performances at home inevitably meant rumours of English club interest in Harry. Although manager George Easton denied any truth in the report, they persisted. Manchester City were said to be particularly keen and were represented at Firhill on a number of occasions, admitting Harry was attracting them. However, the reported interest in Harry was a decoy to City's continuing, but well disguised, interest in Jamie McMullan, who they signed with no competition from other clubs.

Harry's head had been turned, however, by the transfer talk, and in the summer of 1926 he and teammate Alex Donald joined the flood of players leaving Scotland for the United States. Harry and Alex played for a season with Indiana Flooring before returning after hearing that Hearts were interested in signing them. They felt that they were due wages but Indiana withheld the money, reporting the players for having broken their contracts. Hearts signed the players but the dispute with Indiana meant that both players returned to the States without kicking a ball, to sign for the New York Nationals in 1928. After two and a half years Chatton and Donald were discovered to be playing unauthorised football while playing for the Nationals and were banned from playing in the United States.

Again a boat home and a period out of football beckoned.

Harry signed for Shelbourne for a short period where he was capped for the Irish Free State against Spain in Barcelona in April 1931. The Football Association of Ireland had split from the Irish Football Association in Belfast and had begun to play officially recognised internationals. By the time Harry played in the return leg in Dublin Harry had moved back to Dumbarton where he was capped, again against Spain. He was capped for a third time by the Free State, against Holland, by which time he had moved back to Ireland again to play with Cork, before retiring from the game.

Appearances 89, goals 2.
Capped for Ireland v England 1924, 1925; v Scotland 1925.

Other honours
With New York Nationals U.S. Open Cup 1928
With Shelbourne 1 Irish Free State international appearance
With Dumbarton 1 Irish Free State international appearance
With Cork 1 Irish Free State international appearance

JAMES 'CHIC' CHARNLEY

1989 - 2003 (4 SPELLS)

Born 11 June 1963 in Glasgow.

In a modern game reportedly short of genuine characters James Charnley, or Chic as he is better known, stands out from the uniformity of the crowd. A more colourful career, which includes no fewer than four separate spells as a Partick Thistle player, would be hard to find. It all started with junior outfit Rutherglen Glencairn.

Chic making his first step up to the senior ranks when he signed for St Mirren. He subsequently had a spell with Ayr United, terrorising Thistle on one occasion at Somerset Park, but the young Chic was not much for conforming and for a time, a spell at Pollok Juniors aside meant his talent was lost to the game.

It was Clydebank that rescued the career of Chic Charnley but indiscipline continued to haunt his career. A move away from Clydebank saw him come under the charge of John Lambie for the very first time when he signed for Hamilton Accies. The tendency to press the self destruct button would never truly leave Chic, as testified by the number of red cards he received, but working for a sustained period of time with Lambie would prove to be the making of Chic Charnley.

Not that that initially looked like being the case. Lambie left Hamilton to manage Thistle and Chic soon followed Lambie out of the door, typically under something of a cloud. That did though give Lambie the opportunity to once again sign the wayward Charnley and he became a Thistle player for the first time in January 1989.

He would make an immediate impact. John Flood scored a spectacular goal during Charnley's debut against Raith Rovers at Firhill, but it was Chic that stole the show during the 1-1 draw. That set the tone on Charnley's first half season at Firhill. Charnley pulled the strings as Thistle, arguably the form team in the second half of the season, successfully fought against relegation. Chic scored his first Thistle goal during the course of a 4-1 win against Ayr United at Firhill and helped inspire Thistle to a Scottish Cup win against Premier Division St Mirren.

He was in equally sparkling form at the start of the next season. Thistle started the season in impressive form with Charnley, who netted a hat-trick of set pieces against Forfar Athletic, in impressive form and the centre of much media attention and transfer speculation. He did, however, remain at Firhill but Thistle's promotion bid petered out after Lambie returned, briefly, to manage Hamilton Accies.

Lambie was away from Firhill for just a few short months and it was hoped that his return would spark a successful promotion bid during season 1990-91. Thistle though finished the season in fourth spot with Charnley contributing seven goals from 31 games. Although an unsuccessful season Thistle's play at times was most pleasing on the eye. So much so that Charnley was once again the centre of transfer speculation. This time, he left Firhill when he and David Elliot joined St Mirren in a complicated swap deal involving George Shaw, Mark McWalter and a large sum of money.

After a couple of years with St Mirren, a spell on loan with Bolton and a brief period in Sweden with Djurgradens, Chic was back at Firhill in November 1993. He would make his Thistle debut second time around in a Premier Division fixture against Kilmarnock at Firhill. Chic's form on his return home was, as ever, excellent, helping Thistle to avoid relegation. Again transfer speculation mounted with this time strong rumours of a move to Celtic. He did appear in a testimonial match for Celtic against Manchester United but a permanent move never materialised.

Perhaps as a result of that he was less influential the following season despite another successful fight against relegation. At any rate his Thistle career looked to be over when he left Firhill to join Dumbarton. From there he moved to Hibs, then Dundee, before landing once again on the Firhill doorstep in February 1998.

Thistle were at a distinctly low ebb at this time. The future of the Club had been under serious threat and while the Club was in no immediate danger of going out of business dark clouds still circled low over Firhill. Chic was brought in to help the team on the pitch to avoid relegation.

He played just five times as Thistle took the drop. His poor disciplinary record went against him as a couple of bookings meant a lengthy period on the sidelines.

Not an ideal way to end a Thistle career that had delighted many but he was to have one more spell at Firhill. After playing for Portadown in Northern Ireland and junior side Kirkintilloch Rob Roy he returned to Firhill early in 2002-03.

His main remit was to work with young players but he still managed three substitute appearances for the first team. The last of which came on the final day of the season, with Chic just a month or so short of his 40th birthday.

Chic can be currently found, when not appearing on TV in Old Masters tournaments, pulling pints in his Maryhill pub.

Appearances 148, goals 34.

FRANK COULSTON

1967 - 1975

Born 1945 in Stranraer.

Described as a *"first class goal snatcher and tremendous shot"* Frank was the only one of Thistle's attack minded players who didn't plunder a goal against Celtic in the 1971 League Cup Final. That statistical quirk aside Frank is rightly considered as one of Thistle's top performers of the late 1960s and early 1970s.

Sources list Frank's previous club prior to arriving at Firhill as his home town team of Stranraer, he had previously been on the books of Queen's Park, but it was while he was studying to be physical education teacher (once qualified he would combine that job with that of a professional footballer) that he came to the attention of Partick Thistle. Not surprisingly he was a big hit in the Jordanhill College team and with Frank scoring more than his fair share of goals he helped inspire them to victory in the Scottish Amateur Cup Final. In next to no time after that he had progressed to the Partick Thistle first team.

Coulston made his Thistle debut on 22 August 1967 in a Glasgow Cup-tie against Celtic at Parkhead. Thistle would lose that game 0-5 but for Frank it was still a memorable occasion as he explained in an interview in the Thistle programme in May 1995. *"Although we lost it was a memorable occasion because of the personnel in the Celtic team at that time. Earlier that year they had won the European Cup."*

Memorable occasion or not, being part of a side that loses a fixture 0-5 is not the most auspicious of starts to a career at a new club. Thankfully for Frank things would quickly improve. He scored his first goals in Thistle colours when he netted a double in a 2-1 Firhill win against Stirling Albion and he would finish his first season at Firhill with 14 goals, a tally better by only by Tommy Rae who scored 15 times.

Coulston's contribution to the next two seasons though was minimal but that was most certainly not the case in season 1970-71. He played in all 47 of Thistle's League and cup games that season. As Thistle carried off the Second Division championship title Frank scored 26 times and finished the season as Thistle's leading goalscorer.

Goals were marginally harder to come by the following season but with Thistle back among the big boys in the First Division a tally of 15 goals was nothing to be ashamed off. Thistle would finish their first season back in the top flight in seventh position but it wasn't their League form, as impressive as that was, that put Thistle firmly in the spotlight in season 1971-72. Rather it was Thistle's League Cup victory that was the story of the season.

As outlined above Coulston didn't manage to score in the final win against Celtic but his contribution that famous October afternoon and in the previous rounds shouldn't be underestimated.

None more so than in the quarter-final second leg against St Johnstone. Trailing 2-0 from the first leg Thistle marched on to the last four winning 5-1 with Coulston helping himself to two of Thistle's five goals.

Thistle's win taking them to the final took most people by surprise but not, it would seem, Coulston. Commenting some years later he said *"We were convinced that we weren't going into the final as lambs to the slaughter. Although we did have to pinch ourselves at half-time with us 4-0 up."*

The break-up of that highly successful and richly talented Thistle team began within months of the win over Celtic and as such Thistle were unable to build upon that success.

While the likes of Jimmy Bone and Alex Forsyth moved on, Coulston, a little bit older and with a good job outside of football, remained at Firhill for a further three seasons. Although not again reaching double figures in terms of goals scored he continued to make telling contributions to the Thistle cause.

The last of Frank's 273 Thistle games came against Celtic on 1 March 1975. After leaving Firhill he returned to Stranraer before moving on to Stenhousemuir before taking on a coaching role at Falkirk. Highly rated as a coach Frank spent a considerable period at the Scottish Football Association in the post of Assistant Technical Director.

Appearances 273, goals 83.
League Cup winner 1971
Second Division Championship winner 1970-71

TOM CRICHTON

1919 - 1926

Born 28 June 1893 in Sanquhar. Died August 1936.

As Tom Crichton was being stretchered off the pitch at Hampden he heard the Queen's Park players complaining to the referee that play had been stopped to allow a stretcher to remove the prone body of the Thistle right-back. This was in the days when players knocked unconscious would lie until the ball went out of play before treatment could be administered. Many others in the crowd knew how serious the injury was – they had heard the sharp crack of a bone being broken. Sure enough, later in hospital Tom got the confirmation he feared – a compound fracture of his left leg meaning he would be out of action for some time.

It was a bitter blow for the man known as 'the Admirable Crichton'. After six years of consistent performances he was being considered for international honours. Just a few months earlier he had played in a trial match as the SFA selectors tried to pick their best players to play England. He had earlier represented Glasgow on three occasions against Sheffield, and once against Edinburgh.

Tom had played with Nithsdale Wanderers some years before signing and had attracted the interest of Partick Thistle. However, the war intervened and delayed the progress of his football career for a number of years. At the conclusion of hostilities Thistle again offered terms, and this time Tom signed up as a professional footballer in February 1919.

Over the next couple of years Tom began to establish himself in the team playing across the half-back line. He was a neat, tidy player, who prided himself on playing passes into space and along the ground for his forwards to run on to. However, he was unable to secure a regular jersey due to the form of Adam Black, Willie Hamilton and Jamie McMullan, and dropped out as regulars returned.

The following season saw Tom asked to fill in at right-back due to the absence of Walter Borthwick and Tom grudgingly agreed to try the change in position. It took him some time to settle into the full-back position, but the Daily Record a few months later noted that his progress was *"rather wonderful"*.

Although his form, and his partnership with Willie Bulloch, had helped Thistle up the League, to third at the beginning of 1921, it was in Thistle's protracted Scottish Cup campaign, in games against Motherwell, and Hearts in the semi-final, that he came to the attention of those outside Firhill.

> *"This stalwart from 'Kirkonnel Lea' has done wonders during that run. He has played brilliantly. Never flinching, sure of his kicking, strong in his tackling, he gained confidence from his seasoned colleague [Bulloch]."* (Sunday Mail)

Changes to the half-back line for the final against Rangers meant added pressure on the full-backs, and the mercurial Alan Morton gave Tom a nerve-racking first half. However, as the Thistle team gelled Tom gave nothing away, and assisted Thistle to a famous Scottish Cup Final win.

As Scottish Cup holders Thistle were expected to be a force in the following year's competition, and indeed, they reached the semi-final again, facing Rangers. Tom had switched to play left-back due to the absence of Willie Bulloch earlier in the season, and had coped well, being comfortable with both feet. For the Rangers game Tom switched back to the right but Rangers exacted revenge for the previous season's result.

Tom remained at right-back in 1922-23 due to a long-term injury to John Struthers, restoring the Crichton-Bulloch partnership for most of the season, until Willie retired later in the season. Tom switched gain to the left, and Denis O'Hare began a notable Thistle career on the right.

Tales of Tom's fearless tackling and clever passing had reached England, and Middlesbrough expressed an interest in signing him. He decided to stay at Firhill and was rewarded with a benefit match against Liverpool in 1924, which the English champions won 4-1. Tom played in virtually every game for three years. Right or left-back, he could always be relied upon until his career came to a tragically early finale at Hampden Park in October 1925.

There was some encouraging news a few months later that the injury was healing, but in reality Tom would never play football again. A second benefit match was arranged, and the Queen's Park players, perhaps realising their earlier insensitivity, offered their full support. A match between a Thistle/Queens select and a team representing Celtic, Clyde, Rangers and Third Lanark raised £500 for Tom, an amount equivalent to a 32,000 crowd in those days.

Tom remained a popular figure at Firhill for many years, undertaking unofficial scouting jobs for several years.

Appearances 230, goals 0.
Scottish Cup Winner 1921

George Cummings

1932 - 1935

Born 5 June 1913 in Laurieston, Falkirk. Died 1987

George Cummings' early days at Firhill were to be a mirror for the rest of his short Partick Thistle career. George signed for junior team Grange Rovers from Thornbridge Waverley, and accepted an offer from George Easton to train with Thistle's youngsters in 1932. After an appearance for the Scotland Juniors international team, Easton decided to offer George professional terms, pipping Celtic to his signature.

It was an inspired and well timed decision, for Thistle and Celtic weren't the only clubs interested in the promising left-back. Everton, the English League champions, were also tracking George, and they offered Thistle £1,000 for George's transfer – even before he had played his first game for the first team. Liverpool, Arsenal, Chelsea, Aston Villa, Manchester City and Huddersfield were among the clubs who would attempt to tempt George to leave Firhill over his career at Thistle.

If George was hot property before he had kicked a ball, following his debut against Celtic in the Glasgow Cup semi-final, his star had risen further. His *"clean and accurate kicking"* with both feet was praised. The Daily Record was quick to comment *"this youngster was cool as anything, he judges his intervention well, and timed his clearing to a nicety"*.

Thistle had had a poor start to the season, sitting at the bottom of the League. Following his debut, Thistle embarked on a winning run of 13 games, lifting the club to mid-table.

George was ever-present at left-back for the rest of the season, linking well with full-back partner Stewart Calderwood and left-half Eddie McLeod.

While George was admired primarily for his defensive qualities, his stylish tackling and accurate passing, he was also gaining a reputation for getting forward; an unusual thing for a full-back. He scored a 40 yard free-kick to beat Airdrie in 1933, and often surprised his opponents by sprinting out of defence, getting in front of his half-backs, and delivering dangerous deep crosses to his forwards. Johnny Ballantyne in particular benefited from George's forays upfield.

International recognition almost came just a year after turning pro. George was chosen as a reserve for the Scottish League team to play Ireland, and then for the full international team against England in 1934 but didn't make the line-up on either occasion.

However, he was chosen to play against the Irish League in 1934, and followed that up with his full international debut against England, alongside Johnny Jackson, the following year. George played superbly and was picked as 'Man of the Match', a great honour for one still so young.

He then accompanied an SFA Select on a tour of North America in the summer of 1935, playing twelve games alongside Thistle colleagues Bob Donnelly and Willie Miller. Further caps soon followed against England in the Jubilee international, and against Ireland.

Back at Firhill, Thistle had been reaping the benefits of George's improving confidence. His tackling and positional sense, added to his reading of the game meant that he knew exactly what he was going to do with the ball before he had taken it from his opponent. He always liked to beat his opponent with skill rather than just punt the ball upfield. More than once he was warned by his manager for showing off, beating the right-winger again and again instead of clearing the ball. It was a criticism more often applied to forwards than defenders. While League form was a little disappointing Thistle were on fire elsewhere. The finals of the Glasgow Cup and Glasgow Charity Cup were reached without conceding a goal, and both competitions were won, though a goal was conceded in the Charity Cup Final that George missed through injury.

English scouts still watched every Thistle game, and Huddersfield made a *"huge"* bid for George, which was again turned down. Amidst all the transfer talk George signed a new contract, and was rewarded with more money for the 1935-36 season. This didn't stop Aston Villa, and their manager - ex-Thistle player Jamie McMullan - in particular. A number of offers were made, reportedly starting with a world record fee, and then increasing.

The perilous financial situation at Firhill made it difficult to reject the offers, particularly when George announced that he wouldn't be averse to a move to the Midlands, and eventually Thistle agreed to sell. The move was delayed as George extracted a better deal for himself than Villa wanted to offer. The fee was eventually announced as £9,350 – not a world record but a record between a Scottish and English club – money desperately needed to keep Thistle's bank happy. George literally had saved Thistle this time.

George had been signed along with a number of other prominent players, to reverse shocking League form at Villa. That change in fortunes didn't come, and Villa were relegated at the end of the season. He made over 400 appearances for Villa and was a wonderful inspiration as captain after the war. He retired in 1949 to become coach of Villa's third team for a brief spell.

Back at Firhill the Cummings family connection continued. George's brothers Fred and David signed for Thistle, though neither played first-team football, before being signed, coincidentally, by Aston Villa. Management was to follow for George at various non-League clubs, then a spell as a scout at Wolves, followed by retirement. George Cummings passed away in 1987.

Appearances 140, goals 1.
Glasgow Cup winner 1934.
Capped for Scotland v England 1935; v Ireland 1935; v Wales 1935.
Capped for Scotland in Jubilee International v England 1935
Capped for Scottish League v Irish League 1934, 1935.
Other honours: With Aston Villa: 6 Scotland international appearances,
English Wartime League Cup winner 1944, English League Second Division winner 1937-38

PETER CURRAN

1937 - 1949

Born in Saltcoats

Peter Curran signed for Partick Thistle in September 1937 from Kilwinning Rangers, to the considerable disappointment of a number of other top senior sides who had been keeping an eye on the player with the intention of signing him. Peter went straight into the reserve team to play Rangers that same day and made an impressive first appearance. He had two good feet, it was reported – a rare asset for a defender.

In November 1937 Peter replaced the veteran Stewart Calderwood at right-back in the first XI and from that point he was rarely out of the team, missing just a couple of League games till the end of the season. Plaudits were quick to come his way - *"position, poise and punting power"* is what the Daily Record thought Peter brought to the team. The same newspaper reported that Thistle had signed a potential great. *"Not yet is he perhaps the supreme defender, but I can see the day when he will challenge the best in the country."*

Indeed, Peter's step up from juniors to top senior football was swift. In 1941 he played for an SFA XI (effectively the Scottish international team minus those on duty in the war) in a morale-boosting exhibition game against the Scottish Command XI, along with George Sutherland, confirming that in just a couple of years he had indeed become one of the 'best in the country'.

Later that year he played, alongside Alex McSpadyen, for the Scottish League against England. Scotland lost 2-3 but Curran played well, triggering calls for his inclusion in the full international squad for the game at Wembley a few months in the future. He didn't play at Wembley but continued to represent the SFA in games against the army and RAF.

Robert Reid, in The Official History of Partick Thistle, described Peter as *"… a rugged full-back, a no-nonsense type of performer. In those days, before the introduction of fancy formations, the full-back had a very specific, clearly-defined role and that was to remove the threat of the opposing winger, by slightly dubious means sometimes, it has to be admitted. Peter was adept at letting the winger know in no uncertain terms who was the boss."*

One winger that Peter had come up against during the war years was the legendary Stanley Matthews. Stationed in Scotland, Matthews guested for Rangers and was in the line up against Peter in the Charity Cup Final of 1941. Though Rangers won 3-0 Matthews was poor, not getting much of a chance against Peter. Later that year Peter again dominated Matthews, in the game against the English League. Despite being known for his robust play, it was his anticipation of passes to his opponent, rather than his tackling, that caught the eye.

Curran was *"more successful against Matthews than any player I have seen in England,"* said one reporter.

During the war Peter had swapped right-back for the left, and a principle reason for this was the arrival of Jimmy McGowan.

The players went on to form a lasting partnership for eight years, playing more than 200 games as full-back partners, including the final of the 1945 Summer Cup competition which Thistle won, beating Hibernian 2-0.

In 1948, after eleven years, and 399 games, Peter lost his place in the first team after a disappointing start to the season. He was replaced, initially, by Alex Pirrie and later in the season by Bobby Gibb, who was to have a long career at Firhill himself. Peter's last game for Thistle was against Third Lanark in October 1948.

Peter was placed on the open to transfer list at the end of the season and returned to Ayrshire in time for the start of the 1949-50 season, as player-coach of Ayr United, before moving to the highlands for a spell with Inverness Thistle.

Appearances 399, goals 6.

Summer Cup winner 1945
Capped for Scottish League v English League 1941

Jimmy Davidson

1945 - 1960

Born 8 November 1926 in Douglas Water

Jimmy Davidson's illustrious Partick Thistle career, a career that would span 15 years, began in fairly bizarre circumstances. Thistle, as other sides had done before and others would do so later, travelled to play a British Army team still stationed in Germany following the end of the Second World War. Thistle though had a Victory Cup commitment against Clachnacuddin shortly upon their return. With both air transport and the road to Inverness not as advanced as they are now it was decided that Thistle would fulfil their fixture in Germany and send their Reserve team north to Inverness for the first-leg of their Victory Cup-tie. It was a decision that did not go down well in Inverness but it did give Jimmy Davidson the opportunity to make the first of the 411 appearances that he would make as a Partick Thistle player. The Thistle reserve team were held to a 2-2 draw in Inverness but emphatically won the return 7-2 with all their stars back in the team.

After making his debut in fairly unlikely circumstances it would be some time before Davidson could be considered as a first team regular at Firhill. In the two seasons following his debut he made just eight appearances. By the time of the 1948-49 season though he was well on the road to cementing his place in the Thistle team. That season he scored his first Thistle goal in a fixture against St Mirren.

Once firmly established in the Thistle first team he formed a formidable wing-half partnership with Willie Hewitt prompting one observer to comment

"Not since the days of McMullan and Gibson have Partick Thistle been served at wing half as they are by Davidson and Hewitt."

In 1952 the *"shrewd, debonair"* Thistle player came to the attention of the international selectors for the first time. He and Thistle team mate Tommy Ledgerwood played for the Scotland 'B' team against France. Davidson would also be capped for the Scottish League in 1952 against both the Irish League and the League of Ireland. Davidson was also capped against the League selects from both sides of the border in Ireland again in 1954.

In 1954 Davidson won the first of eight caps for Scotland at full international level. In May he was capped twice in fixtures against Norway before travelling to Switzerland with Scotland for the 1954 World Cup Finals. Initially a squad of 22 were selected to go to Switzerland but in keeping with Scotland's shambolic approach to the tournament only 13 players travelled. Two of them, Davidson and Johnny MacKenzie, were Partick Thistle players. Both would play in Scotland's two fixtures and became the first Partick Thistle players to play in the World Cup Finals.

Against Austria, Scotland competed well losing by just a single to goal to nil with Davidson and his half-back partner Cowie *"reigning supreme"*. The fixture with Uruguay, however, was an unmitigated disaster with Scotland losing 7-0.

That wouldn't be the last time that Davidson would be part of a Scotland side that would concede 7 goals in a match. In 1955 he was a member of the Scotland team that went down to a 7-2 defeat at Wembley against England. A much more memorable occasion was the fixture with Hungry in 1954 that was watched by a staggering crowd of 113,146. Also noteworthy was Davidson's contribution to a 2-2 draw with Northern Ireland. It was Davidson that opened the scoring with a free-kick. Indeed Davidson was known as something of a free kick specialist with a glowing tribute paid to his skills.

> *"As an attacking half-back he has few equals and few can put more venom and direction into a free kick."*

Returning to life at Firhill the 1950s were a successful decade for Partick Thistle but with a few disappointments thrown in for good measure. Davidson experienced virtually all the highs and lows that the decade would throw up.

Thistle would win the Glasgow Cup three times, in 1951, 1952 and 1954, and Davidson was part of the victorious Thistle team each time.

Thistle also reached the League Cup final three times in the 1950s. In 1953 Davidson was part of the side that were defeated by East Fife. Thistle were back in the final in 1956, and Davidson chipped in with a vital goal in the semi-final replay against Dundee. Celtic provided the opposition in the final and the first game finished 0-0, despite Davidson being hampered by a cut he sustained above his eye. That cut was so bad in fact that he was unable to play in the replay and Thistle lost 3-0. Thistle reached the final again in 1958 but Davidson's first team appearances by this stage of his career were becoming fewer and fewer and he at least was spared the agony of playing in a match that Thistle lost 5-1.

Jimmy moved to Inverness and played for Caledonians for a few years before returning to Firhill as groundsman.

Appearances 411, goals 46.
Glasgow Cup winner 1951, 1952, 1954.
Capped for Scotland v Austria 1954; v England 1955; v Hungary 1954; v Northern Ireland 1954; v Norway (twice) 1954; v Uruguay; v Wales 1954.
Capped for Scotland 'B' v France 1952
Capped for Scottish League v Irish League 1952, 1954; v, League of Ireland 1952, 1954

Jamie Doyle

1978 - 1984 & 1987

Born 1 October 1961 in Glasgow.

The player that would go on to inspire 'Jamie Doyle Bites' badges arrived at Firhill from boys club Auchengill Star in 1978. Jamie initially served his apprenticeship in the Thistle Reserve side but before too long he made the step up to the First Team. His debut came in December 1978 when he appeared as a substitute in a 0-0 draw with Hibs at Easter Road. Several months would pass before Bertie Auld once again turned to the young midfielder but he did start four of the last five games of the season as he began to emerge as a player rich in potential.

The following season Doyle established himself as a near permanent feature in the Thistle starting eleven, he would miss just six games all season, and it was a similar story the following season as well.

In season 1980-81 Jamie's form in the Thistle midfield brought him international recognition. On 18 November 1980 at Pittodrie, just a few days after having played at the same venue for Thistle, Jamie made his international debut for the Scotland Under 21 side in a fixture with Denmark. Playing in the same side as future Thistle goalkeeper John Brough, Jamie played the full 90 minutes as Scotland recorded a 2-1 win. Subsequent caps would follow in 1982 against Italy in a European Championship Quarter-Final and in the same competition the following year against East Germany. Doyle had prior to his involvement with the Scotland Under 21 side already appeared for the Scottish League in a fixture against the Irish League.

Domestically things weren't going quite so well. By the time Jamie made his third and final appearance in the Scotland Under 21 side Thistle had been relegated to the First Division. A run to the last eight in each of the major cup competitions saw Thistle play an almost unprecedented 56 competitive first team fixtures in season 1982-83 but there was to be no promotion back to the Premier League.

Thistle eventually finished the season in fourth place, five points away from a promotion place. Jamie did though get the opportunity to play alongside his younger brother Gerry in a first team fixture for the very first time. In late September 1982 Gerry wore the number two jersey and Jamie the number six as Thistle defeated Raith Rovers by two goals to one at Firhill.

After failing to win promotion at the first time of asking so too did Thistle the next season. Already in serious financial trouble a failure to return to the top League put further pressure on the Club. During the summer there was a major clear out of those players commanding relatively high wages. Jamie survived that cull but it was obvious that he would rather have been playing his football elsewhere. He expressed a desire to play for Thistle only if he could be guaranteed a free transfer at the end of the season. New manager Benny Rooney wasn't happy at that suggestion and as a result Doyle didn't feature at all in the first few months of the season.

It was late October before he made his first appearance, but within a month he got the transfer he had been wanting when he signed for Motherwell. The not long since departed Ian McDonald returned to Firhill as part of a swap deal, with Gregor Stevens also making the journey from Fir Park to Firhill.

Jamie didn't make as big an impact as he would have liked at Fir Park making just 37 League appearances in his time with Motherwell.

After leaving Motherwell, Doyle made a brief return to Firhill in the 1987-88 season, but was but a shadow of his former self.

He made just two first team appearances for Thistle second time around before departing for Aspell in Australia with Norwell Falcons, before joining Dumbarton. After spending a couple of seasons at Boghead Jamie moved to the junior ranks when he signed for Glenafton Athletic.

Appearances 217, goals 12.
Glasgow Cup winner 1981
Capped for Scotland Under 21s v Denmark 1981; v East Germany 1982; v Italy 1981,
Capped for Scottish League v Irish League 1980

ALEX ELLIOT

1927 - 1940

Born 10 January 1906 in Glasgow

Alex Elliot made his international debut in 1939 alongside the more recognised Peter McKennan and Alex McSpadyen. The Daily Record thought it ironic that *"a player who has consistently played above the average should have to wait so long for recognition"*. Indeed, it had been almost 12 years to the day since Alex had made his debut for Thistle, and during those years he had made his name as a hard working right-half who captained his club to its first taste of victory in the Glasgow Cup competition. Just a year and a half after his international debut he had retired from football – his 'overnight' success brought to a sudden end by the war.

Right-half had been a problem position for Thistle since Jamie Gibson moved from the right to play in the centre of the half-back line. James Richmond had filled in for a season but manager Easton was keen to bring in some extra competition, and had been watching Alex at Glasgow Perthshire for some time. The signing was made over the summer and Alex was regarded as the second choice right-half at the beginning of 1927-28 season. It was a poor start to the season defensively, with twenty goals lost by mid-September, and the half-back line was implicated. Richmond was dropped and Alex given his chance to shine, against Hamilton – and he took it with assurance - helping the team win 5-0. *"Elliot played an eminently useful game,"* said the Daily Record. From that game till the end of the season Alex didn't miss a single match.

Alex wasn't a showy player, but he was very clever on the ball, always looking to create something for his forwards with a clever pass. And he wasn't content just to knock the ball forward. Rather he would follow up, looking for a return pass and the opportunity to develop play further. Several generations of Thistle forwards benefited from his hard work – Davie Ness and Bobby Grove, Johnny Ballantyne, Willie Miller, Lachie McMillan, and McSpadyen plus McKennan, with whom he played some of his best football. And it wasn't just the right-sided forwards that benefited – Alex had perfected the crossfield pass, and was just as likely to set the left-winger in on goal as the one on the right.

As well as partnering with his attackers, Alex became known for his half-back collaborations with Alex Lambie and especially Eddie McLeod, with whom he became synonymous. *"Elliot and McLeod darted into the tackle without ever backing away, they brought the ball on, and their passes were wonderfully accurate,"* said the Daily Record in 1929.

Alex was an integral part of the Thistle team in the late 20s and early 30s, missing just 17 League games between 1928 and 1933, taking part in a Scottish Cup Final defeat in 1930, helping put Thistle to the top of the Scottish League for the first time ever in October 1930, and playing his part in a record twelve game winning run in 1932. The newspapers tipped him for international honours and his star was high.

It shocked Alex, then, and the football world in general, when Thistle offered poor re-signing terms in the summer of 1933. There were problems at Firhill and finances were tight. A number of players refused to re-sign, Alex among them. Willie Miller, prior to his 'Golden Miller' nickname and transfer to Everton, replaced Alex for the opening games, and didn't impress. *"Miller … he hasn't got the spunk of Elliot who goes all out all the time – Alec's a 90 minutes man,"* offered the Daily Record. After five successive losses of three goals in the first five games, Alex re-signed, along with Bobby Johnstone and Stewart Calderwood, and to reward him, Alex was appointed club captain.

Alex's period as captain was a successful one for the club, winning both the Glasgow and Charity Cups in 1934-35, although he did suffer losing his usual first team place to Hugh Baigrie for a spell in 1935, before winning back his place.

His steady, consistent play had begun to receive more considered attention from the selectors.

He had already played for Glasgow against Sheffield in 1928 and 1934, but it was his performances supporting McKennan and McSpadyen that had brought him international recognition. Come the League international against Ireland in 1938, Alex was almost an automatic choice, and a hugely popular one around the country too. Of course, if his rise to international prominence seemed remarkable to those outside Firhill, to those within the club it was just reward for his contributions to the club for over ten years.

McSpadyen and McKennan joined him in the team – Thistle's right-wing triangle would represent the Scottish League at Ibrox. Although Alex didn't get on the scoresheet both his Thistle team-mates did as Scotland won 6-1.

If here was a general impression that Alex had been an overnight international success his career at Firhill did end quickly. Although Jackie Husband was a highly regarded reserve, Alex was regarded as the first choice right-half at the start of the war in September 1939. However, he played just seven more times for the club, eventually completing over 450 games for them and retiring from football.

Appearances 454, goals 17.
Glasgow Cup winner 1934
Glasgow Charity Cup winner 1935
Capped for Scottish League v Irish League 1938.

TOMMY EWING

1955 - 1962 & 1964 - 1966

Born 2 May 1937 in Swinton

Standing at just 5' 6", but with the *"heart of a lion"*, outside left Tommy Ewing joined Thistle from Larkhall Thistle. His Thistle debut came against Raith Rovers in October 1955 and although Partick lost 1-2, Ewing clearly impressed as he was rarely out of the side for the remainder of the season or indeed, providing he was fit, for the duration of his time at Firhill.

The following season Ewing, who contributed some important goals on the way there, was part of the Thistle side that suffered defeat in a replayed League Cup Final against Celtic.

Earlier the same year injury forced him to pull out of the Scottish League side to face the Irish League but just over a year later he gained his first representative honour in the 1957 fixture with the Irish League. The Scottish League, as they invariably did in these fixtures, won easily with Ewing described as being *"anxious to make an impression"*.

He clearly did just that as later the same season he was capped at full international level for Scotland. A victory against Switzerland guaranteed Scotland a place in the World Cup Finals in Sweden but the Scotland performance did little to offer encouragement. So much so that when Scotland faced Wales a week later the introduction of Tommy Ewing was one of six changes that were made. His inclusion in the side was welcomed by all being described as *"small but stocky"* and *"not only clever but thrustful"*.

It didn't turn out to be the happiest of international debuts though. Scotland produced another poor performance and could only manage a 1-1 draw in front of a small Hampden crowd, with Ewing's performance labelled as *"immature"*.

Ewing was given a further chance, while stationed at Ayr with the Royal Scots Fusiliers as part of his National Service, to stake a claim for a place in the World Cup squad when in April of 1958 he lined up for Scotland against England at Hampden Park. Optimism in Scotland for this fixture was not high with an easy English win forecast. Those forecasts were proved accurate as England cantered to a 4-0 victory. Ewing started brightly and was at the heart of one of Scotland's few promising moves but as England took a grip of the game he was unable to make much impact. That would prove to be his second and final cap for Scotland and he didn't make the squad for Sweden.

The next few seasons for Ewing were marred by two cartilage operations and persistent knee problems. Although he played in the 1958 League Cup Final against Hearts his contributions were limited in the last few years of the 1950s.

In January 1962 the Thistle fans were rocked by the news that Ewing was on his way to Aston Villa. It was a bolt totally out of the blue.

~ 51 ~

Earlier in the season Thistle had turned down an offer from Fulham for Davie McParland and it was thought that Thistle weren't interested in selling their 'star' players. An early exit from the Scottish Cup at the hands of Stirling Albion changed all that though. After disposing of Hibs, Thistle had lofty hopes of lifting the 1962 Scottish Cup and were big favourites, though away from home, to eliminate Stirling. Ewing though was injured in the midweek prior to the cup-tie in a bruising encounter with Rangers at Ibrox and wasn't fit to face Stirling. Thistle lost 3-1 and a few days later an offer, thought to be in the region of £20,000, from Aston Villa was accepted and Ewing was on his way down south. Although the Club denied it, it was widely thought that Thistle's defeat at Stirling and subsequent financial pressures hastened Ewing's departure from Firhill.

Ewing spent two seasons with Aston Villa before returning to Thistle in the summer of 1964. If anything Ewing was thought to be an even better player than he had been prior to his departure, a fact borne out by the statistics in his first season back at Firhill. He missed just three games and topped the Thistle scoring charts with 23 goals including hat-tricks against Ayr United and Airdrieonians.

Season 1965-66 was altogether less successful with injury keeping Ewing out of the team for huge chunks of the season. His prodigal return to Firhill lasted just two seasons and the following season saw Ewing line-up in the colours of Morton. From Morton he moved to Hamilton eventually taking up the role of manager at Douglas Park.

Appearances 254, goals 80.
Capped for Scotland v England 1958; v Wales 1958.
Capped for Scottish League v Irish League 1957.

Alex Forsyth

1969 - 1972

Born 5 February 1952 in Swinton.

Full-back Forsyth joined Thistle from Arsenal, where he had been an apprentice professional, in 1969 and made his debut while just 17 in a fixture against Dundee during Thistle's inauspicious League Cup campaign of 1969. That substitute appearance would be his solitary first team appearance in Thistle's relegation season of 1969-70. Indeed he featured only at the very beginning and then again at the very end of the following season as well as the club bounced back to the First Division.

Season 1971-72 though was an entirely different story. Forsyth managed just one start in August of that season but from September onwards he played in all but one of Thistle's remaining fixtures that included, of course, the 1971 League Cup Final. Forsyth wore his usual number three jersey that most famous of afternoons.

Forsyth's consistently excellent form in a Thistle side that were making people sit up and take notice earned him, and team mate Denis McQuade, a cap for the Scottish League when they played their English counterparts at Ayresome Park, Middlesbrough in March 1972. The interest in such fixtures at that time can be reflected in the fact that only a shade under 20,000 saw the Scottish League lose by the odd goal in five.

Back at Firhill it was an exciting time to be a young player.

A Thistle side had played against the Scotland National Team as part of their preparation for a Hampden international fixture and number of Partick players caught the eye of the then Scotland boss Tommy Docherty. In the summer of 1972 Forsyth won the first of four full international caps he would win as a Partick Thistle player. Scotland had been invited to Brazil to participate in the Independence Cup tournament and Forsyth pulled on a Scotland jersey against Yugoslavia as he did a few days later against Czechoslovakia.

The highlight of the South America trip though was a fixture with the then World Cup holders Brazil. A crowd of 130,000 assembled in Rio de Janeiro and were delighted when the home side won 1-0. It was Scotland though that earned most of the after-match plaudits. Forsyth was reported as being *"outstanding in defence"* with the Brazilian press labelling him a superstar.

Forsyth's fourth and final cap as a Thistle player came early the following season when he and Jimmy Bone lined up together for a fixture against Denmark. Both Forsyth and Bone therefore hold the honour of being, to date, the most recent Thistle outfield players to be capped for Scotland.

The break-up of the successful Thistle side that had begun with Jimmy Bone's transfer to Norwich City in February 1972 continued the following season.

Given his obvious admiration of Thistle's young full-back it was hardly a surprise when, in December 1972, Tommy Docherty signed him for Manchester United once he took over at Old Trafford. The reported transfer fee of £100,000, somewhat cushioned the blow of his departure at Firhill.

Forsyth would remain at Old Trafford, a loan period at Rangers aside, until 1978. United though weren't then the force that they later became. Indeed at the end of season 1973-74, Forsyth's first full season at Old Trafford, they were relegated to the Second Division. They bounced back at the first attempt and it was during that season that Forsyth would feature most regularly in the United first team, making a total of 39 appearances. He also featured in the 1976 FA Cup Final when United lost to Southampton.

He, however, missed out the next season when United defeated Liverpool to lift the cup.

While with Manchester United Forsyth was able to further his international career by adding a further six caps to the four he won as a Thistle player. He wasn't selected though as part of the Scotland squad that went to the 1974 World Cup Finals in Germany.

After a loan spell with Rangers he moved permanently to Ibrox in 1979 before playing with Motherwell, Hamilton Accies and, on loan, with Queen of the South. He then moved to the juniors spending a number of seasons with Blantyre Victoria.

Forsyth made a return to Firhill in the 1990s where for a brief period he was Thistle's Youth team coach.

Appearances 110, goals 9.
League Cup winner 1971
Second Division Championship winner 1970-71
Capped for Scotland v Brazil 1972;
v Czechoslovakia 1972; v Denmark 1973; v Yugoslavia 1972.
Capped for Scottish League v English League 1972
Other honours
With Manchester United: 6 Scotland international appearances,
1 Scotland Under 23 appearance,
English League Second Division winner 1974-75.

BOBBY GIBB
1949 - 1957

Born 5th February 1922 in Bo'ness

29 January 1949 was a significant date in the history of Partick Thistle Football Club. Thistle didn't win a trophy that afternoon or indeed win their League fixture with Rangers but that afternoon Thistle boss David Meiklejohn handed Thistle debuts to two players who between them would play a combined total of 625 times for the club. Alex Wright would make 351 of those appearances and the other, Bobby Gibb, 274.

Gibb arrived at Firhill from his local side, Bo'ness United juniors, and the left-back was very much thrown in at the deep end on his Thistle debut. As well as playing in front of 50,000 spectators at Ibrox Gibb was in direct opposition to Rangers' Willie Waddell. Rangers would win the First Division Championship that season and would fail to win at home on just four occasions. The 2-2 draw that Thistle recorded against Rangers on Gibb's debut was, therefore, a more than creditable result. Gibb, who had been performing well for the Thistle reserve side prior to his call up to the first team, was reported to have *"played well"* and *"held up Waddell"*. In fact so impressive was Gibb's debut at left back that the regular defender in that position for the last few months, Alex Pirrie, was unable to get his place back in the side. It was a game that was to make Gibb's reputation and was regularly referred to later in his career.

Gibb, who the Daily Record told us *"kicks attractively with either foot, tackles firmly and judiciously, and is seldom caught off balance"* would remain firmly part of the Firhill scene for the next eight seasons, developing a muscular full-back partnership with Jimmy McGowan. A broken jaw in pre-season training in the summer kept Gibb out of the Thistle side for the first few weeks of the 1949-50 season but once he was fit enough to take up his left-back berth in the Thistle side he was more or less a permanent feature in the Thistle team and was the recipient of frequent praise, being described, amongst other things, as being *"fleet footed"* and possessing *"studied, clean kicking"*.

The 1950s were an exciting decade for Partick Thistle and the name of Bobby Gibb, a *"bold courageous defender"*, is just one that is synonymous with that era. Three times in that decade, in 1951 (for the first time in 11 years), 1952 and 1954 Thistle lifted the Glasgow Cup, with Gibb part of the victorious side on each of those three occasions.

The club equalled its highest ever League position of third in season 1953-54 with Gibb playing 17 times and latterly that season sharing the left-back duties with Andy Kerr. It was in the League Cup though that Thistle had their greatest success and disappointments. Gibb was part of the Thistle side that contested the 1953 final against East Fife and the 1956 final against Celtic; Thistle lost out on both occasions.

In Gibb's Thistle career he scored just two goals. The second of those two goals came in a 3-1 Scottish Cup win against Brechin City in February 1955.

The first was scored six years earlier in a League Cup-tie against Dundee. It was the final sectional match, with Thistle requiring a win to reach the last eight of the competition. A crowd of 30,000, by no means unusual in those days, were at Firhill to witness a tie that was finely poised at 2-2. Gibb was moving up the pitch to support Willie Sharp when the ball broke towards him. The Dundee defenders didn't sense danger when Gibb approached the ball lackadaisically and swung a left boot at it.

The ball fairly screamed into the net and with the Thistle fans in uproar, Gibb danced a jig of delight. Thistle went on to qualify for the quarter finals.

Gibb's final appearance in the Thistle first team came on 23 February 1957 in an away fixture against Dundee at Dens Park. After leaving Firhill he had a spell playing with East Stirling.

Appearances 274, goals 2.
Glasgow Cup winner 1951, 1952, 1954.

JAMES (JAMIE) GIBSON

1921 - 1927

Born 12 June 1901 in Larkhall. Died 1 January 1978.

"Gibson is Partick Thistle and Partick Thistle is Gibson". (Daily Record 7 February 1927)

Jamie Gibson was often known as the saviour of Partick Thistle. Whether as a wholehearted defensive half-back or as a dangerous complement to the forward line, pushing up and letting go with a rocket shot, Jamie was one of Thistle's, and Scotland's best players of the 1920s.

And when Thistle were in financial trouble, struggling to find the money to complete the new stand at Firhill in 1927, the transfer fee from Aston Villa helped to put the club back in the black and on a sound financial footing. Both on and off the field Jamie Gibson was the saviour of Partick Thistle.

When Jamie arrived at Firhill in 1921 he came with a ready-made reputation as the son of

Thistle and Scotland legend Neilly Gibson, who played at Firhill 15 or so years before. Jamie signed from Ashfield at the same time as his brother Neil, as Thistle built on the Scottish Cup success of the previous year by strengthening the squad. After a few games in the reserves Jamie was given his chance in the first team, replacing David Johnstone at right-half, against Aberdeen at Firhill. He made a good impression, getting forward to shoot, and supplying Jamie Kinloch and John Blair with good passes up the right side of the pitch.

Jamie normally played at half-back, either on the right or the left, and as befits the natural footballer he was, able to fit into a number of other positions, covering at both full-back, centre-half, either inside-forward jerseys and centre-forward. From whatever position, Jamie loved to get forward to try his luck at goal, and he scored a remarkable number of goals given his regular position. His shooting from distance in particular troubled goalkeepers, and in a time when free-kicks were generally direct shots at goal, Jamie and his team-mates were clever enough to try variations to trick defences, taking short free-kicks and using space to work better positions for shots. The Daily Record was impressed after a game against Rangers in February 1922.

> *"This lanky son of 'Auld Neilly' made a first rate appearance both in defence and attack. Jamie shoves forward a good ball – he can shoot. What a shock he gave Robb just before the turn-about. Gibson's terrific free-kick almost knocked the Ranger off his feet."*

6' 1" tall, and not heavily built, in defence Jamie relied on timing, and his long legs, but this didn't mean he lacked effort.

"Built like a giraffe but he has a heart of a lion" was one description of him in his early career.

In his early days at Firhill he was often injured, a result of his eagerness to get forward; his physical build meant he was prone to heavy tackles from opponents. However, by 1924 he had brought some needed consistency to his game, teaming up with Jamie McMullan and Alex Lambie along the half-back line, attracting attention for representative games. In September 1924 Jamie was selected for Glasgow's team to play Sheffield. Kinloch and Tom Crichton also played in a 5-0 win for Glasgow. This game was soon followed by calls for international recognition, selection in the international trial in 1925, and a cap for the Scottish League against the Irish League in November 1925 – a 7-3 win for Scotland at Cliftonville.

With the responsibility of the club captaincy in 1925-26 came the need to cover a number of positions, most notably left-back when Crichton and Alex Donald were injured, but it was generally felt that being played out of position was a waste of Jamie's talents. Luckily the SFA selectors knew his best position, and after making a scoring return to right-half in April 1926, a number of months since playing his preferred position, he was selected for Scotland against England at Old Trafford.

Playing alongside McMullan (the players lined up beside each other in the team photo), Jamie looked nervy in the early stages before settling down and playing his normal game, helping Scotland to a 1-0 win in the 50th game between the two sides.

Club and country form inevitably led to interest being shown by English clubs in securing Jamie's transfer.

Newcastle and Liverpool led the swarm of English managers knocking on George Easton's office door, leading the manager to state, *"we are selling no players, and will not sell any meantime"*. The pursuers were persistent, and Everton offered £4,000. Chairman Tom Reid responded, *"that wouldn't pay for the big fellow's boots"*, and in an attempt to scare the English away, quoted a price of £10,000 – a huge figure in those days.

Although Jamie was reckoned to be the highest paid player in Scotland, he couldn't fail to be tempted by the big money that was being offered in England, he was content to continue at Firhill, and at the start of the 1926-27 season he had moved to centre-half to cover an injury to Lambie.

He was a natural in the middle, his height giving him an obvious advantage; playing some of his best football he chipped in with ten goals from his defensive position. He had played one international that season, against Wales, at right-half, but it was testament to his abilities that he was selected for Scotland in his new club position. He played in three internationals in 1927, against Ireland and the English League, and also teamed up again with his old team-mate McMullan against England. Jamie also turned out for Glasgow against Sheffield early in the season at centre-half in a game played at Firhill.

Although Thistle had stated their desire to keep Jamie at Firhill, a new stand was under construction, and money was short at the bank to pay for it. As the season came to an end chairman Reid began to listen to serious offers for his players, and Jamie in particular. When Aston Villa made an offer of £7,500 (a world record at the time) Thistle were tempted, but cheekily asked for a little more. When Villa came back with an £8,000 offer Thistle accepted, and Jamie was transferred to England. The stand was completed, paid for, and opened a few months later.

Jamie became part of a formidable half-back line affectionately known as "Wind, Sleet and Rain" - Jamie, Alec Talbot and Joe Tate were all six footers – that helped Villa finish as runners-up in the English League in 1930 and 1933. Jamie was a stalwart at Villa Park, playing 225 times, and continuing his international career, although he was denied the opportunity of a return to Firhill to play for Scotland against Ireland in 1928 due to club commitments. He did, though, play again for Scotland, most notably alongside McMullan as part of the Wembley Wizards team of 1928.

Villa were relegated at the end of the 1935-36 season, and Jamie took the opportunity to retire from football at the age of 35.

Appearances 204, goals 54.
Capped for Scotland v England 1926, 1927;
v Ireland 1927; v Wales 1927.
Capped for Scottish League v English
League 1927; v Irish League 1925.
Other honours
With Aston Villa
4 Scotland international appearances

JOHNNY GIBSON

1968 - 1975

Born 23 December 1950 in Hull.

Recruited from Clydebank Strollers in 1968, Johnny Gibson's claim to fame was that as Thistle's substitute in the 1971 League Cup final. It would be wrong to single that one afternoon out of a Thistle career that only ended after he had pulled on a Thistle jersey after over 150 occasions.

Gibson made his Thistle debut against Rangers in the opening League game of the 1968-69 season and although he scored his first Thistle goal the following week in a 4-0 win against Clyde he made just three appearances that season. He remained on the fringes of the first team the following season as well and as Thistle won the Second Division title in 1970-71 the bulk of Gibson's contribution came via the substitute bench.

Arguably Gibson's finest performance as a Partick Thistle player came in the opening League game of the 1971-72 season against Rangers. Prior to kick-off, the Second Division championship flag was unfurled in front of the Thistle supporters, but there was better to come for the fans. Rangers took an early lead but inspired by Johnny Gibson Thistle raced to a 3-1 lead. Gibson scored two of those goals and set up the other one for Frank Coulston. Although Thistle would go on to win 3-2 Gibson's contribution was limited to just the first 45 minutes as an injury sustained in the first half resulted in early and enforced substitution.

Injury unfortunately features large in the career of Johnny Gibson and it was another injury, this time sustained in a meeting with Kilmarnock just a few weeks before the League Cup Final, that meant that he had to content himself with a place on the bench during the most famous afternoon in Thistle's history. That match with Kilmarnock came just two days before the semi-final with Falkirk leaving Gibson a major doubt for the game. Johnny in an interview some years later takes up the story.... *"Davie McParland left it up to me to say if I was fit or not and I said that I didn't feel quite right and what happens? Big Denis McQuade comes in and scores two goals."*

Not surprisingly after scoring twice in the semi-final McQuade kept his place in the team and Gibson had to miss out. That's not to say that he didn't still have a role to play in Thistle's victory. With Thistle 4-1 up and with a little over 15 minutes to play Gibson was sent on for Ronnie Glavin. Gibson's involvement in the final may have been a fairly brief one but it was still a significant one. One newspaper, while understandably focusing on Thistle's amazing first half display, felt that Gibson *"contributed to playing out time with his skilful holding of the ball"*.

The strengths in Gibson's game lay in his ability to bring the ball down and beat players and the player admitted once he had retired that an injury sustained in a fixture against

Dumbarton severely impaired his ability to do just that. Although Gibson would remain in the senior game until season 1981-82 his career is one that perhaps didn't quite match its early potential.

His final appearance as a Partick Thistle player came on October 12th 1974 when Thistle played Dumbarton. A few days after that fixture he was off to Ayr United, moving to Somerset Park as part of a swap deal that took Dougie Somner and Dave Mitchell to Firhill.

After leaving Firhill, Gibson enjoyed a somewhat nomadic football career. His first port of call, as we have seen, was Ayr United and he also had spells with St Mirren, Celtic, East Fife, Forfar Athletic and Stirling Albion.

Stirling was his last senior team but not the end of his football career, for he then sampled life in the junior grade with Sauchie before eventually retiring from playing.

Appearances 158, goals 18.
League Cup Winner 1971
Second Division Championship Winner 1970-71

NEIL GIBSON

1904 – 1909

Born 23 February 1873 in Larkhall.

Partick Thistle shocked the footballing world by signing Neil Gibson in September 1904. Gibson had played for Rangers for ten years, having joined from his local junior team - Larkhall Royal Albert. Within a year of signing for Rangers, Gibson had been capped twice for Scotland – an international career that saw him play 13 times while at Ibrox, six of these against England, and many of them alongside Alex Raisbeck (at that time still at Liverpool). In his time at Rangers he gained the reputation as the greatest right half Scotland had ever seen, and won four Scottish League medals, three Scottish Cup winners medals and over 370 first team appearances.

Although he was still a regular in Rangers half-back line as the season ended in 1904, his announcement that he was joining Partick Thistle gave lazy journalists the chance to speculate that Neilly was winding down; looking for an easy way to end his career.

What nobody expected was that Thistle would be getting a player that would continue to develop his career and continue playing at the highest level for a further five years.

Gibson was small for a half-back, almost lightweight, but made up for that with his speed and anticipation. His partnership with full-back Tom Harvey gave Thistle an almost unbeatable defence down the right side for a number of years – his ferocious tackling and recovery skills giving great cover to his defenders.

It wasn't all one-way either, and the forwards who played in front of him were always glad of the accurate passes coming towards them from the middle of the park.

As well as being a tidy, sound player, he played with a cocky edge to his game. He was known for a clever trick – if the ball was too high to be reached with the head, he would allow it to fall behind him, and before it touched the ground, he would back-heel it back over his head with the back of his boot, with a confused opponent running past him looking for the ball.

It had been a poor start to season 1904-05 – Thistle had lost 15 goals in the opening three League games. Neil moved from Rangers in a double signing along with George Gilchrist, and both players made their Thistle debut three days later, in a 2-0 Glasgow Cup win over Clyde in September 1904. Neil was immediately made captain of the team and stopped the rot, before being the inspiration for an eight match winning spell that took Thistle to third top of the League table. The captain and his teammates were presented with gold watches in recognition of the exciting run.

Not content with pushing Thistle up the table, Gibson still had international ambitions, despite being told by the SFA in 1901 that he would never play for his country again after snubbing Scotland to attend a relative's funeral.

However, he returned from international exile when recognition came for his fine club form in the shape of his fourteenth Scotland cap four years after his previous one. Added to the honour was the additional award of the captaincy of his country. Alongside his club goalkeeper Willie Howden the Thistle players helped Scotland to a 4-0 win over Ireland at Parkhead in March 1905.

This was to be Neil's last Scotland cap, but he continued to play a vital role for Thistle. The end of 1905-06 saw Thistle finish in their highest League position ever – fifth and two points off third – helped by two vital goals from Neil to clinch important 1-0 wins over Dundee and Morton. Fans, officials and journalists were amazed to see Neil continue his sprightly style of play throughout the season and into the next in spite of a potentially risky eye operation in the summer of 1906.

However, age was catching up with Neil. Injuries didn't clear up as quickly as they used to, and throughout 1907-08 and 1908-09 he began to miss as many games as he played in due to fitness.

When it was revealed to Gibson that Thistle intended signing Welsh international half-back Maurice Parry during the summer of 1909, Neil decided the time was right for his retirement from first-class football. In a nice display of symmetry Gibson left Partick Thistle for his junior club Royal Albert, and laterally Wishaw Thistle. Neil continued playing at junior level for four years before giving up playing the game.

He continued having a close interest in the game through his three sons. Neil junior played with Thistle and Clyde, Willie won an FA Cup winners medal with Newcastle in 1924, while Neil's third son, Jimmy, signed and played with distinction for Thistle, Aston Villa and Scotland.

Appearances 140, goals 8.
Capped for Scotland v Ireland 1905 (captain).

Other honours
With Rangers
4 Scottish League winners medals,
3 Scottish Cup winners medals,
13 Scotland international appearances.

RONNIE GLAVIN

1968 - 1974

Born 27 March 1951 in Glasgow.

Ronnie Glavin arrived at Firhill from Lochend Rovers and his first introduction to regular first team football was hardly in ideal circumstances. At the end of the 1969-70 season Thistle found themselves relegated from the First Division with the then 18 year old Glavin struggling to make a huge impact in what was naturally a poor Thistle team. He did, however, score the first of his 55 Thistle goals that season netting in successive weeks against Motherwell and Dundee although Thistle lost both of those fixtures.

The following season saw Davie McParland assume the role of Thistle manager and Glavin wasn't the only young star to flourish under his tutelage. Only East Fife presented any real challenge to Thistle's title aspirations that season but Partick still comfortably finished above them as they topped the division. Glavin's contribution, playing in just over half of Thistle's fixtures, was eleven goals.

There was even better just round the corner for Thistle. In October 1971 McParland's largely young team lifted the League Cup defeating Celtic 4-1. Glavin's role that afternoon was to snuff out the threat of Celtic's Jimmy Johnstone - a task he performed with great robustness.

One of the great disappointment's in Thistle's history is the fact that the side that won the League Cup started to break up almost immediately after lifting the trophy. Glavin though remained at Firhill for a number of seasons.

He was Thistle's top scorer in season 1972-73 with 16 goals and topped the scoring charts the following season as well with 13. Rumours abounded though that Glavin would soon be on his way out of Firhill.

The mounting transfer speculation surrounding Glavin finally became something more tangible in November 1974. There was reported strong interest in Glavin from England, but when he did finally leave Firhill it was to a venue much closer to hand. After pulling on a Thistle jersey for the very last time at Aberdeen on 9 November he joined Celtic a few days later. The reported fee of £80,000 was then a Club record fee paid by Celtic. How times have changed in that respect.

While at Parkhead, Glavin was able to add to the medals he won while a Partick Thistle player. He helped Celtic to the Premier Division title in 1977 and was also part of the Celtic side that lifted the Scottish Cup in 1975.

Despite over 200 appearances for Thistle, he appeared to come to the attention of Scotland for the very first time only as a Celtic player, for whilst at Firhill he was neither capped at full or under 23 level for Scotland. Nor did he get the opportunity to represent the Scottish League. While a Celtic player, however, he was capped for Scotland in a fixture with Sweden at Hampden Park in 1977. Lining up in the same side as a former Thistle team mate Alan Rough, Glavin played his part in Scotland's 3-1 win.

Before joining Celtic rumours had been strong that Glavin would leave Thistle to move south to England. In 1978 he did just that when he signed for Barnsley for a fee of £40,000. He proved to be a massive hit in Yorkshire and is still considered as something of a hero by the Barnsley fans. He twice helped Barnsley to promotion and in total he scored 92 times for them - a total that puts him high up in the list of their all time goalscorers.

After leaving Barnsley he spent time in Portugal with Belenenses before returning to England to take up a player coach with old club Barnsley and a similar role with Stockport County, before a short spell with Cowdenbeath.

Ronnie finished his playing career in the USA with St. Louis Steamrollers where he wrote a children's coaching manual *"How to play Soccer."*

He took his first steps into football management as boss of non-League Frickley Athletic in 1991 before moving to Emley in 1994. While boss at Emley he took them on a run in the 1998 FA Cup that took them all the way to the Third Round where they only lost narrowly at West Ham United.

Glavin returned to Barnsley in 2003 as assistant manager before, in 2004 until 2006, becoming manager of Worksop Town.

Appearances 224, goals 55.
League Cup winner 1971
Second Division Championship winner 1969-70

Other honours
With Celtic
1 Scottish League winners medals,
1 Scottish Cup winners medals, 1 Scotland international appearance.

Robert Gray

1896 - 1899 & 1902 - 1907

Robert Gray was a popular inside forward who played 215 times for Thistle over two spells at Inchview and Meadowside, and became a favourite with supporters for his exciting forward play and goalscoring.

Robert was a speedy player who also had excellent ball control and was noted for his shooting from distance. He scored 45 goals during his two spells with the club.

Gray began his career with junior side Lenzie FC, where he played alongside William Ward, who was later to become President of the Scottish League and a director of Partick Thistle. Gray came to Thistle's attention after he played for the Scottish Junior select and joined the club towards the end of the 1896-97 season, making his debut against Kilmarnock in a Second Division match at Inchview Park.

From the start of the following season he was a regular for the club that was playing in the First Division for the first time, having been promoted at the end of the previous season, and he ended that campaign with six goals in ten League games. Gray played in a number of inside and outside forward positions, including making up a successful right wing partnership with veteran Willie Paul, before Everton signed him at the end of the 1898-99 season.

At Everton he joined up with another ex-Thistle favourite John Proudfoot, and played 20 games for the Goodison team, winning a Liverpool Cup winners medal. He also had spells at Nottingham Forest and Southampton during his three years in England.

Robert had come home to Kirkintilloch, and his job as a foundry worker, by the start of the 1902-03 season, and Thistle were keen to have him rejoin the club who had just been promoted again from the Second Division to the First.

At Meadowside he joined up with Tom Harvey, Willie Howden, Andy Wilson and his ex-Everton teammates William Massie and Proudfoot, who were also in their second spells with Thistle.

These important players made up the backbone of the side that brought four seasons of success for the club. After establishing themselves in the First Division they went on to create a club record of eight successive victories in 1904-05, which took them to the brink of the top of the table. The following season saw further improvements and a final position just two points off third place in the League.

Robert's artistic footwork and intelligent passing from inside left particularly helped Sam Kennedy score over 70 goals as they made up a feared partnership. In his two spells with Thistle he had played with and helped the two best centre forwards that Partick had ever seen.

At the end of the 1907-08 season Robert retired from playing football, joining Kirkintilloch Rob Roy as a committee member in 1909.

Appearances 216, goals 45.

BOBBY GROVE

1922 - 1933

Born 10 November 1902 in Shettleston, Glasgow.

Feelings ran high at Fir Park on 29 October 1932 in the game between Partick Thistle and Motherwell. Thistle right-half Bobby Grove was tackled by his opponent and hurt, fell to the ground. As Bobby received treatment from the doctor, unkind comments were shouted from the Motherwell supporters. Concerned team-mate John Torbet was incensed; picking up the ball he volleyed it towards those making the heartless comments. Unsurprisingly this didn't calm the situation, tempers were raised and the police were called to calm things down, but Torbet's worries were justified when Bobby Grove was carried from the pitch with a compound fracture of his right leg above the ankle.

Bobby Grove joined Partick Thistle from his local junior side Shettleston in November 1922 as a big, strong inside forward, capable of playing either on the right or the left of the forward line, but was unable to earn a first team jersey due to the sparkling form of Johnny Ballantyne and Jimmy Kinloch. Bobby spent his first season as a professional footballer learning his trade in the reserve team.

1923-24 season saw Bobby get his chance in the first team due to an unfortunate injury to Kinloch. He grabbed it and helped Thistle to the top half of the League table by the end of the season, scoring seven goals. The following season, with Ballantyne having emigrated to America, Bobby became first choice inside-left.

He combined well with Willie Salisbury on his left, with Davie Ness and Kinloch on his right, and was well liked by players and fans alike for his hard work. His height, too, was an advantage and he was always dangerous when attacking - late runs into the box being his speciality. As well as his hard work and strength, Bobby was known for his skill, bamboozling defenders with feints and shimmys as he ran with the ball at his feet, and he delighted in tricking his opponents with unexpected backheels.

Bobby's club form won recognition from the Glasgow FA, and he was chosen to represent the city in a game against Sheffield in September 1926. He and Davie Ness combined well on the right, and helped Glasgow to a 2-0 win.

Bobby's understanding with, and service to, Sandy Hair helped the centre-forward to an extraordinary goals tally of 49 for the season in 1926-27. Perhaps the pair combined to the best effect in the Charity Cup Final against Rangers in May 1927. Bobby scored one and set Hair up with two of his five goals as Thistle triumphed 6-3 at Hampden.

Consistency had been an important part of Bobby's game, and he had been invaluable across the forward line since his debut, so he was a big miss for the team when he suffered an injury in September 1928. An inflamed toe kept Bobby out of the side for most of the 1928-29 season.

When he regained fitness he returned to a side that now included a returned-from-America Ballantyne and Willie 'Golden' Miller competing for the inside-forward jerseys. For the next few years Bobby had to be content with playing the part of a squad player, filling in when Ballantyne and Miller were unavailable, and also dropping back to good effect to play at right-half when Alex Elliot was injured. His strength was useful, but it was his passing that often caught the eye. His experience of playing as a forward meant he know the value of passing along the ground, and Torbet, and Ness especially, got the benefit of inch perfect passes as Bobby took every opportunity to spread the play around the pitch.

Despite the fact that the leg break that Bobby suffered at Motherwell was a bad one, he retained hope that he would be able to resume his career again. Unfortunately that was not to be, and Bobby was finally forced to accept the end of his playing career during the summer of 1934. Motherwell generously offered to play in a benefit match to raise funds for Bobby, and ungenerously won the game 5-0, but the score was unimportant. It was a sad end to a distinguished career.

Bobby Grove remained involved in football, scouting for Partick Thistle, before retiring from the game.

Appearances 289, goals 60.
Glasgow Charity Cup winner 1927

ALEX (SANDY) HAIR

1923 - 1928

Born 9 March 1898 in Bridgeton, Glasgow. Died 31 May 1970.

Sandy Hair had a veritable career of two halves at Firhill, both of them successful in their own way. In his first spell, between August 1923 and November 1924 he was top scorer and scored six goals in a Scottish Cup-tie. In his second spell, from August 1926 until he finally left the club in October 1928, Sandy was in explosive form, scoring 49 goals in 1926-27 (including five against Rangers in one game), a record for a Partick Thistle player in any one season.

Sandy began his career at Strathclyde Juniors, when he signed as a 14 year old – the club's youngest ever signing. He remained at Strathclyde, making a name for himself as a prolific scorer in the junior ranks, ending the 1922-23 season with 96 goals.

His remarkable scoring reputation had been interesting Partick Thistle for some time and in the summer of 1923 Alex made the step up to senior football.

He made an instant impact on the team at centre-forward, leading the team to three wins in a row, culminating in his first goals for the club – both in a momentous 2-1 win over Celtic at Parkhead. There were perhaps some rough edges to his play, no doubt honed in the juniors, his 'arm play' in particular being penalised by referees, but he was keen and eager, and he combined well with Jamie Kinloch and Johnny Ballantyne beside him, and Willie Salisbury and Davie Ness on the wings. Sandy became known for his unconventional style of passing – he rarely made the easy pass, and always looked for the killer ball to send his team-mates in on goal.

He was a popular player with the fans and his colleagues for his never-say-die perseverance and effort, particularly in September and October when he scored in six consecutive games to lift Thistle towards the top of the League. His finest hour-and-a-half in his first season came in the Scottish Cup. Although the minnows from Dunkeld and Birnam, helped by Thistle legend Frank Branscombe, were not expected to trouble Thistle the goals still had to be scored. And score Sandy did – six times. This was a record for a Thistle player in one game, and at times the entire team appeared to be trying to set Sandy up for another goal. The final score was 11-0.

The season ended successfully for Thistle and for Sandy. The team were in eighth place and Sandy had netted 25 in 40 games, but his team-mates hadn't added greatly to his goals. In the first few games of the following season the Thistle forward line came in for some fierce criticism, with Sandy in particular being singled out. Veteran centre-forward John Miller was signed from Aberdeen, and Sandy's, thus far, explosive Thistle career came stuttering to a standstill.

Sandy was keen to continue playing, and manager Easton could still see the potential, so was keen to retain Sandy's registration. There were a number of clubs interested in having Sandy play for them, but he favoured Queen of the South, then in the 3rd Division, and he went on to have a great impact with the Doonhamers. In helping them to promotion he scored 18 League goals in 19 games, and had managed 30 goals by the time he was recalled to Firhill in time for the Charity Cup competition. Despite a Sandy goal in the semi-final Thistle went out of the competition to Rangers.

His spell in the lower League had done him no harm but he still started the season as the second choice centre-forward. He was given an opportunity to win his place back with a goal against Raith Rovers in the League and a good performance in the Glasgow Cup replay against Celtic in September 1925, creating chances for his fellow forwards. However, a bad injury meant that his stop-start Thistle career was again at 'stop'. After a brief spell of recuperation Sandy was back on the road looking for match practice and a regular game.

In that 1925-26 season, he turned out for Third Lanark, Alloa and Bo'ness, all in the 2nd Division. He returned to Firhill again at the end of the season for his Charity Cup game – with another goal, and another defeat, this time to Celtic.

John Miller departed, back to Aberdeen, and Sandy was again Thistle's first choice to lead the forwards, where he was determined to prove himself again. He began as he continued, with a goal in the first game of the season against Falkirk, and from then the numbers added up to an astonishing 49 goals for the season.

Three in August and five in September were followed by ten goals in October, including four against both Hibs and Dunfermline.

The goals then slowed up, with only four in November and just one in December, then four in January, five in February, three in March and an impressive seven in April. This brought the total to 42 by the time the League season ended, with Thistle in eleventh position, but having scored more goals than all but two other teams. Indeed only Jamie Gibson and Johnny Torbet managed double figures and had Sandy had more support Thistle surely would have totalled over a hundred goals.

Although the League season was over, Sandy's goals hadn't stopped. In his favoured Charity Cup competition he got two against Clyde in the semi, and in the final against Rangers he scored twice again to take the game to extra time, where he added an incredible three more to land Thistle the Cup for the first time. Sandy was presented with the match ball, a trophy and a clock by various grateful supporters after the game.

49 goals in one season is truly a superb feat, but Sandy was quick to point out the support he received from his team-mates. He received great service from his wingers Ness and Torbet, but he especially appreciated the passing through the middle from half-backs Gibson and Jimmy Richmond.

Unfortunately, bad luck struck again in 1927-28 season as Sandy would have been hoping to get amongst the goals again. Injury struck and he missed much of the season, but still managed to score six goals in 13 games.

Fit again at the start of the following season in September, Sandy started as he had done in his golden season – two against Motherwell, four against St Johnstone, five against Hamilton, and another against Clyde, meant that interest was coming from England, and in October 1928 Sandy was transferred to Preston North End for £2,200.

At Deepdale Sandy teamed up with the legendary Alex James, and top-scored for his new team with 19, ending the season on tour in the USA, before a financial dispute meant both players left Preston. Following his time at Preston Sandy joined Shelbourne in Dublin in 1930-31, where he won the League and cup double and was the top goalscorer in the League with 35.

He then moved to Worcester City, Colwyn Bay and Shirley Town in English non-Leagues circles, before retiring from football in 1937, when he returned to Glasgow.

Appearances 120, goals 98.
Glasgow Charity Cup winner 1927

WILLIAM HAMILTON

1911 - 1921

Born 9 October 1889 in Cowdenbeath. Died 16 August 1921.

Willie Hamilton was devastated when he realised he was going to miss the Scottish Cup final in April 1921. An injury sustained against Hamilton the week before was to keep him out of the Thistle side in the most important game of the club's history.

In almost 10 years of service Willie had come close to success on a number of occasions. The big centre-half had been a vital part of the teams that had finished as runners-up in Glasgow Cup finals in 1911, 1915, 1917 and 1919, and in Glasgow Charity Cup finals in 1916 and 1918. Desire was high at Firhill that a final should be won, for a change.

In that charge to Parkhead for the final in 1921, Willie was a steadying force in the middle of the Thistle team, alongside the creativity of long-time teammates Joe Harris and Jamie McMullan. From the start of the season in August 1920 he had been troubled by injury, missing the odd game along the way, but he returned to the side for the second replay against Hibernian in February and looked fit and healthy enough. The Scottish campaign was long and drawn out – the quarter final against Motherwell went to two replays, as did the semi against Hearts, and the extra games couldn't have been good for an ageing centre-half. Willie didn't show it, though, and manager Easton helped by resting him in League matches between the cup-ties.

His form, alongside Harris and McMullan, had taken Thistle to third top of the League, and some serious lobbying of the international selectors was happening – advocating Scotland take on England at Hampden with Thistle's entire half-back line in place. Only McMullan got the call.

Willie was inspirational in the cup games against the more fancied Motherwell and Hearts teams, being named man of the match against Motherwell in the first replay as Thistle battled defensively. He also had a great game in the third playing of the semi final, and there was great relief for the big man when Thistle eventually qualified for the final after 10 gruelling ties.

Joe Harris picked up a knock in the semi, and Willie had to turn out against Hamilton in the League just three days after the semi, despite being tired. There he too picked up an injury. The final was just a week away, Willie didn't recover, and the injury was to keep him out of the Thistle side in the most important game of his life, and the club's history.

Willie watched the final from the stand as Thistle won the cup, no doubt delighted for his replacement Matt Wilson and his teammates, but also deeply disappointed that he wasn't out playing himself.

Willie had joined Thistle from Dunfermline Athletic in September 1911 as a versatile half-back, wishing his Fife mates best of luck in a Qualifying Cup-tie with a lucky black and white horseshoe. He immediately made his debut in a 3-0 win over Celtic, deputising for the injured captain Alex Raisbeck at centre-half. The youngster was signed as cover and expected to play in the reserves for some time, but injuries to Raisbeck and Alex McGregor meant he quickly gained first team experience.

Had Willie played for Thistle in a different era he would undoubtedly have made more appearances, but injuries, and Raisbeck's immovable presence at centre-half, meant that his first team appearances were limited in his early time at Firhill. He was, though, a vital member of the squad, filling in when needed, and leading the successful Thistle reserve team to win the Second XI League Championship in 1912 and the Glasgow Reserve Cup in 1914.

With Raisbeck's retirement in 1915, Willie was finally regarded as the first team centre-half.

He began to form the successful partnership with McMullan and Harris which attracted calls for international recognition six years later.

Willie was becoming a better player as he matured, like a fine wine one reporter suggested, and he was regarded as one of the best *"breaker-uppers"* in Scotland. Thistle showed their appreciation with a benefit match. Newcastle United visited Firhill in 1920 and with Willie at the middle of the team Thistle beat the English giants 3-2 in front of 8,000 people.

After his personal disappointment at the following season's Scottish Cup final, Willie was determined that season 1921-22 was going to be a successful one for him and for the club. He was sent to his family home in Fife to rest and recover over the summer.

However, Willie Hamilton was never to return to Firhill. Over the summer of 1921 he contracted consumption and after a rapid deterioration of his health due to the lung disease, at the age of 31, he died tragically at home in Dunfermline in August 1921.

Appearances 293, goals 15

JOHN HANSEN

1967 - 1979

Born 3 February 1950 in Bridge of Allan.

John Hansen began his football education while at school, moving onto Sauchie Athletic before stepping up to Sauchie Juniors. It was from Sauchie Juniors that John joined Thistle from in 1967. His first months at Firhill were spent in the reserves but not before too long he had graduated to the Thistle first team. His first team debut came against Raith Rovers on 28 February 1968.

John made just one other appearance in his debut season at Firhill but wasted next to no time as establishing himself as a regular in the Thistle side the next season. His versatility proved to be a major asset, with him being described, just a few months after his debut, as being *"a resolute dependable middleman, resilient and responsive who can bring the ball through with sound control almost invariably finding the colleague best placed to develop the thrust"*.

John was part of the Thistle squad that won the Second Division title in 1970-71, although he did miss large chunks of that season with injury, and the First Division title five seasons later. His finest moment in red and yellow was unquestionably though the League Cup Final of 1971 when Thistle hammered Celtic 4-1 to lift the trophy for, to date, the only time in the Club's history. Hansen admitted in a newspaper interview that the closing stages of the game and the after match celebrations were something of a *"blur"* but he recalled spotting younger brother Alan in the crowd.

Bad memory or not Hansen's role in that success was not insignificant and he, and a whole host of exciting, talented players at Firhill came to the attention of the then Scotland National Team manager Tommy Docherty. In a way of a warm up for an international fixture at Hampden against Portugal, Docherty invited Thistle down to the Scotland training camp in Largs for a practice match. The Thistle side clearly impressed the watching Docherty because from that the Thistle side that won that practice match 2-1, two players would be called into the Scotland squad for their next fixture against Belgium at Pittodrie. Alan Rough wasn't pressed into action but John Hansen won his first Scotland cap when he replaced Jimmy Johnstone in the second half of that fixture. In addition to featuring in a Hampden warm up fixture against the West German Olympic XI, Hansen was also included in a number of Scotland Under 23 squads but was never capped at that level.

Hansen was also unfortunate to miss out on a chance to play against Brazil in the Independence Cup tournament in June and July of 1972. John was included, alongside Firhill team mates Alex Forsyth and Denis McQuade, in the squad to travel to South America even though he hadn't long undergone an operation on a damaged cartilage. Unfortunately John further damaged his knee before leaving Scotland and then again after arriving in South America.

He managed just a single substitute appearance when he replaced Alex Forsyth for Scotland's match with Yugoslavia. Indeed that injury curtailed John's involvement with the Thistle side the following season and he made just 14 appearances and missed both UEFA Cup-ties with Honved.

It is more than a little unfortunate and disrespectful to his talents that John is primarily referred to as the elder bother of Alan Hansen. The two brothers first appeared together in the Thistle team in October 1973 when Dundee were the visitors to Firhill. Until Alan's departure to Liverpool in the summer of 1977 the Thistle fans had the pleasure of watching the skills of both brothers in the team at the same time.

John last pulled a Thistle jersey on in a competitive first team fixture against Rangers in 1977 with a knee injury bringing around a premature ending to his playing career.

John didn't retire from playing without a fight and it was only after two years and an abortive comeback with the reserves that he finally admitted defeated in his battle to get back to full fitness. At the age of just 28 John had amassed more than 300 appearances in his time at Firhill and you can't help but wonder just how many appearances he would have made and the influence on the team he would have had had he not been forced to retire.

It wasn't the end of his association with Partick Thistle by any means. John had always had an eye for the future. In 1975 he gave up full-time football, remaining at Firhill as a part-timer, to develop a career outside of football which he began with the Abbey National Building Society. Indeed for a number of seasons the Building Society advertised in the Thistle programme complete with a photo of John Hansen. John's financial experience saw him take up a role in the Club's commercial department and from 1981 – 1987 he sat on the Board of Directors at Firhill.

Appearances 317, goals 14.
League Cup winner 1971
First Division Championship winner 1975-76
Second Division Championship winner 1970-71
Capped for Scotland v Belgium 1971; v Yugoslavia 1972.

JOE HARRIS

1913 - 1923

Born 19 March 1896 in Glasgow. Died November 1933

Joe Harris never gave anything less than 100%. That attitude was never better exemplified than in a game at Dumbarton in October 1913. With Thistle a goal down there was no time to lose, even with a nail sticking into his foot. The nail was attaching studs to the sole of his boot when it pushed through and embedded itself in Joe's foot. Joe played on, literally shedding blood for the cause, for 45 minutes.

Joe Harris signed for Partick Thistle from Strathclyde Juniors in time for the start of the 1913-14 season, and was an immediate success. After his debut, a 2-1 win over Motherwell, the Daily Record reported

> "... he was never beaten out of recovery, there was no guessing or self-consciousness as would have been pardonable from one newly out of the junior ranks. He has the physique to last, and he has the jaw of a man that will never surrender..."

High praise for the teenager. Joe continued as the first choice left-half for some months until Thistle signed another promising half-back – Jimmy McMullan. For the remainder of the season Joe's first team appearances were limited, though he continued to learn his game in the reserves. It was a successful reserve side that season, and Joe finished his first senior season with a Glasgow Reserve Cup winners medal.

The First World War began, and like many young men, Joe joined up to help the war effort. He spent much of his time between 1914 and 1917 away from home training with the army. It was to the detriment of his football career that, just when he was settling into a regular first team game alongside Hamilton and McMullan, he was called up to the Royal Artillery Garrison.

His career was put on hold, though he played a handful of games while on leave, until he returned to Glasgow from service, resuming football in November 1919. Again, he made an instant impact, winning his right-half jersey back from Adam Black. He kept his place for the remainder of the season, the regularity of games settling him down and he improved immeasurably as a player. He was known especially for his tackling and clearances prior to the war, but his game improved to the point that it was felt also that no half-back in Scotland could match him for his passing.

The improvement in his distribution was in no small way attributable to the arrival of the experienced inside-left Jimmy McMenemy, whose partnership with Jacky Bowie, and their intelligent play, gave Joe plenty of options for passing up the field.

Joe's improving performances were noticed by the international selectors, and after a game for Glasgow against Sheffield in 1920, he was selected for full international honours. Along with his Firhill goalkeeper Kenny Campbell, and captain Jamie McMullan, Joe played twice in 1921, against Wales and Ireland. Despite newspaper calls for Thistle centre-half Hamilton to join Joe and McMullan to make up Scotland's half-back line against England, only McMullan was selected.

Although the England selection was a disappointment, Joe had a Scottish Cup final to play in. Joe was the only member of the regular half-back line to play against Rangers; Hamilton and McMullan were both injured, and he was instrumental in leading his inexperienced team-mates in the backs-to-the-wall defence of their one-goal lead. Rangers must have been hopeful when Joe was injured, and had to move to outside-right, but even when limping heavily he fired in good crosses, keeping Rangers busy.

Partick Thistle undoubtedly appreciated Joe's efforts, and designated the first League game after the Scottish Cup triumph as Joe Harris's benefit match. Joe profited from the bumper crowd, and received Thistle's share of a 20,000 gate as thanks for his service of eight years.

1921-22, while not reaching the heights of the Scottish Cup winning season, was again successful for Joe. He was chosen for the Scottish team to play Ireland in 1922 but had to call off injured. He was fit for the Scottish Cup semi-final. This time Rangers took their revenge on Thistle, winning 2-0.

The big English clubs had spotted Joe's abilities, and there had been a number of approaches to sign him that had been rejected by Thistle. However, come 1923, and after ten years of service, Joe was keen to try somewhere new, and successfully negotiated a bumper transfer deal with Middlesborough. Joe became one of the highest paid players in England, and Thistle benefited by £4,200 – a sizeable transfer fee in those days.

Joe played with Boro for two seasons before joining ex-Thistle forward Neil Harris (no relationship) at Newcastle United for six years. After his time at St James' Park Joe joined York City for two seasons before his death in 1933.

Appearances 243, goals 6.
Scottish Cup winner 1921
Capped for Scotland v Ireland 1921; Wales 1921.

JOHN HARVEY

1951 - 1966

Born 21 January 1933 in Clydebank.

John Harvey is a member of a select band, just a dozen in number, of Partick Thistle players to have made in excess of 400 appearances for the club.

Harvey was brought to Firhill by Arthur Dixon as part of a youth policy that also saw the arrival at the club of the likes of Peter Collins, Willie Crawford and Davie Mathers. Harvey, 17, came to Firhill straight from Victoria Drive School and benefited greatly from a spell farmed out to Baillieston Juniors.

His first team debut for Thistle came on Christmas Day 1951 at Firhill against Dundee. Thistle feeling that there was *"enough holiday population"* to justify a Christmas Day fixture. A crowd of *"close on 20,000"* turned up at Firhill to witness a Thistle side, badly hit by injury, hand debuts to both Harvey and Tom McNab who, like Harvey, had played with Baillieston Juniors. It wasn't a happy afternoon for Thistle with injury during the game further disrupting their plans resulting in a move for Harvey to right-half. Thistle lost 1-3 although Harvey did have the consolation of marking his Thistle debut with a goal when *"following a Walker corner which Stott rattled against the cross bar Harvey wasted no time in banging the rebound into the roof of the net."*

Despite that defeat Harvey held his place in the side for the following fixture against Morton, but for the rest of that season, and the following one, it was spent mostly on the fringes of the first team.

Not until season 1953-54, when he made 20 first team appearances, could Harvey be thought of as even a semi regular in the Thistle side. Thistle would reach their first ever League Cup Final that season but Harvey missed out on a place in the side that lost after a replay to Celtic. Indeed Harvey wouldn't appear in any of Thistle three League Cup Final appearances of the 1950s.

He was, however, part of the Thistle side that lifted the Glasgow Cup in 1954 and he was on target in the final as Thistle defeated Rangers 2-0. Thistle would repeat that Glasgow Cup triumph six years later, this time defeating Celtic in the final, and John was again part of the successful Thistle team.

The closest Harvey would get to lifting a major honour with Thistle was in season 1962-63. A win against Dundee United at the start of October started a club record run of 10 successive victories with Harvey playing in each and every one of those ten games. Not surprisingly such a run had Thistle challenging at the top of the First Division but the worst winter for many a year plunged football into cold storage for the best part of two months and Thistle's title hopes drifted away.

Third spot in the League though earned Thistle a spot in the following season's Fairs Cup, and Harvey, who was perhaps a little unlucky not have been recognised by at least the Scottish League selectors (he did represent Glasgow in the then annual Glasgow v Sheffield fixture), lined up in all four of Thistle's games against Glentoran and Spartak Brno, even managing a goal against Glentoran.

John Harvey played his last game for Partick Thistle on 20 November 1965 in a 2-0 defeat at Love Street against St Mirren. After leaving Firhill he spent six months with Third Lanark before retiring at the end of the 1965-66 season.

After retiring, publican John re-established his links with Partick Thistle firstly on the management side of the Social Club before serving the Club for several years in the role of the Jagspool promoter. John is still a frequent, and most welcome, visitor to Firhill.

Appearances 433, goals 21.
Glasgow Cup winner 1954, 1960.

BOBBY HENDERSON

1937 – 1951

Born 4 October 1917 in Maryhill, Glasgow. Died May 2006.

When Bobby Henderson was at school he read about Kenny Campbell, the great Partick Thistle goalie of the 20s and 30s. He was enthralled because Campbell had inspired Bobby's Thistle hero, Johnny Jackson, to become a goalkeeper. Bobby desperately wanted to be a goalkeeper like Jackson, despite being a little on the short side. He began by becoming a ballboy at Firhill, demanding the spot behind Jackson's goal – all the better to learn how to be a top-class goalkeeper.

Bobby played in the same church and Boys Brigade teams that Jackson had done, and Jackson shared tips with his young admirer.

A few years later Bobby signed for Glasgow Perthshire, and a short time after that he realised his boyhood dream by signing professional terms with Thistle, although he realised the path to the first team would not be an easy one. Bobby Johnstone had been established as Thistle's number one for four years, having replaced Jackson on his departure to Chelsea.

Johnstone had shown to be a solid 'keeper, one of the best in the country. In the public trial match Johnstone lined up for the likely First XI, while Bobby stripped for the hopefuls that were expected to play in the reserves. *"A great young goalkeeper who will disappoint me if he does not develop into a real top-notcher,"* said one reporter after the game. It wasn't to be the last that the two 'keepers would be rivals for the jersey.

Bobby had to be content with playing in the reserves for a couple of seasons with the odd game in the first team, but he continued to impress those who watched him. *"I liked young Henderson in goal. Maybe on the small side, but big enough to stop everything that came to him in this game,"* said the Daily Record after one reserve match. He continued to be patient while he received perhaps the ultimate compliment. *"Watching him last night I was struck by his resemblance in action and appearance to Jaiky Jackson when the latter arrived at Firhill"*, said one commentator.

He must have thought his chance was coming in February 1939 when he was given the nod ahead of Johnstone for a game against Celtic. Johnstone felt he was being unfairly treated and asked for a transfer. Manager Turner turned the request down and explained that his decision was purely to take the chance of giving his young reserve goalie a chance to get some experience. Johnstone was back in goals a couple of games later.

At the outbreak of the war Johnstone discovered he would be unable to play regularly, and Bobby was handed the jersey, turning out in all but one of the games until the end of the season. If this, sadly, was an enforced end to Johnstone's Thistle career, it was a great chance for Bobby, and one he grabbed.

He missed just five games in a possible 229 games through the early 40s until he was called up for national service in February 1945. He remained in the services for two years until demob in August 1947. On his return to Glasgow one of the first things he did was walk round to Firhill to sign a contract for the new season.

International football was shelved during the war, which was unfortunate for a player on the top of his game, and Bobby undoubtedly missed out on the chance of representing his country. He was selected as a reserve for Scotland's unofficial fund-raising games against England in 1942 and 1943, but didn't play in either game.

When Bobby reported for pre-season training after his demob he found a promising young goalkeeper called Tommy Ledgerwood holding the goalkeeper's jersey. In those days goalkeepers wore heavy jerseys. After one game the jersey that Bobby had been wearing was soaked through. The jersey was weighed at the end of the game and found to be eight times as heavy as it had been at the start of the game.

Ledgerwood began the season in goal, and Ayr United made Bobby an offer to sign for them. Although unable to dislodge Ledgerwood, Bobby chose to remain at Firhill, and was rewarded when he took over in goals in October 1947 and remained there until the end of the season.

There then began a couple of seasons that saw the 'keepers share duties. Most clubs would have been delighted to have two such talented men on their books. Bobby began 1948-49 in goal before Tommy took over in December. Bobby returned towards the end of the season and played in the team that beat Rangers in the Charity Cup Final.

He began the following season in possession, but after cnoceding nine goals in two games in August, was dropped for Ledgerwood until the turn of the year. Among Bobby's games in the second half of 1949-50 was a Scottish Cup-tie which is fondly remembered by those who were there. Hibs had the most feared strikers in the game - the 'Famous Five'. Bobby stopped every effort they tried, and there were many, from every angle and distance possible. Thistle snuck a goal at the other end and were through.

The pattern followed again at the start of 1950-51, when Bobby turned out for the first seven games before Tommy took over. This time, however, Tommy's brilliance meant that Bobby didn't play again for Thistle. At the end of the season he was given a free transfer in recognition of his great service to the club.

Dundee snapped Bobby up, making him an excellent personal offer for him to sign for them. While at Dens Park Bobby played, and lost, in the Scottish Cup Final of 1952 before signing for Dundee United, then subsequently retiring from the game.

Appearances 324, goals 0.
Glasgow Charity Cup winner 1949

JOE HOGAN

1955 -1966

Born 24 February 1938 in Armadale

Although Joe Hogan would play a large proportion of his 295 appearances for Partick Thistle in the right back role he first exhibited his obvious football talent as a goalscorer. While a pupil at Bathgate Academy he represented - alongside another future Partick Thistle player Joe McBride - Glasgow and District Schools in a fixture against their counterparts from London.

After leaving school Hogan joined junior side Newtongrange Star for whom in one season alone he scored over 60 goals. That kind of form in front of goal naturally brought him to the attention of senior scouts and in season 1955-56 the then Thistle manager David Meiklejohn managed to lure Hogan to Firhill.

At the age of 17 he made his Thistle debut in a fixture against Clyde at Firhill on 2 January 1956. In total Hogan would make five appearances in the Thistle first team during his debut season but the following campaign he began to really establish himself as a regular in the Thistle side. His first goal came during the course of a 2-1 win over Falkirk in December 1956. He also scored later in the season in a 3-1 win over Celtic as Thistle defeated their Glasgow rivals at Firhill for the third season in a row.

That win though was scant consolation for defeat against the same opposition in the final of the League Cup.

Still just 18, Hogan played in both the first game that finished 0-0 and in the replay that Celtic won 3-0 just a few days later.

Thistle would be back in the League Cup Final in 1958, losing again, this time to Hearts, and Hogan would once more be part of the defeated Thistle side. This time though he appeared not as a centre but as right back. He first appeared at the back for Thistle in a League game against Queen's Park in January 1958 and played in the same role in a fixture with Tottenham Hotspur just a couple of months later.

Thistle lost both those games 4-1 but Hogan must have done something right in that position as in season 1958-59, playing at the back, he missed just a handful of games. He performed too with no little success. Although not capped by the Scottish League he was on one occasion listed as a reserve. He did, however, get the opportunity to represent Scotland at Under 23 level against England in March 1961.

Hogan's opportunity may not have come had there not been a series of Scottish Cup replays scheduled for the same midweek as the Scotland Under 23's trip to Middlesbrough. Although Thistle were in action the same night at Ayr United, the call-offs due to the cup replays led to give Hogan his chance. The depleted Scotland side though was given next to no chance of winning. It was a major surprise therefore when the young Scots ran out 1-0 victors, Denis Law scoring the winning goal with Hogan and his other 'reserve' full back Beattie described as *"playing very well"*.

Sadly Hogan wouldn't be given any further opportunity to represent either his country or the Scottish League. At Firhill too he missed out on any major honours. Being part of the Thistle side, playing as a striker that lifted the 1960 Glasgow Cup was hardly consolation for defeat in two League Cup Finals. Hogan and Thistle were to be denied also in the League in season 1962-63 when the weather intervened with Thistle challenging at the top of the table.

Although converted to a defender for much of his time at Firhill, Hogan was still able to chip in with the odd goals, few more memorable than a long range effort that helped Thistle to a 2-0 Parkhead win against Celtic. Hogan would go on and score the following week against Airdrieonians as well.

Nor was Hogan employed exclusively as a defender. He started the 1960-61 season playing up front and scored three times for Thistle in the first four games of that season. When, in subsequent seasons, he was moved up front he enjoyed no little success either. In February 1965 he scored twice against Third Lanark before hitting another double a few weeks later against Dundee in a 4-4 draw. Later the same year Dundee would suffer again as Hogan once more scored twice against them. While at Firhill Hogan combined playing with studying at University and after he retired he became a physics teacher.

Appearances 295, goals 26.
Glasgow Cup winner 1960
Capped for Scotland Under 23s v England 1961.

BOBBY HOUSTON

1971 - 1979

Born 23 January 1952 in Glasgow.

Bobby Houston or, as he affectionately came to be know by Thistle fans, 'Badger', started his football career playing for his school teams. It was while playing with St Margaret Mary's Secondary School in Castlemilk that this talented young lad really started to make people sit up and take notice. His stepped up to the junior ranks when he joined Rutherglen Glencairn and it was from there that he joined Thistle in 1971. His debut for the Thistle Reserves would soon follow.

Season 1973-74 was his first full season as a member of the Thistle first team squad and Houston played a total of 39 games that season as, to quote a Thistle programme of the time, *"an inside man, midfield player and latterly as a full back."* The article continued. *"Although this is his first season as a regular first team choice Bobby has shown commendable skill in each of the roles he has been asked to play."*

Versatile or not it is as a flying winger that Houston the Thistle player is first thought of. Johnny Gibson's transfer to Ayr United saw Houston move more or less permanently to an attacking role in the Thistle side. A role he filled with no little skill.

It was a little disappointing therefore that Bobby's undoubted skills were never recognised at international level. Twice he was called into the Scotland Under 23 squad but on neither occasion did he get to make an appearance. He was, however, capped by the Scottish League in a fixture against the Irish League in 1978.

The biggest disappointment, though, in Houston's Thistle career was unquestionably defeat in the 1979 Scottish Cup semi-final. Thistle lost a Hampden replay 0-1 to Rangers but it was a replay that Thistle fans swear to this day should not have been necessary. With the score tied at 0-0 and with time rapidly running out Bobby Houston looked to have headed the goal that would have taken Thistle to the final for the first time since 1930. A raised flag though ended Thistle celebrations. In an interview in the Thistle Programme in 1989 Houston took up the story.

> *"We all thought that we could beat them (Rangers), and we did 'beat' them. The goal I scored was never offside. We had practised the move leading to the goal at training and I can remember that when I started my run I was behind Ally Dawson. The ball came to me at head height and I just had to nod it into the net. I started running about delirious only to see the linesman chalk it off for offside. I met Stan Anderson, who was the Rangers coach at the time, a couple of weeks after the game and he told me that when the ball went in the Rangers bench thought the game was over as there were only ten minutes left."*

Houston's Thistle career came to an end in the first few months of the 1979-80 season, his final appearance for Thistle coming in a fixture against Dundee United on 22 September.

By the time the following weekend's fixtures came round Houston had joined Kilmarnock in a deal that saw Ian Jardine move to Firhill.

Now at Rugby Park, Houston came up against his old side for the first time just a couple of months after his departure from Firhill. Thistle won the fixture 1-0, as they often seemed to do at Rugby Park in those days, with Houston's involvement in the match fleeting to say the least. Sent on as a second half substitute the story goes that Houston received a less than friendly welcome from his old teammates.

"Still aff yir heid then Badger?" is one of the comments alleged to have made in Houston's direction. At any rate the red mist came down, a yellow card was swiftly followed by a red one and off he went. Houston had been on the park for only a handful of minutes.

Despite that indiscretion Houston would serve Kilmarnock well for a number of years. After leaving Rugby Park Houston spent a number of seasons with Morton before retiring at the end of the 1983-84 season.

Appearances 274, Goals 29
First Division Championship winner 1975-76
Capped for Scottish League v Irish League 1978

Other honours
With Morton: First Division Championship winner 1983-84

Willie Howden

1901 – 1908 & 1909 – 1910

Born 28 March 1875 in Glasgow.

By the time goalkeeper Willie Howden arrived at Meadowside in 1901 to begin his Thistle career, he already had experience, having played with Benburb and Rutherglen Glencairn and had also played a trial match for Rangers. He signed for Second Division Thistle as an amateur.

After a number of weeks playing in the reserves Willie's chance for first team football came, thanks to regular 'keeper John Wilkie's illness. The game was away to Port Glasgow Athletic and Willie played well enough to retain his place for a further two games before Wilkie returned. The two 'keepers alternated for the remainder of the season and the Thistle backs were happy having two top-quality stoppers behind them. Thistle ended the season in second place and were elected to the First Division for the 1902-03 season.

The season started with a trial match – possibles versus probables. Willie played with the possibles and began the season again in the reserves, although the Evening Times advised the Thistle selectors that playing Howden was less of a risky option than Wilkie in goal. After a 0-9 defeat to Rangers, Willie returned to the first team, results improved thanks to his performances, and Thistle moved away from the bottom of the division.

While Howden was reckoned to be more than a substitute for Wilkie, the more experienced goalie returned later in the season, and the 'keeper rotation system began again.

The system worked, for 1902-03 was the club's most successful season since League football had begun in 1890 and the final League position was eighth.

Thistle returned the following season with a new goalkeeper, but one with the same name – Wilkie, and again Willie was reckoned to be the new 'keeper's understudy. However, he displaced his new rival and once back in the first team, Howden was not for moving. Between October 1903 and January 1907 Willie missed only a handful of games and was instrumental in the club continuing to improve League positions. By the end of 1903-04 seventh was achieved, in 1904-05 sixth, in 1905-06 fifth (just two points off third). In late 1904 Willie was part of the team that achieved a record eight League wins in a row – the team were awarded gold watches as thanks for their efforts. In February 1905 the Daily Record reckoned Willie's performance against Hibs in the Scottish Cup was a *display "never bettered by any Partick goalkeeper"*.

A reputation for being consistent, cool and safe meant that representative honours were on their way to Willie. A full international cap for Scotland was awarded for his performance in a 4-0 win over Ireland at Parkhead in 1905. Willie's captain that day was his Partick Thistle captain Neil Gibson. Following the full international there was a chance to represent his city when Willie was picked for Glasgow to play against a Sheffield select – Glasgow lost 2-3 in October 1906.

When Willie was injured during a Scottish Cup-tie against Dundee in 1907 he would have been forgiven if he worried about the future of his career. Later hospital tests showed a broken collarbone, but with his arm hanging limp from the shoulder, Willie bravely played on. He saved a number of shots by flinging his body in the way of the ball, but when he tried to save with the injured arm and damaged it further he was forced to go off.

A benefit match was to be arranged for him in January 1908, but after such a major injury Howden went into semi-retirement after just a few games of the 1907-08 season. However, an injury to Lee Massey in November 1907 saw him recalled to the team and play for most of the remainder of the season, and the benefit was forgotten.

Willie's desire to take things easy eventually led him to ask for, and receive, a transfer to Abercorn in the Second Division in October 1908. Thistle quickly realised that Willie was playing below his standard, and when a 'keeper was needed in an emergency for a Cup-tie against Queen's Park in 1909 Willie came back – "for just one more time".

Against his better wishes he was once more tempted out of retirement and back to the Thistle first team at the start of the 1909-10 season, and he became the first Jags goalkeeper to play at Firhill Park, playing regularly throughout the season. This time, at last, he received that long-promised benefit match in April 1910. Celtic were the opposition in a drawn 1-1 game, but Willie didn't play, having injured himself the previous week. He did benefit to the sum of £50.

Despite his return to top-flight football Willie remained unconvinced that he wanted to play there, and despite starting the 1910-11 season as first choice, he was unhappy. Although the criticism was mild, when it was suggested in the newspapers that his display against St Mirren in October 1910 was not up to his normal standard, Willie took the opportunity to once again announce his retirement and left Partick Thistle for the last time.

Abercorn again signed Howden in 1911, and the veteran 'keeper had a good spell at the Paisley club, winning the Qualifying Cup in 1913. Willie ended his career, after a period at Beith, by playing for Arthurlie well into his 40s.

Appearances 244, goals 0.
Capped for Scotland v Ireland 1906.

JACKIE HUSBAND

1938 – 1950

Born 28 May 1918 in Dunfermline. Died May 1992 in Glasgow.

Were it not for a brief period as manager of Queen of the South in the mid-1960s Jackie Husband would have spent his adult life at Firhill. From his signing for the club in October 1938 to his death in May 1992, Jackie was a great servant to Partick Thistle, as player, captain, trainer, coach, physiotherapist, kitman, masseur and mentor to players young and old, for 52 of his 74 years. Jackie signed for Thistle in October 1938 after Donald Turner watched him over a period of weeks playing with Yoker Athletic.

As other clubs started to show interest, Easton signed the big half-back with an eye to the aging half-back pair of Alec Elliot and Eddie McLeod – Jackie could play on the left or the right. McLeod and Elliot were vastly experienced, with 23 years service between them, and they weren't about to give up their first-team places easily. Jackie bided his time, and learned the ropes in the reserves for most of the season before replacing first Elliot and then McLeod for the last five League games of the season.

It was an entertaining and unpredictable Thistle team that Jackie joined – he took part in a 4-0 win over Hibs on his debut, followed by a 0-7 defeat to St Johnstone, a 4-1 win over Third Lanark, a 0-4 defeat at Arbroath, and then a 2-0 win over Falkirk on the last day of the season.

Jackie was a tireless worker from the half-back line, and he loved to get forward and support his forwards. Peter McKennan surely would have developed a legendary partnership with Jackie had he not been called to the war. Alex McSpadyen did, as did Sammy Picken, Willie O'Donnell, and Willie Sharp. In his debut against Hibs the Daily Record reported, *"He did impress with his intelligent interpretation of half-back play. He believes in devoting a big measure of his energy to attack"*.

The trial match in August 1939 saw Jackie line up in the 'A' team – the likely starting team for the first game – and the veteran Elliot was in the 'B'. However, when the season started Jackie had to stand aside. However, when war was declared, with Elliot unable to play on a Saturday, Jackie again had his chance, and didn't miss a game until the end of the season, mostly at right-half, and occasionally at left-half.

Jackie worked on a farm and was exempt from military service during the war, and remained at the heart of the Thistle team through the war years, on the right, the left, and as centre-half, when George Sutherland was called up, guiding the team to two Southern League Cup semi-finals and a Glasgow Cup Final. However, it was in the Summer Cup (a replacement for the Scottish Cup) of 1945, as war came to an end, that Jackie's finest hour as a Partick Thistle player came. Captaining a team containing greats such as Peter Curran, Bobby Parker, Willie Sharp, Jimmy McGowan, Hugh Brown, and guest Bill Shankly, Jackie lifted the Summer Cup as Thistle beat Hibs through goals from Jack Johnston.

Jackie wasn't a fancy player. What you got was ninety minutes of effort, that and two distinctive aspects to his game. The first was a strong shot from a dead ball. In 1945 the Daily Record wondered if anyone in football had a stronger shot after a free-kick from great distance. Jackie would shoot from any distance, and the fact that the muddy ball would be as heavy as a medicine ball made no difference. The weight of the ball made no difference to his ability to throw the ball long distances also. Jackie would propel the ball forty yards, sending Thistle into attack when the opposition little realised the danger.

Jackie had begun his career as a goalkeeper and had practised his throwing techniques, and had continued developing the throws long after his team-mates had finished training. It was from throw-ins that he got most success from his practicing.

The end of the war saw international football return, and Jackie was tipped for a cap. He was chosen as a reserve for Scotland's game against Wales in 1945, and travelled with an SFA select, along with Jimmy Walker and

Jimmy McGowan, to play two exhibition games in Germany against a Combined Services team that included Peter McKennan. He was one of Scotland's heroes in a 1-0 win over England in the Victory International, as the Daily Record reported. *"Not so colourful as his colleagues, or so apt to stealing the limelight, yet made of solid dependable stuff. Always there when wanted and taking a trick with his tremendous length in his throw-ins."* Jackie went on to play against Switzerland, and England again, in games that were classified as unofficial internationals. He was eventually rewarded with his first cap against Wales in 1946, and played again soon after against the English League in 1947.

Jackie remained a loyal club servant, always the first to sign a new contract when the previous one ran out. He remained a steadying influence alongside Hugh Brown, Willie Hewitt, and Adam Forsyth, occasionally filling in for the injured Peter Curran at left back, until the start of the 1948-49 season. Injury cut his appearances to just seven. The following season he was back and fit, but his place had been taken. Ironically Jackie had spent his recuperation the previous year coaching the youngsters at Firhill, particularly Bertie Thomson. Bertie had taken Jackie's place as long-throw expert and regular right-half, but no-one was more delighted for Bertie than Jackie.

Kilmarnock, in the Second Division, made Jackie an offer to sign but it was quickly turned down. *"No, I started with Thistle and I would like to finish with them. I might be able to help with the reserve team."* Jackie filled in for a handful of games in 1950 when Jimmy McGowan was injured, but it was with the reserves initially, and then the first team, that Jackie's new career as trainer and coach began at the end of the 1949-50 season.

Jackie's playing career had been a distinguished one, and his career after playing was no less enjoyable. Jackie was a constant at Firhill, assisting (and seeing out) 17 managers in a variety of roles. If something needed done at Firhill, Jackie would do it. Jackie was still at Firhill a matter of days before he died in May 1992, just two days before Thistle clinched promotion. It was a fitting tribute to a wonderful man that the East Stand at Firhill was named in his honour.

If one man deserves to be called a legend of Firhill it is Jackie Husband.

Appearances 371, goals 12.
Summer Cup Winner 1945
Capped for Scotland v Wales 1946.
Capped for Scotland in Victory Internationals v England April 1946, August 1946; v Switzerland 1946.
Capped for Scottish League v English League 1947.

Johnny (Jaikey) Jackson

1926 - 1933

Born 29 November 1906 in Ruchill, Glasgow. Died 16 June 1965.

Young Johnny Jackson didn't look like a goalkeeper. He was slightly built and wore spectacles, but his hero was Partick Thistle's international 'keeper Kenny Campbell. Johnny played whenever he could - for the North Kelvinside school team on Saturday morning, then for the local 69th Boys Brigade in the Church League in the afternoon. He would practice with his mates, always in goal, and when his mates went home he would practice on his own – kicking the ball off the gable end of Ruchill Hospital and diving to save it.

Johnny was rewarded for such dedication with a professional contract for his favourite team when Thistle signed him from Kirkintilloch Rob Roy in the summer of 1926, after he turned down the chance to sign for Ayr United following a trial. Thistle hadn't satisfactorily replaced Campbell in goal since his departure in 1922, and had signed Tommy Gibbs from Dunfermline, as well as Johnny, to wear the goalkeeper's jersey. Gibbs started the season as first choice, but after spilling five goals in a 4-5 defeat to Morton, Johnny was asked to play the next game.

Johnny's first game for Thistle was away at Ibrox, and this began a remarkable run of games. Johnny was a model of consistency and reliability. In seven years Johnny missed just one game, and that was tolerable – he was playing for Scotland against England that day. Johnny's modelling of himself on Campbell paid off and he gathered admirers quickly. The Daily Record enthused:

"Jackson was in the Campbell fashion; swift to catch the ball and elusive when in possession of it. He was most graceful in action, and his body, when he threw himself to right or left for a high shot, was swallow-like in motion."

A safe pair of hands and good anticipation are required for any good goalkeeper, and Johnny combined these qualities with a coolness under pressure and calculated bravery. He wouldn't dive into any dangerous situation, but knew instinctively when it was worth the risk to deny the opposition. Johnny wasn't tall, but he had a great spring and clutched high balls confidently.

In Johnny's first season, League form wasn't great, but the cup competitions suited Thistle's cavalier play better. The semi-final of the Scottish Cup was reached, although narrowly lost to East Fife, but Johnny and his mates wanted a trophy. In an exciting Glasgow Charity Cup Final Rangers were beaten after a perfect display of all-out attack from both teams. Johnny was beaten three times but Thistle scored six to win 6-3, lift the trophy, and Johnny had a medal in his first season.

Over the following seasons Johnny was to develop a bond with Denis O'Hare and Stewart Calderwood, and a reputation for saving penalties, which was to lift Thistle up the table. In 1930 consistent League form was coupled with Scottish Cup success, of a sort.

The final was reached, but Johnny couldn't recreate Kenny Campbell's success of nine years previous. Thistle lost a replayed final to Rangers after Johnny had kept the Rangers forwards at bay in the first game.

Good club form had meant Johnny appearing on the radar for international selection. Selection for the Glasgow Select to play Sheffield in 1929 was quickly followed by a Cap for the Scottish League against the Irish League. Three further League Caps followed, including one against the Irish at Firhill in 1930, and full international recognition wasn't far away. Johnny was selected to tour Europe with Scotland in 1931, where he played three games, against Austria, Italy, and Switzerland. His final game for Scotland whilst still a Thistle player was against England in a momentous 2-1 win in front of 134,170 people in 1933.

It had been Johnny's Thistle form that saw him capped. Following the Scottish Cup disappointment in 1930, the Jags concentrated on the League. Johnny was part of the proud team that was the first Thistle team to top the Scottish League, after beating Cowdenbeath in October 1930.

From that pinnacle it was inevitably downhill, though Thistle retained consistent League form, finishing fourth in 1931 and sixth in 1932. 1933-34 started well, and Thistle went on a record-breaking run of twelve League wins in a row, but when form dipped, Johnny felt that it was time he moved on, despite being due a benefit match later that year.

Thistle reluctantly agreed to the transfer request and in the summer of 1933 Johnny signed for Chelsea for what was believed to be a world record fee for a goalkeeper. Johnny didn't forget his old mates though, for he sent money back to Firhill, and the players celebrated his big-money transfer with a slap-up meal.

An unfortunate kick to the head in one of his first games for Chelsea saw Johnny carried off unconscious, and when he returned from a stay in hospital he had lost his place to future England internationalist Vic Woodley. He struggled to regain his place throughout his Chelsea career, often making do with reserve team football, but this didn't affect his international career. Indeed he was chosen to play against England in 1934 while playing for Chelsea's second team.

At the end of his career at Chelsea, he guested with Brentford, Portsmouth and Bath City during the war, before retiring from football, and becoming a golfer, taking part in the British Open on a number of occasions, first as a professional at Wyke Green in Ealing and laterly in Canada.

Not bad for a speccy wee boy from Ruchill.

Appearances 334, goals 0
Capped for Scotland v Austria 1931; v England 1933; v Italy 1931; v Switzerland 1931.
Capped for Scottish League v English League 1931, 1932; v Irish League 1929, 1930.
Glasgow Charity Cup Winner 1927

Other honours
With Chelsea 5 Scotland international appearances (1 a Jubilee international)

BOBBY JOHNSTONE

1933 - 1940

Born 6 November 1911 in Wishaw

When Bobby Johnstone joined Partick Thistle from Blantyre Celtic in the summer of 1933 he also joined a legacy of great Thistle goalkeepers, such as John McCorkindale, Willie Howden, Kenny Campbell and Johnny Jackson. While it was no doubt flattering for Bobby to be compared to these greats, it was to be a bit of an impediment too in his formative months at the club.

Bobby was signed as cover for junior internationalist Archie Gourlay. He found himself in the first team following an injury to Gourlay and following his debut, a 0-3 home defeat to Falkirk, the Daily Record unkindly suggested that he was *"not exactly a Johnny Jackson"*. However, the evidence points to problems elsewhere, for an unsteady defence (with either Gourlay or Bobby in goal) shipped 34 goals in the first two months of the season, until Stewart Calderwood and Alec Elliot returned to secure things.

The instability in front of Bobby didn't help his early performances; his preference to use his feet instead of his hands, and to punch rather than catch, gave the Thistle fans some bracing moments. As Gourlay regained his fitness, the newspapers expected Bobby to return to the reserves, but he had done enough to merit a run in the first team. Bobby was ever-present from September 1933 until the outbreak of the war in 1939, missing less than 20 League games in the six year period.

Although only 5'9", and slight for a goalkeeper, Bobby was strong and fearless. At a time when forwards were allowed to challenge goalkeepers physically Bobby gave as good as he got, and often it was the bigger forwards who ended up on the ground as Bobby cleared the ball upfield. His height meant that he had to punch the ball more often than catch it, but once he realised that using his hands was a better option than his feet the Daily Record changed their minds about him. In January 1934, just five months after his debut, the newspapers reckoned there were not many better goalies in the country, and were touting him for international honours – the League international against England was coming up. Bobby wasn't selected but his star was high at Firhill - he was now reckoned to be as good a 'keeper as Jackson. High praise indeed.

When Bobby hurt his left hand in a game against Rangers in September 1934 he was determined to play through the pain despite only being able to use his right hand, but Rangers won 4-0. After the game an x-ray showed Bobby had broken his wrist, and he was forced to sit out seven League games to recover, although he was brought back before fully fit, for the Glasgow Cup Final against Rangers. He was rewarded with a shut-out, and a goal from Willie Miller gave Thistle the City trophy for the first time.

After another week off Bobby returned to the team for the remainder of the season, which tailed of perfectly with another cup final win – this time in the Charity Cup. This was perfect compensation for Bobby and his mates, who had lost the same competition the year before to Rangers after a draw, having conceded more corners than their opponents.

Bobby played behind some excellent full-backs but craved the consistency that a regular full-back partnership would have given him. It was only in 1934 and 1935, when Calderwood and George Cummings played together that he had that stability in front of him. However, Bobby liked to cover for his defenders, and became known for a fondness for anticipating forward passes and charging from his area to thump clearances up the field. Opposing forwards were exasperated, having foxed their direct defenders.

Almost a prototype sweeper, it was an unknown tactic in Scotland, and helped compensate for the inexperience of some of his defenders.

In January 1937 Bobby again showed his commitment to Thistle. He had suffered a leg injury against Clyde but limped up to Firhill to be told he was unfit and was sent home as the call went to reserve 'keeper McNair. When it was discovered that McNair was ill and couldn't leave his bed the search went out for Bobby. He was found, hobbling down Maryhill Road on his way home, and returned to Firhill where he turned out in a 0-1 defeat to Rangers.

Bobby finally received international recognition in 1937 (he had previously turned out for Glasgow against Sheffield in 1934), when he played in a trial match along with Peter McKennan and Alex McSpadyen, for the Scottish League team to play against England. McKennan was the only one of the trio selected.

Although known for his penalty-saving abilities, and his red gloves, it was his consistency for five years that saw him appointed club captain in 1938. Goalkeeper/captains were unusual, and Bobby took his position seriously. He was one of the first goalkeepers to direct his defenders, always talking and advising them on the play from his vantage point.

In 1937 Thistle had signed a young 'keeper called Bobby Henderson, and he began to push for the first team. When Johnstone was dropped in February 1939 he was upset and immediately asked for a transfer. Thistle could have commanded a high fee, but manager Turner placated Bobby, explaining that it was simply a good time to blood a young player.

Bobby returned to the team soon after, and played until the war broke out in September.

During the war Bobby was required to work as a steelworker, and his shifts meant that he was unable to play for Thistle, Henderson taking his place.

Bobby was frustrated with the lack of football, and left Firhill in January for Motherwell. After a spell at Fir Park, Bobby moved on to St Mirren and finally Albion Rovers, before the requirements of his wartime job saw him retire from football.

Appearances 255, goals 0.
Glasgow Cup winner 1934
Glasgow Charity Cup winner 1935

David Johnstone

1920 - 1923

David Johnstone was a reluctant centre-forward with only four months experience of playing in the position when he turned out in the 1921 Scottish Cup Final. Thistle had struggled to fill the position since Neil Harris had departed to Newcastle United at the start of the season and had tried a number of players without great success. At least David was the right shape for a centre-forward, tall and strong, and when he played his first game, leading the forward line against Third Lanark on Ne'erday 1921, he scored his first League goal for the club. He netted another, three days later, against St Mirren. Thistle fans hoped that the club had found their new centre-forward.

It was in the later stages of the Scottish Cup that David showed his real worth as a forward. In the first semi-final against Hearts he was a constant problem in the early stages. After 30 minutes David was clear with only Sandy Kane to beat, but the 'keeper dived on the ball at his feet, and as he tried to clear the ball he only succeeded in kicking it directly to David. The ball was volleyed back with power and accuracy but the 'keeper again saved with a full-stretch save.

A minute later David was back in, from a Willie Salisbury pass, but again the 'keeper saved. A little more strikers' composure might have helped, but David couldn't be faulted for his efforts.

Thistle eventually progressed to the final after two replays, and in the interim David returned to play at right-back, and showed he was more comfortable in the defensive position.

He was pressed back into the forward role in the final against Rangers and constantly harassed the opposition, never allowing them to fully concentrate on attacking the Thistle goal and giving respite to his harassed teammates. Indeed, just before halftime he launched himself at a cross from Jimmy McMenemy and almost connected. Goalkeeper Robb grabbed the ball as David ended up in the back of the net himself. Although he didn't score, the makeshift centre contributed hugely to the success of the makeshift team that won the cup.

David was signed as a right-back from Beith in the summer of 1920 as a replacement for Tom Adams, but struggled to make an impact after a short spell in the team in September and was replaced by Tom Crichton at right-back. However, Thistle's problem position was centre-forward. A number of players were tried, including Jamie Kinloch, but none were satisfactory.

Thistle were struggling to score goals and Spurs legend Jimmy Cantrell was approached, but was too expensive. David became the sixth player to be tried, and he quickly became manager Easton's preferred choice, despite him being unhappy in the position. He returned to defensive duties as injuries throughout the team meant the team was shuffled weekly and despite his place in the Cup Final as a forward, he played almost as many games in defence as he did up front.

The start of 1921-22 season saw David line up in another position, moving into the half-back line on the right beside Matt Wilson and

Joe Harris, and the Daily Record felt that now he was *"... surely in his right place at right half, for beside his good defence, his feeding was splendid"*. He played regularly in the intermediate line, helping take Thistle to third place in the League in January 1922, but by now his place in the team was being threatened by a young protégé. Jamie Gibson had arrived at Firhill, and was beginning to stake his claim for a regular game at half-back.

David continued playing at right-half until the end of the season, but 1922-23 saw him play just three games, and he decided to leave senior football at the end of the season, when he rejoined Beith in the Third Division in 1923.

David was an important part of the Beith team that remained in the League until it was disbanded in 1926.

David continued playing with Beith, in the Alliance League, until 1934 when he retired from playing. Thistle marked David's contributions to both clubs by travelling to Ayrshire to play in a benefit match, following which David Johnstone continued his service to Beith as club secretary.

Appearances 60, goals 3
Scottish Cup winner 1921

SAM KENNEDY

1902 - 1910

Born 8 April 1881 in Girvan.

Tall and straight-backed, blond with a handlebar moustache, Sam Kennedy looked every inch the late Victorian/early Edwardian gentleman. However, Sam was a plumber who came from Girvan and was a battering-ram centre-forward for Partick Thistle.

Sam joined Partick Thistle in August 1902 from Ayr, where he was regarded as the best centre-forward in Division 2. He played for the probables in the pre-season trial match at Meadowside, impressing enough to replace the previous season's main striker Alex McAllister in the opening League game.

The Ayrshire boy faced Kilmarnock in his first game in the big League and had a great game, scoring the equaliser, and then setting up William Massie for the winner as Thistle won 2-1.

This win augured well for the rest of the season, and thanks to Sam's 14 goals and partnerships with Massie and Robert Gray, meant that Thistle finished the season in their highest ever League position - eighth.

Sam was an individual type of player. When the fashions of the time dictated that the centre-forward should be a pivot for the rest of his team, receiving the ball from his mates and playing it wide to the other forwards, Sam liked to do things differently. Strong and fast, he loved to take opposition defences by surprise, using his fancy dribbling skills as well as his muscle to attack directly. He was often criticised in the press:

> *"Kennedy is a clever, able, player, but really he tries too much. A little less dribbling and trying to beat the defence single handed would result in greater efficiency all round, and more goals to the club."*
> (Daily Record)

But he was efficient, scoring eleven goals in 18 League games in 1902-03. Would he change to suit the whims of the press?

He didn't; Thistle's wide men were happy for Sam's characteristic rushing game to continue, and results and Division One positions continued to improve – seventh in 1903-04, sixth in 1904-05, and fifth in 1905-06, two points off third, with Sam captaining the team.

The SFA selectors were happy, too, and Sam was a surprise choice to lead the line for Scotland against Wales at Wrexham in 1905.

Representative honours didn't come regularly to Sam – his other 'cap' was alongside his Division One peers against a Division Two select in 1907. Sam found his position in the forward line at Firhill regularly under threat as the club tried to persuade Sam to change his style, or be dropped. And he was dropped, regularly, but always came back between 1906 and 1909 to make the jersey his again.

Whether it was the trend for more inclusive centre-forwards, or age catching up, things were tough for Sam. No matter how resolute he was, the criticism from press and supporters must have been difficult to take. In 1908-09, when Thistle were homeless and waiting for Firhill to be built, the Daily Record reported on some Thistle fans who felt that the club would be unlucky for as long as Sam was playing at centre. Ironically the Record felt that Sam was the best of the Thistle forwards in a difficult season.

As Thistle moved into Firhill, the curtain fell on Sam's Partick Thistle career. He was replaced by Sid Smith, one of a number of signings from England, after an early season injury, and this time Sam couldn't bounce back. In October 1910 Sam returned to his first love – Girvan – where he continued to play, and keep an interested eye on Firhill. For years it was felt that Thistle had never adequately replaced Sam Kennedy.

Appearances 254, goals 95.
Capped for Scotland v Wales 1905.

ANDY KERR

1952 - 1959

Born 29 June 1931 in Lugar. Died December 1997 in Aberdeen.

Andy Kerr came to Firhill from his home town team of Lugar Boswell. Although perhaps lacking a little in inches at 5' 10" he arrived at Firhill as a centre-half and it was in that position that he made his Thistle debut against Aberdeen in September 1952, the opening League game of the season. Kerr was unable to mark his Thistle debut by being part of a winning Thistle team, the final score being a 1-1 draw, but he was singled out for some, qualified, praise in the press in the games aftermath.

> *"It was simple for Kerr, Thistle's centre half, to allow Dunbar to lose himself in a labyrinth of mistakes and the young Lugar man had better not get the impression that this was any test of his prowess. He merely had an airing."*

It turned out to be something more than just an airing. While by no means a permanent fixture in the Thistle team he did mark his debut season by playing 19 games in the Thistle first team. His time as a centre-half though was soon to be at an end. That lack of inches was perhaps a hindrance to a career in the heart of the defence and it was a shrewd move indeed to move the young Kerr to the position of full-back. He first appeared in that position as Thistle, who would finish the season in third spot in the League, defeated Dundee in November 1953.

He did, however, still appear as centre-half on occasion and indeed played in that role in the 1953 League Cup Final defeat at the hands of East Fife and the 1954 Glasgow Cup Final win over Rangers.

Kerr's form for Thistle was such that he soon came to the attention of the international selectors. He won the first of his two caps for the Scottish League in 1955 against the English League. The Scottish League lost 4-2 with Kerr's performance being described as *"a mixture, sometimes he was the icicle and sometimes far out in his timing of the tackle."*

He had more success two years later as part of a Scottish League side that hammered their Irish League counterparts 7-0 at Ibrox. Kerr was drafted in to replace the injured Alec Parker. The Glasgow Herald was fulsome in its praise of Kerr's performance.

> *"At full-back Kerr outshone Caldow, which is not to say that the Rangers player was not a success. It was noticeable, however, that whenever an ominous gap appeared between Evans and Caldow, the Partick Thistle player was quick to intervene."*

Sandwiched between those two League caps Kerr was capped at 'B' level for Scotland against England. Scotland drew 2-2 after reportedly having *"no chance"* of avoiding defeat.

At full international level Kerr was capped twice inside ten days for Scotland. In May 1955 he was part of the Scotland side that defeated Austria 4-1 in Vienna during a game marked by fist fights on the field and pitch invasions from the terracing. Ten days later 102,000 spectators saw Scotland lost 3-1 to Hungary in Budapest.

There would be no further caps for Kerr although there were frequent calls for him to be brought into the side and he accompanied Scotland to Wembley in 1959 as reserve.

Back at Firhill Kerr remained as part of Thistle's arguably best ever side until virtually the end of the 1950s but not exclusively as part of the Thistle defence. Already converted from centre-half to full-back, he moved further upfield in December 1957. A Thistle team entertained a Glasgow Select in the Jimmy McGowan benefit match and Thistle took the opportunity to try Kerr as centre-forward. In the admittedly low key surrounds of a benefit match the experiment had an almost instant reward.

Thistle won 3-2 with Kerr helping himself to two of those three goals. A few days later Kerr again lined up as a centre-forward, this time in a League match against Queen of the South, and again scored twice.

He scored the following week against Raith Rovers, seven days later against Celtic at Parkhead as Thistle won 3-2 and again the next week against East Fife.

The goals dried up after that burst of goalscoring but the following season, his last as a Partick Thistle player, he topped the Thistle scoring charts with 25 goals.

That kind of form was bound to bring him to the attention of others and he started the following season as a Manchester City player with Thistle receiving a reported £11,000 transfer fee for him.

His stay in Manchester was a brief one though, making just 10 League appearances for City before returning to Scotland to sign for Kilmarnock. He proved to be a huge success at Rugby Park averaging only a little less than a goal a game in 4 years with Killie. In 1960-61 he equalled a Kilmarnock record by scoring 34 times in the one season.

He left Kilmarnock in 1963 to join Sunderland, this time for a fee of £22,000, before once again coming home to Scotland this time to Aberdeen the following year. He rounded off his senior playing career with a spell in Northern Ireland with Glentoran.

Appearances 253 goals 44.
Glasgow Cup winner 1952, 1954.
Capped for Scotland v Austria 1955; v Hungary 1955
Capped for Scotland B v England 1956
Capped for Scottish League v English League 1955; v Irish League 1957

James (Jamie) Kinloch

1920 - 1928

Born 14 April 1898 in Govan. Died November 1962.

Jamie Kinloch was a Firhill institution for 42 years, as a clever attacking player, reliable captain, and long-serving director. From the day he was signed from Queen's Park in August 1920 to his death in November 1962 he served the club with distinction and dignity.

He had joined Queen's Park from Parkhead Juniors as an inside left, but was quickly converted to the right, from where he scored 21 goals in his two seasons, including a hat-trick against Thistle in 1919. Thistle obviously noticed this performance. Inside-right had been a problem position since the days of John McTavish during the war, and Thistle moved to bring Jamie to Firhill in the summer of 1920.

Jamie made an instant impact, scoring on his debut against Dumbarton plus the following week against Clydebank, and all agreed that manager Easton had got himself a clever little forward. Jamie was top scorer come November, but Thistle were having problems at centre-forward, and Jamie was asked to try the central position. Although he scored a hat-trick, ironically against Queen's Park, it was agreed that at 5' 6" he was too small for a centre-forward, and he returned to inside-right.

Although goals weren't abundant for Thistle they had still reached third in the League by the time the Scottish Cup started in February 1921, and Jamie found scoring easier in the cup.

Doubles against East Stirlingshire and Hearts in the semi-final second replay helped Thistle to the Scottish Cup Final. Although he didn't score in the final against Rangers he was a vital member of the forward line, especially when Jimmy McMenemy was forced deep to help the half-backs.

Jamie's first season at Firhill had been a great success. He wasn't a tough player, and in fact was described as *"dainty"*; his success came in reading the game cleverly, and making sure his passing was accurate, though he wasn't afraid to drop back to win the ball from the opposition. In front of goal in those early days he was an opportunist who believed in shooting hard and shooting often, and he ended his first season as top scorer.

He was rewarded with selection for Glasgow against Sheffield, and was the best forward on show in the game at Brammall Lane, and that game was followed up by being chosen for his full international debut in March 1922 against Ireland – a 2-1 win at Parkhead alongside Kenny Campbell. By all accounts Jamie was a little below par – he *"lacked punch and craft"*.

At Firhill he wasn't lacking punch and craft, and ended his next two seasons again as top goalscorer, teaming up particularly well with John Blair on his outside. However, Thistle fans were left to imagine just how much more effective Jamie might be was he just a bit bigger.

He had a knack of swaying one way then changing direction, leaving defenders behind. However, at just ten stone there was only so far his balance and tricky footwork would take him before defenders would just knock him off the ball.

Further games saw Jamie represent Glasgow in the annual match with Sheffield in 1922 and 1923 (when Thistle were also represented by Harry Chatton, Alex Lambie and Tom Crichton). Jamie scored a goal in each game, but his representative and club form wasn't enough to win him further international honours. He did play again for Glasgow, though, in 1924, a 5-0 win against Sheffield.

Jamie's career had come to an unexpected stop through injury in October 1923, and he was greatly missed for much of the League campaign until he returned later in the season, but it wasn't till the start of the 1924-25 season that he was able to play regularly. Davie Ness had joined the club, and he and Jamie formed a successful right wing partnership, providing much of the service for John Miller's goals for two seasons.

Illness again stalled the Kinloch career at the start of the 1926-27 season, and it wasn't until December that Jamie was able to make his first start.

By now Jamie didn't have the energy he once did, but throughout the remainder of the season he masterminded the Thistle attack, prompting Ness and Bobby Grove forward, and feeding Sandy Hair with enough chances to help his goals tally to almost 50 for the season.

Indeed, it was form that prompted Tottenham Hotspur to enquire about Jamie's availability after it was reported that he had not signed a new contract as the new season approached. Spurs were told that there was a mutual unwritten understanding between the club and the player; a few days later Jamie signed a new contract.

Yet just a few games into the season Jamie was forced to rest up, with an *"irritating and painful rash"* that kept him out of the team. Initially it was expected that after a few weeks treatment he would return, but after a few months passed Jamie announced that he was retiring from playing football.

In March 1928 Jamie was appointed a director of Partick Thistle, and the directorship was a post that he filled with dignity and distinction until he passed away in September 1962.

Appearances 241, goals 72.
Scottish Cup winner 1921
Capped for Scotland v Ireland 1922

ALEX LAMBIE

1921 - 1931

Born 15 April 1897 in Troon.

With an acknowledgement of the lack of cover at centre-half for the previous season's Scottish Cup Final, and to the tragic death of Willie Hamilton, burly Alex Lambie was signed as cover for Matty Wilson, and when he played his first games it was simply to deputise for Wilson. However excellent performances in late December 1921 meant that he retained his place in the first team for the remainder of the season, missing just two games out of 26 and remaining as first choice centre-half for all but one of his ten seasons at Firhill.

Alex was signed from Troon in 1921, and had already acquired a reputation for being a solid dependable centre-half, having played with local clubs Dreghorn and Kilmarnock Juniors before his local club. It was felt in some quarters that a step up from the Ayrshire juniors to the top of the Scottish League (Thistle were third from top in December 1921) would be a step too far for Alex. However, the big man didn't look out of place, and helped by Joe Harris beside him, with Willie Bulloch and Kenny Campbell behind, he quickly made the position his own.

Alex wouldn't go down in history as a cultured centre-half like Alec Raisbeck or creative like Jamie Gibson. He was a defensive centre-half in the days when that position was part of the midfield – but his job to defend his goal and the players behind him.

"Lambie, a big chap with a lot to learn, knows his limitations, and acts accordingly. His aim is not to link up the Firhill middle with the attack. He knows that job is too big for him yet. Instead he lashes out at everything, and very much oftener than not gets what he goes out for."
(Daily Record)

He was a spoiler, but a spoiler that was to become a great reader of the game. In those early days at Firhill his main assets were his height and weight. At 6'1" he was powerful in the air and on the ground, although not the quickest, his enthusiasm helped him make tackles when his opponents thought they had him beaten. *"Lambie may not be poetry in motion, but he was at least a man and a half. Lambie seemed to spread himself all over the field,"* said the Daily Record.

Although he had made a name for himself as a reliable centre-half in less than a year, Alex was asked to try a few games as centre-forward in late 1922. It was felt that his power and height could help out at a time when Thistle were struggling badly for a regular scoring centre. The experiment worked, for a while. Alex scored three goals in three games, against St Mirren, Kilmarnock, and Raith Rovers, but after a heavy defeat to Hamilton it was felt that Alex was better used in defence. After that foray up front he returned to centre-half, only to play four times in an alternate position in over 250 games. He truly was a stalwart centre-half.

The Glasgow FA selectors weren't slow to notice Alex's potential. He was selected, along with teammates Harry Chatton, Jamie Kinloch, and Tom Crichton, for the Glasgow team who beat Sheffield 2-0 in 1923 and again in 1927. His partnership with internationals Chatton and Jamie McMullan had helped his game immensely, and the first rumours of Alex's own international recognition came towards the end of the 1925-26 season.

Unfortunately, a mystery injury struck Alex while in pre-season training. At one point there were concerns that he would have to give up the game, never mind international hopes. He did return, but it was only for a handful of games towards the end of the 1926-27 season, though one of them was the Charity Cup Final in which Thistle beat Rangers 6-3.

Alex returned to the team, fitter and stronger, in August 1927 and set about re-affirming his reputation as one of Scotland's best centre-halves, and establishing a new half-back line. Along with Alec Elliot and Eddie McLeod they were to be at the centre of the Thistle team for a good number of years.

An international opportunity finally came Alex's way later in the season. In March 1928 he was uncharacteristically missing from the Thistle team when he was selected for the Scottish League team to play England at Ibrox. England won 6-2 and Alex's direct opponent, the legendary Dixie Dean, scored twice.

It was felt that Alex hadn't shown his true form, despite being up against Dean at the top of his form, and Alex was given a second chance the following week. In the trial match for the Scotland team to play England - what would become the famous Wembley Wizards team – Alex played for a Home Scots team against an Anglos select, but was not selected for the Wembley side.

Alex was awarded the captaincy of the team in 1929 and led Thistle out at Hampden in the Scottish Cup Final in April 1930. He had an outstanding individual game, stopping single-handedly many Rangers attacks and taking the game to a replay. In the replay another good defensive performance was not enough as Rangers won 2-1. Two weeks later Alex was rewarded for his loyalty to Thistle with a benefit match against Liverpool.

After his time at Thistle ended in 1931 Alex moved south to play for Chester and Swindon Town for a spell. He then moved to Ireland and joined Distillery before retiring from football.

Appearances 325, goals 17.
Capped for Scottish League v English League 1928.
Glasgow Charity Cup Winner 1927

Bobby Law

1984 - 1995

Born 24 December 1965 in Bellshill.

Recruited from junior outfit Stonehouse Violet, Bobby Law had a turbulent time at Firhill with the Thistle support quite often split between those that loved Bobby and those that were less keen on his skills.

During the close on eleven years that Bobby spent at Partick he played under no fewer than seven different managers (including those in temporary charge). It was the first of these, Benny Rooney, who handed Law his first team debut just a few months after arriving at Firhill. On 27 October 1984 he wore the number six jersey as a Thistle side very much struggling at that point went down 2-1 at home to Brechin City.

It certainly wasn't the most auspicious of starts to his career at Firhill. Indeed Law would spend the rest of that season in the Thistle reserve side and would make just one other first team appearance in a low key Glasgow Cup-tie at home to Clyde.

The following season though Law began to establish himself as a regular in Thistle's first team squad. He would play in each of Thistle's first six games of the season and at Dumbarton he scored his first ever Thistle goal. Far from a prolific scorer, he would net just eight goals in Thistle colours from over 300 appearances. He did have an eye for the spectacular and his first Thistle goal certainly came under that heading – his long distance volley was the Thistle winner in a 2-1 win.

However, after a bitterly disappointing 0-5 reverse at Rugby Park, six months would pass before Bobby would again feature in the Thistle first team.

As that season drew to a close Thistle, who were involved in a real relegation dogfight, replaced manager Benny Rooney with Bertie Auld and he helped steer Thistle to safety with Bobby Law more than playing his part. Now firmly back in the first team plans Bobby scored in successive games against Ayr United and Clyde.

The 1980s were an almost constant struggle for Partick Thistle with a whole host of players coming through the doors at Firhill. Many of them soon left having made the barest minimum of contributions. While Bobby Law may have had his detractors amongst the often hard to please Thistle support he and Kenny Watson were often the only constants during a bleak period for the club.

With that in mind, few were entitled to as vigorously celebrate promotion at the end of the 1991-92 season than Bobby Law. Thistle's promotion achieved on the last day of the season following a 0-0 draw with Forfar Athletic was by the narrowest of narrow margins. Few cared though when the final whistle sounded and thousands of Thistle fans spilled onto the Firhill surface. While most of the Thistle squad headed for the dressing room legend has it that Bobby ran in the opposite direction and straight into the arms of the jubilant Thistle support.

Once promoted to the Premier Division, Thistle were expected to make a rapid return to whence they had come and many predicted that Law wouldn't be able to make the step up either.

Both predictions were to be proved wrong as Thistle spent four seasons in the top flight with Bobby in the team far more often than he was out of it. He also played his part in notable wins against both halves of the Old Firm.

At times it appeared that his relationship with John Lambie was a little strained. Bobby for all his commitment and application wasn't without his impetuous moments and he often incurred the wrath of referees and, as a consequence, his manager. Who that saw it will forget Lambie's reaction to a Law red card in a Scottish Cup-tie with Falkirk at Brockville?

As already mentioned Bobby was hardly noted for his goalscoring exploits but he did net one unforgettable goal in a fixture against Hamilton Accies.

Or did he? On 11 November 1989 Hamilton, managed by a not long departed from Firhill John Lambie, came to Firhill and soon found themselves trailing 1-0 when a Law thunderbolt struck the post before hitting Accies' 'keeper Andy Murdoch on the back of the head before entering the net. Bobby's delight at scoring was clear for all to see with the TV cameras also present to record the moment for prosterity. Bobby was also on target during Thistle's famous 11-1 win against Albion Rovers.

Bobby's final Thistle appearance was on Boxing Day 1994 when he came on as a substitute towards the end of a 3-0 defeat at Tynecastle. After leaving Firhill, Bobby played with St Mirren, Ayr United and Stenhousemuir before going back to the juniors with Kilsyth Rangers.

Appearances 305, goals 8.

BOBBY LAWRIE

1969 - 1975

Born 1947

The Bobby Lawrie story is similar to many who played in the most famous of Partick Thistle teams on 23 October 1971.

He arrived at Firhill from Irvine Meadow in 1969 and his introduction to first team football at Firhill was hardly in ideal circumstances. After the gloriously exciting decade that the 1950s were for Partick Thistle, the 1960s, aside from the title challenge of season 1962-63, were a downward spiral for Partick Thistle. The last full season of the decade had seen Thistle finish fifth from bottom. Not relegated since the start of the century, the writing was nevertheless on the wall for the club.

The 1969-70 season was an unmitigated disaster for Thistle from start to finish. The League Cup threw up the humiliation of an 8-1 defeat at the hands of St Johnstone and early League form wasn't exactly providing much room for optimism either. It was in these bleak circumstances that winger Bobby Lawrie was handed his debut against Clyde at Shawfield in September 1969. It would be nice to report that Lawrie helped turn the tide in Thistle's favour but it didn't happen that way. Thistle lost their fourth straight League game that afternoon. Indeed in a season where Lawrie would play 21 times for Thistle he was part of a winning Thistle team on just three occasions. Not surprisingly given that kind of form Thistle were relegated at the end of the season.

Better times though were just around the corner and Lawrie, and a whole crop of young players, would have time to develop in the Second Division in 1970-71. Davie McParland took control of first team matters and under his influence players like Bobby Lawrie really started to come to the fore.

There were a few hiccups along the way, particularly in the opening few months of the season, but once Thistle got going there was no stopping them. Promotion was clinched with four games of the season still to play with the title following just a couple of weeks later.

Lawrie's contribution to that success was significant. Described as a *"direct, fearless winger"* with *"two good feet"* and *"promise and power on the wings"* he played over 30 games and chipped in with a more than useful nine goals including one of Thistle's two in the title clinching fixture against Queen's Park at Firhill. The following season he would score an even more high profile goal.

The story of Thistle's League Cup win of 1971 hardly needs to be recounted but Lawrie's contribution to the 4-1 victory needs to be highlighted. It was Lawrie's 15th minute goal, perhaps with a deflection off Celtic defender, that gave Thistle a 2-0 lead. It was also his free kick that led to Thistle's fourth towards the end of an amazing first half.

Lawrie's contribution to Thistle in the first half of the 1970s though was much more than a goal and an assist in the League Cup Final. In the League Cup winning season he played in all but two of Thistle's 34 League games and he remained a regular squad member for the next three seasons as well.

Lawrie appeared in the Thistle first team for the last time in September 1975 as a substitute in a win against Kilmarnock at Rugby Park. After his departure from Firhill he had a spell down the west coast with Stranraer. After leaving Stranraer he joined Ardeer Thistle and re-established a relationship with junior football in Ayrshire. It was a relationship that would last for a further 25 years.

After a spell at Troon, in 1995, he became manager of Whitletts Victoria, one of Ayrshire's least fashionable - in an unfashionable world - junior teams.

Based in Ayr they received next to no support and resources were frequently stretched to breaking point. So much so that as late as 2001 and at the age of 54 Lawrie would still pull the boots on to help out on the field. Not that his commitment stopped at playing.

At the height of Thistle's financial problems in season 1997-98 he auctioned off his prized League Cup Winners medal from 1971, the proceeds of which were split equally between the 'Save the Jags' campaign and Whitletts Victoria. For that gesture alone Bobby Lawrie deserves the title of a 'Thistle Great'.

Appearances 226, goals 24.
League Cup winner 1971
Second Division Championship winner 1970-71

TOMMY LEDGERWOOD

1946 - 1959

Born 23 February 1923 in Coldstream. Died February 2006.

Partick Thistle have, throughout their history, been blessed by the presence of a number of extremely talented goalkeepers. Tommy Ledgerwood would certainly come under that heading.

Former guardsman Ledgerwood was brought to Firhill by manager Donald Turner from East of Scotland League side Coldstream in 1946. After impressing in the Thistle reserve team he was given his opportunity to impress in the first team when he was handed his debut in Thistle's penultimate League game of the season against Motherwell at Fir Park in April 1947. Ledgerwood may have conceded three goals in his debut fixture, a 3-3 draw, but his performance impressed not just the *"good contingent of Partick partisans"* that saw the game but the Evening Times reporter of the time as well. Ledgerwood was described as the *"personality of what had become a raging contest"*. That wouldn't be the last good review that Ledgerwood would receive in a Thistle career that spanned 13 years.

After impressing at the tail end of the 1946-47 season, Tommy found himself sharing the goalkeeping duties with Bobby Henderson for the next few seasons before firmly establishing himself as first choice custodian at the start of the 1950-51 season. William Smith would challenge for his place in the team, most notably in the 1955-56 season, but for the most part of the 1950s Ledgerwood would be the last line of defence in a very good Thistle side and one that challenged for honours throughout the decade.

Although Tommy would play in the Thistle side that would win the Glasgow Cup in 1951 and again in 1954 major honours eluded both him and Partick Thistle. Three times in the 1950s Thistle were to reach the final of the League Cup but on each occasion, against East Fife in 1953, Celtic in 1956 and Hearts in 1958, Thistle were defeated.

In addition to being denied the chance to win a major honour, so too was Ledgerwood denied the chance to win a full international cap for Scotland. Morton's Jimmy Cowan and Tommy Younger of Hibs and Liverpool would dominate the goalkeeping position for Scotland in the 1950s. Tommy was though capped for Scotland at 'B' level against France in Toulouse in November 1952 and kept a clean sheet as Scotland drew 0-0. He was also capped later that season for the Scottish League in a 5-1 win over the Irish League.

In over 300 appearances for Thistle, Tommy produced countless excellent performance and innumerable top class saves. Arguably his best came in a fixture with Hibs at Easter Road in October 1953. At this time the famous Hibs forward line of Smith, Johnstone, Reilly, Turnbull and Ormond was at its peak. The prospect of facing them was enough to give any goalkeeper a few sleepless nights. It had been a pretty even game when Hibs were awarded a penalty kick, which Eddie Turnbull took, hitting it with plenty of power and venom straight into the top right corner, or so everyone thought.

Everyone that is with the exception of Tommy Ledgerwood, who somehow managed to get a hand to the ball and kept it out.

For all Ledgerwood's exploits in the Thistle goal there is a certain irony that one of his most famous games was when he was forced to play outfield. On 4 November 1950, Thistle faced Hearts at Tynecastle and during the course of a first half that would finish with Thistle trailing by three goals to one, Ledgerwood picked up a nasty injury. So nasty in fact that he had to leave the field leaving Thistle, in the days before substitutes, to battle on with just ten men.

Ledgerwood returned to the Thistle goal for the remainder of the first half but the second half started with him lining up in the outside left position. Thought no more than a nuisance, it was Ledgerwood who fired Thistle back into the game with a goal to make it 3-2. That goal helped inspire a famous comeback with the team emerging victorious by five goals to four.

Tommy's Thistle career ended on the final day of the 1958-59 League season.

Tommy sadly passed away in February 2006.

Appearances 338, goals 1
Glasgow Cup winner 1951, 1954.
Capped for Scotland 'B' v France 1952.
Capped for Scottish League v Irish League 1952.

JOHNNY MACKENZIE

1948 - 1960

Born 4 September 1925 in Dennistoun, Glasgow

Johnny MacKenzie has no shortage of highlights to consider when he thinks back on his football career. From appearing in front of 90,000 in one of the three League Cup Finals he appeared in, to winning three Glasgow Cups, from his debut for Scotland in 1949 to becoming the first Thistle player to play in the World Cup (along with Jimmy Davidson), Johnny's Thistle career was a distinguished and successful one. Perhaps the crowning moment for the tricky winger, though, was after his appearance at Hampden in 1954 against Hungary. At the time Hungary were regarded as the best team in the world, and had just beaten England 6-3 and 7-1. Johnny ran rings around the full back, Mihaly Lantos. Afterwards the legendary Ferenc Puskas said he had never seen wing play of such a high standard.

Robert Philip of the 'Daily Telegraph', many years later, pointed out how much of a compliment this was – there were a number of great Scottish wingers around at that time.... *"MacKenzie … was unfortunate to play in the same era as Willie Waddell, Gordon Smith and Billy Liddell."*

Johnny signed for Thistle in October 1944 as Thistle looked to rebuild a side ravaged by the war – player after player were called up to the services. Johnny was to remain with his junior club Petershill for the remainder of the season before joining Thistle, filling the gap that the likes of Alex McSpadyen and Peter McKennan's absences had created.

However, before he could play even once for Thistle he too was called to represent King and Country, and Thistle again had to look elsewhere for players.

While serving in the Scots Guards at Windsor he signed for Bournemouth, in August 1947, on loan. He stayed for the whole of the 1947-48 season, making 38 League appearances and scoring nine times as Bournemouth finished as Third Division (South) runners-up. He was demobbed, and returned to Glasgow in July 1948 to resume his Thistle career.

That Thistle career started the following month with a 2-8 defeat by Queen of the South, but he soon became a favourite of the supporters - *"Partick Thistle fans needn't be alarmed at losing one who has played himself into their hearts,"* commented the Daily Record after reports of Wolverhampton Wanderers interest. The press were equally impressed by Johnny's performance. *"MacKenzie's resourceful play on the right wing suggests that in this young man Thistle have a coming internationalist,"* gushed the Daily Record after just a few months.

The papers were correct, and just a few months after his debut, he was turning out for his first cap against the English League at Ibrox. A month later he was chosen to join the SFA select team who were touring North America. The Daily Record again was quick with the praise.

"MacKenzie's lovely action, his 'fluid action drive' is at the moment your soccer gourmet's delight, and is such as to enthral the American soccer connoisseur, if there is such a thing."

Johnny returned a much more confident player and he was in great form at the start of his second season. Unfortunately he was struck by a mystery illness, and unable to shake it off and was forced to recuperate at his mother's home in Tiree for most of the season. It was a severe setback to a career that had promised riches. He returned in April and created two goals against Queen of the South again. *"Johnny's footwork was as captivating as ever,"* said the Evening Times.

Johnny was tall, 5'10", for a tricky winger, but tricky he was. His was not the speedy way past a defender. Rather he would dribble close to the full-back, tempting the defender to tackle, then Johnny would flick the ball sideways and he was away, with the defender still looking for the ball. He was also an expert crosser of the ball from wide positions, and a range of Thistle centre-forwards including Bert Kinnell, Willie O'Donnell, Alex Stott, Willie Sharp, Gordon Smith and Andy Kerr all benefited from his pinpoint passes.

"He was as swift as a greyhound, a mazy dribbler and, if you think David Beckham can cross the ball, you should have seen Johnny in his pomp," said Robert Philip in the Telegraph.

Perhaps the only thing missing from his game was reluctance to shoot – a flaw that certainly cost Johnny more than a few caps, and also the chance of a move to England. Manchester City were impressed by his *"ability to slink by a defender by a flick and a feint, his tremendous pace and accuracy in the beating of a man."*

"They knew of his shooting timidity," said the Sunday Mail. Thistle valued Johnny too highly, and he stayed at Firhill.

A couple of years later came the opportunity that few players ever get – the chance to play in the World Cup Finals. Unfortunately, the SFA's incompetence meant that the 1954 World Cup in Switzerland was a nightmare for all the Scottish players. Not taking the tournament seriously, Scotland travelled with 13 players, though the rules allowed 22. Not used to summer football, the heavy winter jerseys were completely unsuitable, where Johnny reckoned he lost half a stone in the defeat to Uruguay.

At Partick, Johnny was a regular in the Thistle team that was perhaps the best ever seen at Firhill. In the League, third place was reached in 1954, but it was in the cup competitions that the best results were produced. Johnny helped Thistle reach the League Cup Final in 1953, 1956 and 1958, though all the finals ended in defeat, while the Charity Cup Final was reached in 1951 with his help, though also lost., The Glasgow Cup, however, did bring success and medals for Johnny. 1954 was particularly special – in the semi-final Thistle were 0-3 down to Celtic in a semi-final second replay at Parkhead when Johnny turned the game on its head with a virtuoso performance of passing and wing play. He created five goals as Thistle reached the final with a 5-4 win. In that final Rangers were defeated 2-0. The Cup was also lifted in 1951 (3-2 v Celtic) and the following year (3-1 v Rangers) with a rare goal from Johnny.

Johnny had a short spell at Fulham in 1958, returning in the same year for a second period at Firhill. *"I am glad to be back in Glasgow as my heart has always been here. I'm looking forward to once again wearing the Thistle colours."*

He joined Dumbarton in 1960 for a couple of seasons, before moving to Ireland where he joined Derry City for a successful spell before retiring from playing, taking up a coaching role at Third Lanark in 1967.

Appearances 393, goals 53.
Glasgow Cup winner 1951, 1952, 1954.
Capped for Scotland v Austria 1954, 1956; v England 1954, 1955;
v Finland 1954; v Hungary 1954; v Norway 1954; v Uruguay 1954; v Wales 1953.
Capped for Scottish League v English League 1949; v Irish League 1953.

Other honours
With Derry City: Irish League Championship winner 1965,
IFA Cup winner 1964,
Gold Cup winner 1963.

Ian McDonald

1975 - 1989

Born 26 December 1958 in Glasgow

When midfielder Ian McDonald arrived at Firhill from Eastercraigs BC as a raw 16 year old at the start of the 1975-76 season he began an almost unbroken 14-year association with Partick Thistle.

Not surprisingly for a young player, McDonald didn't go straight into the first team upon his arrival at Firhill. His first season at Partick was spent exclusively in the reserve team where he quickly earned a reputation as a clever and versatile (he played a number of games as centre forward) player. He was among the most talented players of his age group and that ability was recognised when he was selected to play for a Home Scots XI against an Anglo Scottish XI at Love Street. He also accompanied a Scotland Youth team to the Festival of Youth at Cannes although an out of date passport nearly meant that the young McDonald had to stay behind in Scotland.

A breakthrough into the Thistle first team came at the start of the 1976-77 season when he appeared as a second half substitute in Thistle's very first Premier Division fixture against Ayr United. That though would be one of just three substitute appearances that McDonald would make that season, his football education continuing with the Thistle Second XI.

Hopes that season 1977-78 might mark a significant breakthrough into the first team squad were dashed when a knee injury required surgery. Not until March of that season would McDonald return to action.

The competitive nature of the Premier Division was such that it wasn't always considered the right environment to introduce young talent and although now fully fit McDonald was again restricted to only a handful of substitute appearances in the 1978-79 season.

That, however, was soon to change, for in the second half of the 1978-80 season the name Ian McDonald started to appear on a Thistle team sheet on a regular basis. His long awaited first start came against Hibs in December 1979 and that had been preceded some weeks earlier when he came off the bench to score his first goal against Aberdeen. Of the last eleven games of that season McDonald played in ten of them. From now on till McDonald's departure from Firhill in May 1989 he was in the side far more often that he was out of it.

It wasn't the happiest of eras for Thistle though. The club survived another Premier Division season with McDonald playing 32 times in 1980-81 but relegation would follow 12 months later. Although twice Thistle would come close to returning to the Premier Division.

In season 1982-83 McDonald would play 47 times and score three goals, including a vital late strike in a League Cup-tie at Brechin City, but Thistle could manage no better than fourth in the First Division. When Thistle's next promotion challenge ended in failure McDonald's Thistle career looked to be over.

In the summer of 1984 he moved to Motherwell but spent just a few months at Fir Park and by December he was back in the fold at Firhill. Jamie Doyle moved to Motherwell, coming to Firhill in exchange for him were McDonald and Gregor Stevens.

McDonald's debut second time around came against the same side, Ayr United, against whom he had made his initial Thistle appearance, back in September 1976. Seven days earlier, Thistle had lost 7-3 at home to St Johnstone, but with McDonald back in the side Thistle defeated Ayr 2-0.

The remainder of that season and also the next few would present real struggles. McDonald, was a midfielder more of the creative nature rather than a ball winner often bore, unfairly, the brunt of the Thistle fans' frustrations despite making quite often telling contributions.

In season 1986-87 Thistle made a quite miserable start of the season and not until the eleventh game when McDonald scored the winner against Brechin City, did they record a victory. In the next campaign McDonald added goalscoring to his repertoire and scored nine goals including a run of four in six games across October and November.

Season 1988-89 would be his last as a Partick Thistle player. He had a spell on loan at Stranraer and although he appeared as a substitute in John Lambie's first match as Thistle manager, he would make only a further five appearances, the last of which came on the final day of the League season against Raith Rovers.

McDonald started the next season at Morton and after a number of seasons in their midfield he joined the club's coaching staff.

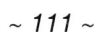

Appearances 329, goals 34

Jimmy "Whitey" McGowan

1941 - 1956

Born 10 June 1916 in Whiterigg, by Airdrie. Died 24 July 1989.

"If they commissioned a bust of the player who typifies Partick Thistle's fighting spirit the model will be Jimmy McGowan."

So said the Sunday Mail in 1952 after the news that McGowan had turned down two dream moves that would have set the McGowan family up for life. Offers were made from both Canadian club Van City FC and US team Detroit, for Jimmy to immigrate to North America and become a player coach. Jimmy was tempted but turned down the excellent terms to stay in Glasgow. *"I want to finish my playing days with the Thistle. They've always been good to me at Firhill, I wouldn't be happy anywhere else"*, said McGowan.

This was typical of the man who had signed for Thistle at the age of 25, after spending a number of years at Maryhill Juniors, and had never sought to play for any other club, stayed for 15 years at Firhill. Jimmy played his first game for Thistle as a trialist against Celtic in April 1941 and signed professional terms just a few days later. The full-back positions had been a problem for Thistle since the war started, but from the start of 1941-42 Jimmy made right-back his position. Peter Curran, who had played both on the right and the left, settled into the left-back role and so started a partnership that lasted through the forties, in front of Bobby Henderson, until Curran was displaced by Bobby Gibb. The McGowan/Gibb collaboration with Tommy Ledgerwood then lasted well into the fifties.

Jimmy McGowan truly was the rock that Partick Thistle was built on for fifteen years. There were only two periods when Jimmy wasn't automatically chosen. In 1944 an injured knee kept him out of the team for 18 games, while in 1950 an appendix operation sidelined him for ten games. Outwith these two spells of unavailability, Jimmy's name was virtually the first on the teamsheet every week – he missed very few games in a decade and a half of top-class football.

In 1945, after helping Thistle win the Summer Cup, Jimmy was selected to travel with an SFA team to play morale-raising games for the troops in Germany at the end of the war. Effectively a Scottish international select of those players not in the services, Jimmy played in two games alongside Jackie Husband and Jimmy Walker. On his return, McGowan turned out for Scotland in games against Belgium and Northern Ireland – again unofficial internationals. Full international honours nearly came for Jimmy in 1948 when he was chosen to be a reserve for Scotland's games versus England and Belgium, but selection in the team didn't happen.

McGowan was described as being *"big and robust"*, and it's true that he wasn't a showy player. Rather, he was known for *"swooping tackles"*, *"lusty kicking"* and *"thundering clearances"*. While perhaps not a fancy player with fancy touches, Jimmy was very good at the basics of defending. *"Here was craft, speed, and tenacity representative of the defensive skill and a treat to witness,"* enthused the Evening Times after a typical McGowan display. Playing against Jimmy was a nightmare for wingers. They never had time to settle – Jimmy was always quick to the tackle. Not for nothing was he known as 'Tiger'.

The one thing that Jimmy could be relied on for was his effort. McGowan *"nearly fell over his own heart it bulged out of his shirt so far"*, said the Sunday Mail after a typically colossal McGowan effort to level the match when Thistle went down 1-2 to East Fife in the 1949 Scottish Cup semi-final. Sadly Jimmy's efforts couldn't bring an equaliser, and the opportunity of playing in a Scottish Cup Final was missed.

However, cup success was achieved in the Glasgow Cup competitions of 1950-51 (Celtic 3-2), 1952 (Rangers 3-1) and 1954 (Rangers 2-0), and Jimmy was proud to captain the team to all three successes. The Charity Cup was also won in 1949 (Celtic 2-1), although there was also a Cup Final disappointment in 1953 when Thistle lost to East Fife 2-3.

At the age of 40 Jimmy played his last game for Partick Thistle in March 1956, before taking a well deserved retirement due to injury. He was awarded a testimonial match against a Glasgow Select in 1957.

Appearances 542, goals 1.
Summer Cup winner 1945
Glasgow Cup winner 1951, 1952, 1954
Glasgow Charity Cup winner 1949
Capped for Scotland in Unofficial Internationals v Belgium 1946, v Northern Ireland 1946.

PETER McKENNAN

1935 - 1948

Born 16 July 1918 in Airdrie. Died September 1991.

Of all the hardships that Partick Thistle fans had to endure during the dark days of the second world war – bombings, rationing, conscription – it's a fair bet that you would have found a few who would have said that the worst part of the war was the way it ruined Peter McKennan's Thistle career.

Peter was the darling of Thistle fans in the period directly before the war, loved for his individual style of play and determination to play entertaining football. He was regarded by many as the best inside-forward in Scotland, and the international selectors agreed, having capped him at League level. When Peter received his conscription notice in April 1939 it was effectively the end of his career, although he went on to have short spells with eleven other clubs during and after the war.

The youngster had been tracked by a number of clubs while with Thorniewood Juveniles and then Whitburn Juniors and Thistle manager Donald Turner had heard good things. He organised a private trial for Peter in December 1934, concerned about alerting others to Peter's availability, and signed him immediately after the try-out. *"I've just signed a boy who, I promise, will be a great player,"* whispered Turner to the other players after the game.

Peter stayed with Whitburn till the end of the season, and it was Turner's intention to let him further develop in the reserves at Firhill.

However, after a good performance in the public trial in August 1935, poor displays by John Wylie, and Turner's belief in Peter's ability, saw him hastily promoted to the first team for two months. His first goal came at the age of 17 years and 60 days (likely the youngest player to score for the club) and was regularly described as the only Thistle forward that was any good.

After that short spell, where he impressed all watchers with his skill but confounded them with his failure to pass when play required it, he was returned to the reserves to rest and develop – the plan all along.

When he returned to the first team, at the start of the next season, he was a changed player, physically at least. Gone was the boy and in his place was a much stronger youth. He scored in the first game of the season against Queen of the South and didn't look back, netting a further 23 times from inside forward. His position, though, was in title only, for Peter would drift around the field, asking for the ball at all times, hence the nickname 'Ma Ba'.

The supporters loved him for his direct attacking style, driving runs and powerful shooting, as did many in the press, though he divided the critics, as can be seen from that written about him in his first real season:

"spearhead ... too greedy ... individual brilliance ... would rather beat three men than pass ... solo stuff ... needs to pass ... directness ... dilly dallying ... none of the square crossing of the pitch ... makes a beeline ... holds the ball too much ... compelling close dribbles ... colourful ... useless manoeuvring ... the youngster's feet twinkled ... clever dribbling and bullet-like shooting ... cannonball shots ... entertainer-in-chief."

However, the Thistle fans, and Donald Turner, were willing to forgive the frustrations of Peter's insatiable appetite for the ball for the occasions when things worked out, such as a game against Third Lanark when one sway of his body sent the whole Thirds team the wrong way. He then set off on a mazy run that took half the opposition to stop him. Or a one-man show against Albion Rovers which Peter directed, scoring four and setting John Wallace up for another two goals. *"He could not get enough of the ball to satisfy"*, said the Daily Record.

Peter wasn't just an individualist, and his partnership with right-winger Alex McSpadyen was blossoming, to the extent that they became known as the Two Macs. They played together for Glasgow against Sheffield in November 1936 and both were suggested for the 1937 internationals, despite the youth of both. The trial match for the game against the English League saw the two selected, Peter making a good enough impression for he played against the English in a 1-0 win at Ibrox. Alex didn't impress enough and had to wait a year for his international chance, when the Macs teamed up in Scotland blue against the Irish League. Both players scored in a 6-1 win that also featured Alex Elliot.

Peter was already on the radar of the English before the international. There were always English scouts watching him, and Arsenal, Spurs and Newcastle in particular expressed interest in signing him. Rumours circulated that Manchester United offered £12,000 for the Two Macs.

Over and over again Thistle rejected the offers, though they could have earned a lot of money. A rumour was jokingly started by a Thistle director that McKennan was going to Huddersfield, and the papers ran the story, not realising that Peter and his team-mates were going to Huddersfield to play a friendly, returning to Glasgow immediately afterwards.

If Peter's critics hoped that maturity would make him more of a team player they were consistently disappointed. They pointed to a game against Hamilton in 1937 when he passed the ball regularly to McSpadyen and John McMenemy and was rewarded with good passes back, and the opportunity to score four goals, as an example of what could be. But he constantly exasperated those who wanted to see football played like chess. Peter had no time for the tactical nuances. He would waltz his way around the pitch, up and down, from side to side, looking for the opportunity to burst towards the goal.

Apart from his skill with the ball he was so big and strong that his physical attributes alone had an upsetting influence on opposing defences. And when he found sight of the goal he loved to let fly, with distance little object. *"I can't name another who can kick the ball with such force when in a shooting position,"* said trainer Jimmy Kennedy. The Daily Record summed up Peter's style of play after the game against Queen of the South in September 1938.

"The star piece was McKennan's goal. McKennan does some things we don't always agree with. His holding of the ball, and losing it, is his fault – no doubt the outcome of his eagerness is to do the utmost for the team. But when he succeeds in his intention, he registers high marks. Several times he attempted to bore through by himself and failed. Failure seemed to urge him the more. This time, he beat man after man, and when he finished by planting the ball in the net Firhill heard a cheer that must have resounded down the Cowcaddens."

In April 1939 the SFA were looking for players to travel to the USA to represent Scotland, and McKennan and McSpadyen were immediately suggested. However, because Peter hadn't signed a new contract with Thistle he was ineligible, and the SFA saw the two Macs as 'a team', and didn't select Alex on his own. Peter's signing dispute with the club was over financial terms and he suggested he might consider looking south for a new club. Thistle fans were aghast…. *"The Thistle forward line without McKennan is like whisky without soda – no fizz in it!"* Disappointed with the offer, Peter refused to play in the final game of the season against Queen's Park.

Donald Turner stated his desire to keep Peter at Firhill, but the onset of war meant that the player suddenly became less desirable. With conscription came the lack of opportunities to play regular football, but Thistle still wanted Peter to sign a new contract. Relations had broken down, and Peter agreed to the new contract, but it was only a convenient way for Peter to get a move south, and Thistle to make some money from a transfer fee.

So it was a further blow when war was officially declared. The transfer system was annulled and player registrations relaxed. Peter guested with Wrexham, Glentoran, Linfield, West Bromwich Albion, Chelsea and Brentford during the war, before he was sent to Germany. Peter also represented Scotland in army internationals and the British Army in representative games.

On his first spell of leave in December 1939 Peter arrived at manager Turner's office with minutes to spare before a game against Celtic, and asked with a smile *"Any chance of a game?"* Needless to say Peter stripped and played, scoring one of the goals in a 4-2 win. Peter and Partick Thistle had solved their differences and when Peter was home on leave he would always make an appearance for Thistle; and these games were eagerly anticipated. On one occasion Clyde man-marked Peter so tightly that the Thistle fans were given the unusual sight of Peter McKennan asking not to be given the ball.

Another treat for the fans came in 1944 when both Peter and McSpadyen were on leave at the same time. Firhill saw its biggest crowd of the season for the return of the Two Macs.

Peter was demobbed from the army in January 1946 and immediately returned to the Thistle team. Normal service was resumed – goals, international rumours and interest from English clubs. However, a groin injury sustained in the army re-asserted itself at the start of the 1946-47 season, and he missed much of the campaign. A further injury at the start of the following season kept him out for the first few games, and when he returned he discovered that new manager David Meiklejohn was unwilling to let Peter play the way he was accustomed to. Peter handed in a transfer request.

West Bromwich Albion knew Peter from the war, and won the race to sign him from Thistle, for a fee reported to be between £10,000 and £12,000. After an injury-hit spell at West Brom Peter joined Leicester City in a swap deal involving Johnny Haines, then moved to Brentford, and Middlesbrough and Oldham. At the end of his career he moved to Ireland, managing and playing at Coleraine until his retirement in 1955.

His post-war career was disappointing, as Peter failed to settle with any of his clubs. We can only speculate what Peter might have achieved had his career not been so disrupted by the war.

Appearances 198, goals 113
Capped for Scottish League v English League 1937;
v Irish League 1938.

ARCHIE McKENZIE

1905 - 1915

Died April 1950

It's unlikely that Archie McKenzie was feeling optimistic about his football career at the end of 1905-06 season. He had made his Thistle debut in a 1-0 win over Aberdeen in August 1905, being brought in from Bo'ness with a view to replacing Andrew Wilson at left-back. However, after a handful of games Archie lost his place and played the rest of the season in the reserves, before being loaned back to Bo'ness for the start of the 1906-07 season. It wasn't an auspicious start to his senior career.

However, when an emergency struck in February 1907 and Thistle found themselves without cover at left-back on the day of a Scottish Cup replay against Dundee, Archie received a desperate telegram asking him to report to Dens Park. After a dramatic rush from Bo'ness to Dundee, Archie met his teammates for the first time that year and turned out for the Jags. However, his day became even more remarkable for after an injury to Willie Howden during the game, Archie was asked to deputise in goal.

Despite a valiant effort, Dundee scored five goals and Thistle were out.

Archie was back in at Firhill, though, and he remained the first choice left-back for most of the rest of the season. Indeed he was one of the first on the teamsheet for a further eight years, equally comfortable on the left or the right.

Football in those days was less sophisticated than nowadays, and the full-back's job was a simple one. Tackling and kicking the ball a long way in a straight line were the main requirements, and Archie was good at both. He *"kicked a good length and tackled fearlessly"*, but it wasn't just these qualities that endeared him to the fans at Firhill. The Daily Record remarked *"McKenzie can shoulder the men freely off the ball. The Thistle Mac is the best back the club have had for several seasons"*, and it was this attribute that earned Archie the nickname 'Rattler'.

The Rattler's consistency, at either full-back position over a period of years, meant that he had the chance to develop partnerships with a number of players, most notably with Neil Gibson and Harry Wilson, his half-back partners. When Willie Bulloch arrived they formed a full-back pairing that combined Archie's energy and Willie's coolness, helping Thistle through the 1910-11 season without losing a game at home, and to a Glasgow Cup Final. In front of 58,000 Rangers beat a weakened Thistle team 1-0; Rangers' goal was scored while Archie was off the field receiving treatment for an injury.

A receding hairline combined with an abbreviation of his name saw Archibald McKenzie with a new nickname – 'Baldy', and Baldy began to receive recognition for his strong and aggressive, sometimes rough-and-ready, defensive play. He was chosen, along with teammate Branscombe, for a trial match to pick a Scottish League team to play England in 1910. Despite a good show, he wasn't picked for the international. A couple of years later Baldy was selected to play for Glasgow against a Sheffield select but had to withdraw from the team due to an injury.

It was for Thistle, though, that Baldy McKenzie was happiest playing, and the tribute he received from Thistle, in the shape of a benefit match (a 1-2 defeat to Rangers in 1910) meant more to him than narrowly missed representative recognition.

The arrival at Firhill of Tommy Adams, and an increasing susceptibility to injury meant that come the end of the 1912-13 season the Thistle fans no longer saw Archie as a first choice full-back, but when selected he never gave anything less than full effort.

When he returned from a lengthy period through injury at the start of the 1913-14 season the Daily Record *said "it was delightful to see the 'father' of the Thistle team. 'Rattler' McKenzie as virile as ever and even safer than usual"*.

However, another injury halfway through the season again lost Archie his place to Adams. Archie played on, passing his experience to the youngsters in the Thistle reserve team, and helped them to a 2-0 win over Rangers in the Glasgow Reserve Cup Final in April 1914.

Games in 1914-15 were even fewer, though on the occasion that he was able to help out his old team mates he was greeted warmly by the crowd, who remembered the sometimes tousy but always wholehearted defender, if a little less bulky in his earlier days.

Archie made his last appearances for Thistle towards the end of that 1914-15 season, having helped Thistle to a Glasgow Cup Final (a 0-1 defeat by Clyde), providing cover as Bulloch recovered from an injury.

The evergreen old servant played his final game for Partick Thistle at Ibrox in April 1915, helping the Jags to a famous 1-0 win over Rangers, before retiring gracefully from a club and a game that he had served with credit and distinction for ten years.

Appearances 265, goals 1.

DONNIE McKINNON

1959 - 1973

Born 20 August 1940 in Glasgow.

Although born in Glasgow Donnie McKinnon spent his formative years in Stornoway after being evacuated from Glasgow during the Second World War. Indeed when he returned to Glasgow five years later he couldn't speak English - only Gaelic!

That didn't seem to hamper his development as a footballer, or that of his twin brother Ronnie, who would play for both Rangers and Scotland.

Donnie progressed through his school team onto Govan Juveniles before joining junior outfit Rutherglen Glencairn.

It was from Glencairn that Thistle plucked a still raw but clearly talented central defender in 1959. Donnie first wore a Thistle jersey in November 1959 in a reserve game against Celtic. Fourteen months would pass before, after continuing his footballing education in the reserves at Firhill, Donnie made his debut at first team level.

St Johnstone provided the opposition at Firhill on 4 March 1961 with Thistle running out 3-0 winners.

Donnie would hold his place in the Thistle side for the remainder of the season and the following season missed just two games as Thistle finished the season in a respectable seventh position in Division One. Season 1961-62 was McKinnon's best in terms of number of appearances.

The following season Thistle spent the season challenging at the top of the league, and the fans who witnessed those games still claim that Partick would have won the League had football not gone into cold storage for the best part of two months during a particularly harsh winter. McKinnon though missed most of the fun. He didn't feature in the Thistle first team until March by which time Thistle's title hopes had already started to recede.

Partick eventually finished the 1962-63 season in third position, which qualified them for participation in the Fairs Cup. Although Donnie would miss both legs of the second round tie with Spartak Brno he did play in the first leg of the first round encounter with Glentoran. After Thistle's exit from the competition, a further nine years would pass before the Jags would again be involved in European football by which time McKinnon was the only survivor from their squad of 1963. When he played against Honved in 1972 McKinnon became the first, and to date only, player to have played for Thistle in European competition in separate seasons.

Thistle's qualification for the 1972-73 UEFA Cup came as a result of their triumph in the 1971 League Cup Final. The fact that he missed the most famous of those games, indeed he played just once that whole season, was unquestionably the biggest disappointment of his time at Firhill. Featuring in the Glasgow Cup Final of 1967 was hardly compensation especially as Thistle lost 4-0 to Celtic. He did, however, play in 28 of the team's 36 League games when they won the Second Division title in season 1970-71.

28 September 1968 marked a landmark in Donnie's Thistle career. In a fixture with Hibs at Firhill Donnie scored the second, winning, goal in a 2-1 victory. In over 300 appearances for Thistle that would be his only goal.

In November 1973 a star studded Manchester United team including, among others, George Best, travelled north to Glasgow to provide the opposition in Donnie's testimonial match. In the programme for that fixture the then Thistle boss Davie McParland paid tribute to McKinnon.

"In the present climate when players throughout the country are continually asking for transfers, Donnie McKinnon is every Manager's dream. At the end of each season, Donnie has put pen to paper without question or argument and his dedication to the game is the perfect example to all young players."

McParland continued:
"While he gives the appearance of being the quiet man of Firhill, his sense of humour and practical jokes can be of great help to the young players when at times tension builds up in the dressing room."

10,000 people turned out at Firhill to honour McKinnon and to watch United record a comfortable 3-0 win. By the time his testimonial came round McKinnon had retired from playing.

His final first team appearance came on 27 January 1973 when Thistle lost 1-2 at home to Ayr United. McKinnon's association with Partick though would last for some time to come. Long before he retired from playing Donnie had clearly more than half an eye for the future.

He enrolled as a trainee physiotherapist and after three years he became fully qualified.

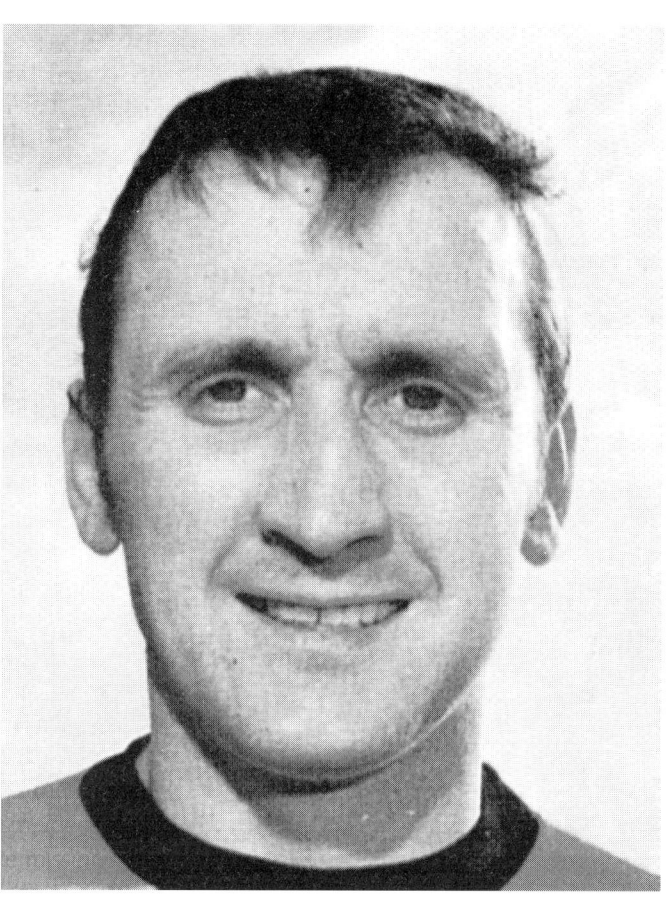

He duly took up a post in this role at Firhill, at first assisting the existing man, Willie Ross, and before long McKinnon established himself as one of the most respected football physios in the business. In addition to carrying the sponge for Thistle he also did so for Scotland, accompanying the Scotland National Team to the World Cup Finals of 1978 and 1982.

Appearances 321, goals 1.
Second Division Championship 1970-71

EDDIE McLEOD

1926 - 1940

Born 28 July 1907 in Springburn, Glasgow.

In the first few decades of the twentieth century Partick Thistle began a policy at odds with many of the clubs at the top of the Scottish game. Rather than taking advantage of other clubs' ability to groom young players by making an offer that couldn't be refused, manager George Easton, and later Donald Turner, preferred to find the talent for themselves at junior level.

While the net was cast wide – Ayrshire and Lanarkshire were exploited – it was Thistle's relationships with the local clubs that reaped the best rewards. Ashfield, especially, have provided players that have represented Thistle with distinction, such as John Ball-antyne, George Boardman, Alex Lauder, Alex McGregor, and in more recent years Craig

Nelson, but one ex-Ashfield player particularly stands out for his contribution to Partick Thistle – Eddie McLeod.

From his signing as a raw 19 year-old in 1926, with a huge act to follow, to his enforced war-induced retirement in 1940, Eddie was to play almost 500 games for Thistle. Only five players have appeared more times for the club. In that time he was to partner with Alex Elliot and Alex Lambie, thus forming a formidable half-back line.

Eddie's hard act to follow was to replace the incomparable Jamie McMullan, who had left Firhill for Manchester City a few months earlier. A number of experienced players had been tried in McMullan's left-half position, including Irish internationalist Harry Chatton, but it was to an inexperienced junior that Thistle turned at the start of the 1926-27 season. It was a gamble for manager Easton, but boy did it pay off!

Eddie was thrust into the team for the first game of the season and missed just one game from then to the end of that campaign. He was soon favourably compared to McMullan. Eddie's intelligent style of play – he was known for his ground passes to the outside-left – was vital in taking Thistle on two cup runs.

One was a success – a Charity Cup Final win over Rangers, while the other ended in semi-final disappointment against East Fife. It was an auspicious first season for the boy from Springburn.

The following season saw Eddie join up with the two Alexs' to form their half-back line for the first time, and this partnership helped Thistle finish to the top six for the following five years. Lambie was a demolisher at centre-half, but Eddie and Elliot were much more.

"Elliot and McLeod darted into the tackle without ever backing away, they brought the ball on, and their passes were wonderfully accurate," said the Daily Record. For someone who was known for his accurate passing and vision, Eddie was incredibly one-footed. Indeed after his retirement he admitted that his right one was only needed for standing on!

In 1930 Eddie represented The Scottish League in a 5-0 win over the Irish League at Firhill, and he again faced the Irish the following year, this time in a 2-3 defeat in Belfast. Eddie came close to full international honours, being selected as a reserve for games against England, Wales, and Ireland, but never played a full match. He did play for Glasgow v Sheffield in 1932 along with his outside-left partner John Torbet.

Eddie and Alex Elliot continued to turn out for Thistle and were asked to partner up with new centre-halves after Lambie left for Chester. Bob Donnelly and George Sutherland were notable colleagues for the two long-serving players.

In 1932 the final of the Glasgow Cup was reached, and lost, but two years later Eddie won his first football medal when Thistle, this time, won the Glasgow Cup Final with a 1-0 win over Rangers at Hampden.

For the first time in his career, Eddie struggled to hold down his place in the team at the start of the 1937-38 season. Relegated to the reserves, and believing he could still play at a higher level, Eddie asked for a transfer, and Thistle agreed.

However, before any offers were made for him, injuries struck the team, and Eddie was back in, in his usual left-half position.

There were doubts again, at the start of the 1938-39 season, over whether he was fit enough to play. Suspected appendicitis while playing for Thistle in Huddersfield had sown concerns.

However, Eddie was in great form, playing some of his best football. *"What a great comeback is Eddie's. Thistle should be grateful that he didn't make use of the free transfer they gave him a wee while back,"* said the Daily Record.

The war curtailed Eddie's opportunities to play football regularly, and at the end of the 1939-40 season, he decided to join up, and retire from football. *"Imagine, I'm too old to play football but not too old to fight,"* he said ruefully on his departure from Firhill.

Appearances 498, goals 7.
Capped for Scottish League v Irish League
1930, 1931.
Glasgow Cup Winner 1934

JIMMY (NAPOLEON) McMENEMY

1920 - 1922

Born 23 August 1880 in Rutherglen, Glasgow. Died 1965

When manager George Easton was faced with injury problems immediately before the Scottish Cup Final in 1921, he turned to the vastly experienced Jimmy McMenemy for advice. *"Play me"* said McMenemy confidently, despite having missed seven recent games through injury himself. The veteran inside-left played the game of his life, helping out a young half-back line as Rangers attacked constantly, still finding time to support his fellow forwards and combine with Willie Salisbury to give Rangers problems at the other end.

Exhausted at the end of the game, Jimmy was delighted. *"I'll value the Scottish badge beyond anything I've ever won,"* he said after the medal presentation. For a player who had won every honour available to him in Scotland to say this shows the extent of the achievement.

Jimmy was a Celtic player for 18 years, receiving two benefit matches from his club and earning a reputation for being a tactical genius, hence the nickname of 'Napoleon'. He was part of the famous Celtic team that won six League titles in a row between 1904 and 1910, and played 515 times, scoring 168 goals, and winning seven Scottish Cup medals.

In his time at Parkhead he played 12 games for Scotland, and it was in a Victory international in 1919 that he teamed up with Jamie McMullan for the first time.

Thistle manager George Easton instantly saw that the partnership would work for Partick Thistle, and in Napoleon he saw the perfect player to develop the exciting young forwards at Firhill.

When Jimmy was given a free transfer from Celtic, the wily Easton was quick to move in, successfully offering a playing contract augmented by an informal position as trainer/coach as opposed to the big money offers from other clubs north and south of the border.

Jimmy immediately made a difference, providing a tactical element to Thistle's play that had never been seen before. In the past the centre-forward linked play, but now that was Jimmy's job, and Salisbury, John Blair and Jimmy Kinloch in particular took advantage of Napoleon's strategic knowledge. Time and again the Thistle youngsters surged forward to get on the end of intelligent passes from deep. But it wasn't just as a provider of chances that Jimmy contributed. Lying deeper than a conventional inside-forward meant that he could help out his half-back line, acting almost as an extra man. It was one of the first tactical changes to the traditional 2-3-5 line-up employed by teams during the previous 40 years.

That subtle change, providing assistance for the inexperienced Thistle team, was one of the main reasons for Thistle's win in the Scottish Cup Final, and his intelligence over Rangers' raw effort was another, as the Daily Record recognised:

"McMenemy was the master man. With him it was a case of mind rather than matter, but when the necessity arose, 'Napoleon' did not scruple to take his man. Jamie was both a half back and a forward."

When Jimmy returned from a summer tour of Canada and the USA, as part of a Scottish select team, with Willie Bulloch he was *"stouter, and perhaps a shade slower"* but continued to show his flexibility, filling in on the right and in deeper roles when required, but always with the intelligence and awareness of the players around him, until the end of season 1921-22.

In the summer of 1922 he was officially appointed coach at Firhill but he was keen to continue playing, and spent a spell at Stenhousemuir before age and fitness finally caught up with Nap. later that year when he retired from playing at the age of 42.

Jimmy remained at Firhill until 1934, as a trusted adviser to managers Easton and Donald Turner, and as a coach and trainer to many grateful players who were lucky to have the assistance of one of Scottish football's greatest players. He left Firhill, returning to Celtic for a spell and training the international team, whilst the his son, John, signed for Thistle in 1936. Jimmy retired from a near 40 year football career in 1940.

Appearances 73, goals 4.
Scottish Cup winner 1921

Other honours
With Celtic
11 Scottish League winners medals, 6 Scottish Cup winners medals, 14 Scotland international appearances (2 in Victory internationals), 14 Scottish League international appearances.

Jamie McMullan

1913 - 1921 & 1923 - 1926

Born 26 March 1895 in Denny. Died 28 November 1964.

When 18 year-old Jamie McMullan signed for Partick Thistle little did he know that in his career he would captain teams to Cup Finals in Scotland and England, lead his country to the greatest win over the Auld Enemy at Wembley, and be transferred for a world record fee being regarded as the greatest Scottish half-back of the twenties.

Manager George Easton did. He had Jamie in his sights since watching him play for Denny Hibs the year before in the Scottish Junior Cup Final at Firhill. He was signed in October 1913 but was promoted to the first team after just five weeks in the reserves, and made an impressive debut against Kilmarnock, setting up Frank Branscombe for Thistle's first goal in a 4-2 win.

McMullan joined a team in transition. A number of players were coming to the end of notable careers while others were starting illustrious ones themselves. A handful of games alongside the legendary Alex Raisbeck, and in front of Baldy McKenzie helped young Jamie settle down quickly, and he was immediately a regular part of the team. In a matter of a few months he was a favourite of the supporters, and regarded as an international prospect. *"He is [James] Gordon and [Alex] Bennett rolled into one, and is an immense favourite with the crowd"*, said the Scottish Referee.

Jamie wasn't tall for a left-half but he was sturdy, and made up for it with terrier-like energy.

His anticipation of play made him defensively strong, covering his defenders, but it was as an inventive player that he was lauded. His touch and ability to send his forwards free with a well-placed pass, often spectacularly from one side of the field to the other, and his willingness to move out of midfield and support his forwards soon saw him recognised for representative football.

Alongside Willie Hamilton and Dougie Morrison (and later Joe Harris) Jamie was part of a half-back line that was capable of spoiling and creating in equal measure, lifting Thistle to excellent League positions. Players playing alongside Jamie suddenly became better players for his influence. Willie Salisbury, Neil Harris and Jacky Bowie benefited from his distribution, Willie Bulloch gained from having Jamie just in front of him.

As the war came to an end Jamie was in line for international honours, and was selected for the Scottish team to play Ireland in March 1919. His train was delayed and he missed the start of his international debut by eight minutes. He made his international name that day with a good performance and played the remaining three Victory internationals, against Ireland and England. It was in the games against England that Jamie first played alongside Jimmy McMenemy. The pair combined well for Scotland, and they were to reproduce that partnership to great effect for Thistle in years to come.

While Jamie was honoured to continue his international career, playing for Thistle was his main focus. His contribution to the club was recognised with a benefit match at Firhill against an International Select XI in 1920. The start of the decade saw a real determination to win real honours. In Jamie's time at Firhill, Glasgow Cup finals in 1915, 1917, 1919, and Glasgow Charity Finals in 1916 and 1918 had been reached, and lost. There was a real desire to bring silverware to Firhill. Internationalists Kenny Campbell, and Jamie's friend McMenemy had been signed. Thistle, and McMullan, meant business.

The new players had helped Thistle to third in the League by the time the Scottish Cup started in 1921. After a gruelling series of cupties there was nobody more proud when Thistle reached their first Scottish Cup Final than captain McMullan. And no-one looked forward more to the final than McMullan – his chance to translate his international success to club football.

Before the Cup Final though was the small matter of the Scotland v England match. There were calls for Jamie to play alongside Thistle team mates Harris and Hamilton, but in the end it was only Jamie that played, and starred, in a 3-0 win. It was to be the first of seven games against England.

Jamie thought nothing of the ankle knock he picked up in the international, but in the week leading up to the Cup Final it started to give him problems, and remarkably he was forced to sit out the final, watching Thistle win from the stands. It was terribly hard luck for the man who had led Thistle to that day.

Despite the Scottish Cup victory Thistle were struggling financially, and established internationalist and club captain McMullan was asked to take a pay cut, along with all the other players for the 1921-22 season.

Jamie furiously refused the terms and Newcastle offered £5,000 for his transfer. Jamie again refused and opted to sign for non-league Maidstone FC meaning that Thistle missed out on a sizeable fee. At the Kent club Jamie was player/manager and signed a number of well-known Scottish players, but his international career stalled.

After two years in England, Jamie returned to Firhill and received a warm welcome, although it was suggested that he perhaps hadn't been training down south as much as he might have. It took him a little time to get fit again, but when he did, again it was Salisbury, and also now Johnny Ballantyne, who took advantage of the master's passing, while Tom Crichton and Alex Lambie got the benefit of Jamie's experience at the back.

Jamie also returned almost immediately to the international fold, playing twice for Scotland in 1924, including captaining his country against England at Wembley in a 1-1 draw. This was the first (and only) time a Partick Thistle player captained Scotland against England.

Jamie was ambitious, and Thistle had acquired a reputation for thriftiness. The club's policy of signing promising youngsters instead of established players didn't match Jamie's dreams. After more than 350 games for the club and a real emotional attachment, Jamie was in tears when he signed for Manchester City in January 1926 for a reported record fee of £8,000. He travelled down to Kilmarnock a day later to say a sad cheerio to his old team mates before a League game.

City were in a peculiar situation; bottom of the League, but on their way to the FA Cup Final. City wanted Jamie to concentrate on them, and he was immediately withdrawn from the Scotland team to play Ireland. Come the end of the season Jamie had returned to the National team, playing in a 1-0 win over

England at Old Trafford, alongside old mate Jamie Gibson. He had also captained his new team to a 0-1 defeat to Bolton in the Cup Final and had been relegated to the Second Division.

City didn't manage immediate promotion, but McMullan's international career continued with huge success while at Maine Road. He was due an emotional return to Firhill, host to Scotland v Ireland in 1928, but was withdrawn again due to club commitments. However, he was released to play against England, this time at Wembley. Jamie captained the team that were to become the greatest Scotland team ever – the Wembley Wizards. Scotland won 5-1.

After over 200 appearances for City, two FA Cup Final defeats and a further Cup semi reached, Jamie retired from playing football at the end of the 1932-33 season.

He was appointed manager of Oldham Athletic before becoming Aston Villa's first manager, where he brokered the transfer of George Cummings from Thistle to Villa shortly before taking over at Notts County and then Sheffield Wednesday as manager. The Second World War brought an end to his illustrious career in football.

Appearances 354, goals 16.
Capped for Scotland v England 1921, 1924, 1925; v Ireland 1921, 1924;
v Wales 1920, 1921, 1926.
Capped for Scotland in Victory Internationals v England April 1919, May 1919;
v Ireland March 1919, April 1919.
Capped for Scottish League v English League 1919, 1921; v Irish League 1919, 1921.

Other honours
With Manchester City
8 Scotland international appearances, English Second Division Championship 1928.

DAVIE McPARLAND

1953 - 1974

Born 5 May 1935 in Larkhall.

The contribution that Davie McParland made to Partick Thistle, in an association that lasted 21 years, is without parallel. As a player he scored 110 goals from 587 appearances, in his role as assistant manager he was responsible for the implementation of a youth policy that produced arguably the most talented crop of young players in the Club's history and finally, as manager he led Thistle to their greatest ever triumph.

All of which was some way off when McParland stepped onto the Firhill pitch for the first time on 7 November 1953 when he appeared as a trialist in the Thistle reserve team in a fixture against Airdrie reserves. Thistle won 3-1 that day with McParland scoring one of the three goals. His performance was such that the watching Thistle manager David Meiklejohn signed him after the game.

It had been no easy task in getting McParland to Firhill. While a pupil at Our Lady's High School in Motherwell he represented both Scotland and Great Britain at schoolboy level and he quite naturally came to the attention of the senior scouts. It would be to the juniors though that the youthful McParland would go, when he signed for Larkhall Thistle, and from there to Firhill.

After a just a few months after his first appearance for Thistle against the Airdrie reserve team McParland made his full debut. An injury to Joe McInnes gave McParland the opportunity to make his first team debut when Stirling Albion visited Firhill on 6 March 1954.

McParland, with *"stockings down over his boot tops"*, made an almost immediate impact. Partick won 3-1 with McParland getting his name of the score sheet when he *"squeezed in a third goal for Thistle in 28 second half minutes after McKenzie and Sharp had made the opening. The winger just got the ball in at the post."*

That would be the only first team appearance that McParland would make in his debut season but he wasted no time at all in firmly establishing himself in the side the following season. In a remarkable Glasgow Cup semi-final against Celtic, McParland scored a last minute winner in a 5-4 Thistle win. He was on target again in the final as Thistle defeated Rangers 2-1.

That Glasgow Cup success plus a similar triumph in 1960 - McParland on target again this time in a 2-0 win over Celtic - were the only trophies that McParland would get his hands on as a player with the club. McParland suffered the disappointment of playing in the Thistle sides defeated in the League Cup Finals of 1956 and 1958.

It is impossible to do true justice to McParland's contribution in just shy of 600 first team appearances; his total of 110 goals included two hat-tricks. The first was netted at Love Street in April 1960, the second at Firhill against Hibs in October 1960 during a season when McParland scored 17 goals. In season 1957-58 he netted five goals in the first four League games of the season and would finish the season as joint top scorer alongside Tommy Ewing with 14 to his name.

His form for Thistle earned McParland international recognition. In 1955 he was capped for Scotland in their very first under 23 international fixture. It didn't have a happy ending, however, as Scotland went down to a 0-6 defeat at the hands of their English counterparts.

In addition to that cap at under 23 level for Scotland, McParland also represented the Scottish League on three separate occasions. In November 1962 he played against the Italian League in the Olympic Stadium in Rome and then a fortnight later was part of the Scottish League side that hammered the League of Ireland 11-0; he was capped again versus the Irish in 1964.

McParland's playing career at Firhill came to an end on 19 April 1969 when he was part of a Thistle team that drew 2-2 with Falkirk, but it was far from the end of his association with the club.

After gaining his SFA Coaching Certificates he combined playing with his duties firstly as a coach and then as assistant manager to Scott Symon. He was handed the special responsibility for the youth policy at Firhill, when he and the then chief scout Jimmy Dickie formed Partick Thistle Amateurs which would produce a whole host of talented young players.

McParland himself benefited directly from the hard work put into Thistle's youth development programme. Following Thistle's relegation at the end of the 1969-70 season, McParland succeeded Scott Symon as Thistle's manager. In his first season as Thistle boss he led his talented young team back to the First Division at the first time of asking. Better was to follow the next season, with Thistle gaining their first major honour in 50 years when Celtic were defeated in spectacular fashion in the League Cup final. The bulk of the victorious Thistle team were either still in their teens or in their early twenties.

McParland would remain as Thistle manager until 1974 when he left Firhill to take up the position of assistant manager to Jock Stein at Celtic. He returned to management in his own right when between 1978 and 1982 he was manager of Hamilton Accies.

After leaving Hamilton his obvious talent in terms of developing of young players saw McParland take up the role of Youth Development Officer at a number of Clubs most notably Motherwell.

Although 23 years may have passed since his last official involvement with Partick Thistle he remains a frequent and welcome guest at Firhill.

Appearances 587, goals 110.
Glasgow Cup winner 1954, 1960.
Capped by Scottish League v Italian League 1962; v League of Ireland 1962, 1964.

Denis McQuade

1969 - 1978

Born 6 January 1951

In BBC's 'Cult Heroes' series a few years ago 48% of Thistle supporters that took part voted Denis McQuade as Thistle's all time cult hero. There are certainly few, if any, Thistle players that engender as much affection as Denis McQuade did and still does. And that affection is a result of more than just having played over 300 times for Partick Thistle. It's more about the way that McQuade played the game.

McQuade's route to Firhill was traditional enough. Stepping up from the junior ranks, in his case St Rochs, is now something of a rarity. In McQuade's day though that was very much the norm. If that was traditional, then very little else about Denis McQuade was.

The man who would one day become known as 'The Enigma of Firhill', at one stage was studying for the priesthood. The church's loss was very much Partick Thistle's gain. He was also considered as something of an intellectual, by no means normal in a football club's dressing room. Alan Rough in his autobiography can remember McQuade replying to a half-time tirade administered in his direction by then boss Bertie Auld in somewhat untypical fashion. As Auld cursed and raved over the role McQuade was playing in the team Denis piped up, *"Well, Mr Auld, I thought that my raison d'etre was to be the catalyst for our attacking forays, so what do you think is wrong with my modus operandi?"*

Whether that story is apocryphal in nature or not is largely irrelevant as it helps create the image of a player who was, to say the least, just that bit different from other footballers. The stories of him beating six players before falling on his backside when faced with an open goal are legend.

McQuade's playing career at Firhill though would span the best part of ten years during which he would clock up well in excess of 300 appearances. Clearly there was much more to Denis McQuade than an unpredictable talent.

He made his debut on the Firhill stage at a time when Partick Thistle were at a fairly low ebb. He sat on the bench as barely 1,000 people turned out to watch an already relegated Thistle side slide to yet another defeat, this time 1-2 against Morton in April 1970. Even at this low point in the club's history there were signs of better times to come. Also making his debut that night was Alan Rough. Less than two years later both would play a major part in Thistle's 1971 League Cup triumph.

Before then though, the team had the small matter of hauling themselves out of the Second Division. McQuade played no small part in helping them to do just that. In his first full season at Firhill he made 43 first team appearances and scored 15 times. Not bad for a winger and a total bettered by only Frank Coulston and Jimmy Bone.

There was even better to follow the next season when McQuade was once again a virtual ever present in the Thistle team playing in over 40 games.

His goal tally was reduced slightly to eleven but included in those eleven goals were some really important ones. It was two that helped see off Falkirk in the League Cup semi-final and it was Denis who scored Thistle's third goal during the 4-1 win against Celtic in the final. He also scored all three of the Thistle goals in a 3-1 home win against Dundee United just a few weeks after the team lifted the League Cup.

To complete a memorable season for McQuade he was capped for the Scottish League against the English League, scoring one of the Scots goals in a 3-2 defeat at Middlesbrough. That came just a couple of months after he represented Scotland at under 23 level in a match against Wales, with McQuade coming on as a second half substitute. However, despite being named in a number of squads and accompanying Scotland to the Independence Cup in Brazil in the summer of 1972 he was never given the opportunity to display his unique talents at full international level.

For both Denis McQuade and Partick Thistle, topping the achievements of season 1971-1972 would prove to be an impossible task. McQuade's Thistle career though didn't end at the completion of that season. Quite the reverse, for he would continue to entertain and, it must be said, exasperate the Thistle fans for many years to come.

The good far outweighed the bad. He would in another three seasons top the 40-appearance mark and in season 1974-75 he helped himself to 15 goals including his second Thistle hat-trick when he bagged three against Hearts in September 1974.

All good things must come to an end and McQuade's Partick Thistle career reached that point in the early stages of the 1978-79 season. His final appearance in a Thistle jersey came against Hearts in an Anglo-Scottish Cup-tie in August 1978. A few weeks later he became a Hearts player when he and John Craig moved to Tynecastle with Donald Park moving to Firhill in exchange.

He didn't quite make an immediate impact at his new club - his first game as a Hearts player was against Thistle - but he didn't have to wait too long before doing so. He scored his first Hearts goal in only his second game and in his first Edinburgh derby fixture in November he scored the winner in a 2-1 victory.

Despite McQuade's contribution of four goals, Hearts were relegated at the end of his only season at Tynecastle. The next season he once again teamed up with Davie McParland, the man who led Thistle to the League Cup win in 1971, who was now manager at Hamilton Accies, before retiring at the end of the 1979-80 season.

Outside football McQuade made a successful career in IT working in Bermuda and Australia, and back in Scotland Denis is a frequent and popular visitor to Firhill.

Appearances 333, goals 82.
League Cup winner 1971
First Division Championship winner 1975-76
Second Division Championship winner 1970-71

Alex (Spaddy) McSpadyen

1935 - 1943

Born 19 December 1914 in Holytown. Died October 1978.

Alex McSpadyen became used to making dramatic progress during his football career. The speedy winger made the jump from playing juvenile football to playing at a senior first team level in two weeks, when he signed for Thistle from Holytown United in 1935, and his elevation from raw talent to international footballer in two and a half years was notable for the fact that he had lost a year of his embryonic career to influenza. There's no doubt that Spaddy would have gone on to reach the very top of his career had the war not disrupted things.

In the second half of 1934-35 there was no shortage of right-wing talent. Although David Ness was coming to the end of his Firhill career, Thistle already had cover in the shape of Bobby Regan and John Neish. However, when the opportunity presented itself in March 1935 to sign the most promising player in juvenile football, Donald Turner was quick to move, and Alex McSpadyen moved from his young team-mates in Holytown to begin training with experienced pros and internationalists.

Alex was a natural winger with the juveniles, quick and strong with his crosses, but no one expected him to graduate from the reserves for a few months. However, after just one reserve game he earned his chance of a first-team debut as Regan moved to the left wing to accommodate the teenage prodigy. It was a debut to remember; Alex set up Sandy McLennan for a goal and the jersey was his for the remainder of the season. The Daily Record was in no doubt of his quality.

"I fancy this boy McSpadyen has come to stay. He plays the game like a natural footballer, controls the ball deftly and is quick away. When he takes his head to the ball he can give it direction, which is something few young players can do."

A remarkable season of international honours and professional football was rounded of when Alex helped Thistle to win the Charity Cup Final against Queen's Park.

The following season saw Alex as firm first choice outside-right, but the team had a significant change. Peter McKennan had signed for Thistle, and the teenage partnership began to develop into one of the most potent ever seen in Scotland, never mind Firhill. Alex responded to Peter's passes, and Peter found a willing outlet outside him in Alex. They would interchange their positions and Alex would take advantage of the confusion by speeding past unsuspecting defenders to shoot at goal.

It was a setback to Alex, and to Thistle, when he was struck down by influenza in October 1935 and missed the remainder of the season, making a brief comeback in the reserves after he recovered from his illness. However, he had to wait until Bobby Regan was sold to Manchester City, missing just three games in 1936-37 once back in the team at the end of August. It was a game against Clyde in September 1936 that the Thistle fans realised that Spaddy had returned to form. In a blistering seven minute spell he scored twice and created another goal as Thistle ended the game 6-0 winners.

Attention wasn't just coming his way from inside Firhill. English clubs, particularly Birmingham and Leicester, began sniffing round. Alex was touted for international games against Ireland and Germany, and Alex and Peter McKennan now christened the 'Two Macs' played for Glasgow against Sheffield. Alex scored Glasgow's goal in a 1-2 defeat; the two players were becoming synonymous with each other.

Alex had always been a dangerous provider due to his speed and accurate crossing, but he also began to weigh in with goals of his own. In particular he took advantage of deep crosses from William Gray with late runs from the opposite wing and diving headers.

In late 1937, Thistle recognised the fact that Alex could be a target for English clubs. *"... McSpadyen is impressing as one who would be suitable for the South. He is recognised as just about the fastest thing in football this side of the border. So far as I can gather no approaches have been made ..."*. Indeed Leicester soon had an offer turned down, while Manchester United were rumoured to have unsuccessfully offered £12,000 for the Two Macs.

Both players were selected for the Scottish League's game against the Irish in 1938, and Alex was exceptional – the best player on the field – scoring one goal in the 6-1 win. Following the League international, Alex was handed his full international debut against Hungary at Ibrox, and he ripped the visitors' defence wide open. Another notable success.

His form was such that a call-up for the foremost game of the season, the international against England, was expected to be a formality when Celtic's Delaney called off. His mixture of skill, strength and speed made him one of the outstanding right-wingers in the country.

As the ultimate international honour approached Alex was injured against St Johnstone, two weeks before the game. As the nation held its breath the newspapers ran daily fitness reports. Alex made his comeback a week later to huge cheers from the Thistle fans, and inspired them to a 4-1 win over Third Lanark. He duly received his international call two days later.

Sadly his performance against England was too inconsistent and too individualistic, though he wasn't helped by terrible weather conditions that reduced the Hampden pitch to a ploughed field. His international career wasn't ruined by the England game, and the Two Macs were selected to travel to Canada for the SFA's tour in 1939. Unfortunately, Alex's partnership with Peter, normally a positive, was to be a failing. Peter hadn't signed a contract for the next season and was ineligible; the SFA didn't want one Mac without the other, and Alex didn't travel to Canada.

Wartime hindered normal football and Thistle were affected by the loss of several of Alex's team-mates, called up to aid the war effort. Indeed at the age of 25 he was regarded as the old man of the forward line, suffering from a niggling knee cartilage injury. His wartime work meant that he was unable to schedule an operation. He continued to play, with occasional absences for rest, until he was called up in 1943, his characteristic speed earning him the nickname the 'Firhill Flyer' some years before Jimmy Walker took the title.

Whilst undertaking army training, Alex played some games for Aberdeen, but when he was on leave he found his jersey waiting at Firhill for him. In March 1944 his leave, and that of McKennan's, coincided, and a huge crowd of 38,000 flocked to Firhill to see the Two Army Macs run out for Thistle again.

It was to be Alex's last game for three and a half years. He returned to Glasgow after the war, in the summer of 1947, a shadow of his former pacey, powerful self, and only lasted a handful of games before succumbing to his knee problems in late August, never to play for Partick Thistle again.

Alex was placed on the transfer market in May 1948 and had spells with Millwall and Portadown before returning to Inverness Caledonian to end his career.

Appearances 297, goals 33.
Glasgow Charity Cup winner 1934
Capped for Scotland v England 1938;
v Hungary 1938.
Capped for Scottish League v English League 1941; v Irish League 1938, 1939.

DAVIE MATHERS

1950 - 1959

Born 25 October 1931 in Glasgow.

Davie Mathers first came to the attention of Partick Thistle, while still a pupil at Govan High School, when he was spotted by Thistle manager Davie Meiklejohn playing in an inter-schools fixture in 1948. A year later, and still at school, he featured in a Thistle team for the first time when he was fielded in a reserve fixture with Hibs.

Mathers was eventually handed his first team Firhill debut, a broken ankle sustained in a reserve fixture keeping him out of action for a period, at right half on 25 February 1950.

Thistle won 2-0 and thus an illustrious Thistle career could really get off and running. It was one that would see Mathers make a little under 300 appearances and be capped at full international level.

Like so many Thistle players from the 1950s Davie Mathers was denied any tangible reward for his role in arguably the most talented sides in Thistle's history. He missed out on a place to face, and ultimately lose, to East Fife in the 1953 League Cup Final. He did, however, make final appearances in the same competition against Celtic and Hearts but they would also end in defeat.

Thistle's silverware haul of the 1950s was restricted to Glasgow Cup triumphs in 1952 and 1954, but injury rather cruelly denied Mathers the opportunity of playing in either of those two victories.

In 1954, Mathers form at Firhill was described by one contemporary source of the time as the *"best left half in Scotland"*, such that he was capped at full international level for Scotland. Although Scotland had qualified for the Word Cup Finals in Switzerland, Mathers debut came during something of a low ebb for the national team. In their final home match before the World Cup Finals Scotland had been booed from the field following an insipid 1-0 win over Norway. Shortly after that game an 18 man party, including Mathers, travelled to Norway and Finland for two warm up games that would decide the make up of the squad to go to Switzerland.

Mathers didn't feature in the 1-1 draw with Norway in Oslo but he and Johnny MacKenzie were included in the side to play in Helsinki.

Playing in Lord Rosebery's colours, Scotland won 2-1 with Mathers described as *"using the ball shrewdly"*.

There would be no place at the World Cup Finals for Mathers, since for some inexplicable reason of the pool of 22 selected prior to the Finals only 13 made the trip to Switzerland. Despite the fact that Thistle's Chairman Tom Reid was also Chairman of the Selection Committee, Mathers was one of eight players that remained in Scotland on standby. Thistle, though, were represented by Jimmy Davidson and Johnny MacKenzie.

Mathers would gain one further representative honour two years later. In September 1956 when he was picked as part of the Scottish League side to face the Irish League. The Scottish League cantered to a 7-1 win but Mathers, perhaps because the game was so one sided, was unable to make much impact on proceedings.

After leaving Firhill Mathers spent a short spell with East Stirling before retiring.

Appearances 272, goals 11.
Capped for Scotland v Finland 1954
Capped for Scottish League v Irish League 1956

DAVID NESS

1923 - 1935

Born 15 August 1902 in Irvine.

It was a tall order. To replace John Blair - the man who scored the goal to win Partick Thistle the Scottish Cup for the one and only time. That was exactly the task given to Davie Ness when he joined Thistle from Nithsdale Wanderers in 1923. Davie was small, at 5' 6" just the right size for a tricky right-winger, and the fact that *"The Dancing Master"* spent twelve years at Firhill suggests that Davie Ness did help the Thistle fans forget about Blair.

Davie began his footballing career with his local junior team Irvine Meadow, where he was capped for junior Scotland, before joining non-League Nithsdale for a short spell, and he spent no time in grabbing the right wing place for himself, dispossessing Blair and installing himself as the regular winger for the rest of his time at Firhill. His liveliness, speed and good crossing, all requirements for a winger, were present. Davie had a preference for placing his crosses on the head of his centre-forward, that first season it was Sandy Hair. *"Dinky"* crosses they were called. The Sunday Mail was an early fan, enthusing after a handful of games:

> *"Partick Thistle have picked up a gem. He doesn't waste too much time getting the ball over, neither does he part with it like the proverbial hot potato."*

In that first season he combined with a number of inside partners such as Jamie Kinloch, Johnny Ballantyne, and Bobby Grove, but in the following years it was Kinloch that he was to team up with regularly, forming a much admired right sided attack.

Davie was also making a name for himself as a goalscorer, and he finished season 1925-26 at second top, and it was this combination of scoring and providing that alerted the Glasgow FA selectors. Davie was chosen to play for Glasgow against Edinburgh and Sheffield in September 1926. Glasgow won both games and Davie scored one of the goals in the 3-0 win over Edinburgh. Further games followed against Sheffield in 1927 and 1928. Davie was justifying the claims in the Daily Record of December 1928 that he was *"the best outside right wing forward in the country"*, but international honours still eluded him.

By 1927 Grove had become his partner of choice and this pairing helped Davie again improve as a player. Previously a wide man pure and simple, he learned to cover space inside when Grove dropped back to help the defence. This was the kind of intelligent outside-forward play that lifted Thistle to top six League finishes five years in a row between 1928 and 1932, and a Scottish Cup Final in 1930, with Davie literally on the fringes of the team, but in essence at the heart of the side.

Davie had his best season until then for Thistle in 1928-29, and it coincided with the return of Ballantyne from America. Davie blossomed as a player, eagerly accepting probing passes and finishing the season with 18 goals from his wide position. Rumours abounded that Davie would be the next high profile Thistle player to move to England. He was happy to stay at Firhill, but was struck by illness over the summer of 1929 and didn't play until the end of October.

This season was different, for he played more as a provider and entertainer. *"He toyed with the defenders, juggling the ball and feinting in mystifying fashion,"* raved the Daily Record. Davie was rewarded for his seven years at Firhill with a benefit match against Rangers in August 1930.

After ten years of continuous outstanding service at Firhill Davie was eventually recognised by the international selectors who considered him for the Austria and England internationals in 1933 and 1934. He wasn't selected then, but did get the call for the League international against the Irish League at Firhill in October 1934, alongside George Cummings. Davie was one of the few that looked as if they could play at a higher international level as Scotland won 3-2 thanks in part to a goal from Davie himself.

Although Davie had been recognised at international level, at club level things weren't so rosy. He had fallen out with the management, who were dis-appointed that he wasn't able to adapt to new tactics. Just a fortnight after his cap for Scotland he was dropped by Thistle, his place taken by Bobby Regan. Towards the end of the season Thistle signed highly rated winger Alex McSpadyen, and it was felt that the writing was on the wall for Davie's Firhill career.

In recognition of his service to the club Thistle were quick to offer a free transfer to allow Davie to get fixed up easily with a new club, but he took the opportunity to retire from football, despite a number of offers. On leaving Firhill Davie returned to Ayrshire, opening a pub in Saltcoats.

Appearances 424, goals 97.
Glasgow Charity Cup winner 1927.
Capped for Scottish League v Irish League 1934

GEORGE NIVEN

1962 - 1968

Born in Blairhall.

Goalkeeper George Niven joined Thistle in the latter portion of the 1961-62 season when Willie Thornton signed him from Rangers.

Niven had started his career with Rangers, joining them from Coupar Angus, in 1947 and in addition to having won every honour available to him while at Ibrox he had been capped three times by the Scottish League prior to his arrival at Firhill. His move though was seen very much as a chance for the player to rebuild his career. At the age of 32 he hadn't featured at all in the Rangers team in season 1961-62 and had been largely inactive in the months in the lead up to his arrival at Firhill, following surgery on an injured knee. Niven though couldn't wait to get started and on the morning he signed for Thistle he asked manager Thornton if he could *"go to Firhill tonight and put in a spot of work with the part-time players"*.

His first appearance in a Thistle jersey came in the low key surrounds of a friendly match at Queen of the South. Thistle lost that fixture 1-0, but Niven's manager described his new player as having played *"extremely well"*.

His full debut followed seven days later, on 24 February 1962, when Dundee visited Glasgow. Dundee arrived at Firhill as League leaders and would finish the season as champions. A tough debut for Niven was predicted and sure enough he was called into action inside the first 30 seconds, but by full-time Thistle had put a massive dent into Dundee's title hopes by running out 3-0 winners. Niven even had the good fortune of watching a Dundee penalty smack against the post thus helping him on his way to a debut clean sheet.

Had there been doubts surrounding Niven's fitness prior to his arrival then they were soon dispelled. After his debut against Dundee he played in all eight of Thistle's remaining fixtures in season 1961-62 and he played in all but two of their 49 League and cup games in 1962-63. The following season again he missed just one game, however, he wasn't immune to injuries. On New Year's Day 1963 Thistle preserved an unbeaten League run that went all the way back to September with a 2-1 win over Clyde at Shawfield. It was a victory that was not achieved without cost however, for on a frozen surface Niven broke a bone in his wrist and a lengthy period on the sidelines was predicted. He was, however, back in the Thistle goal for their very next League fixture against St Mirren. The hardest winter for many years dictated a long two month gap between those fixtures. While football was in cold storage Niven missed just one game, a Scottish Cup-tie with Morton.

While that enforced break did no harm to George Niven it had a major, negative, impact on Thistle's season. At the turn of the year Thistle had looked well placed to repeat Dundee's title success of the previous season, but the inevitable fixture pile up - Thistle played a total eight League games in the month of April - took its toll and Thistle eventually finished third behind champions Rangers and Kilmarnock.

That third place finish though qualified Thistle for European competition for the very first time and George Niven played in all four of Thistle's Fairs Cup-ties in September and November of 1963, against Glentoran and Spartak Brno.

He also remained very much the first choice 'keeper at Firhill for the next few seasons. Only in season 1965-66, when James Gray - the man Niven had replaced in goal back in February 1962 and featured in 18 matches - was his place ever in serious jeopardy. Indeed in his final season he missed just two games and in February and March kept a clean sheet in five successive League fixtures.

At the end of the 1967-68 season Niven, now 38, called it a day. The final game of a career that had spanned 21 years came on 27 April 1968, when Thistle travelled to play Airdrieonians. It was somewhat apt that Niven kept a clean sheet as the two teams rounded off the season with a 0-0 draw.

Appearances 257, goals 0

Honours: With Rangers: 5 Scottish League winners medals,
1 Scottish Cup winners medal, 7 Scottish League international appearances.

ALEX O'HARA

1977 - 1984

Born 21 October 1956 in Glasgow.

Signed for a then Thistle record fee of £25,000, Alex O'Hara became a Partick Thistle player in October 1977 when he signed from Rangers. Rangers had recruited O'Hara from Glasgow Amateurs and handed him his first team debut, while still just 16, and he wasted next to no time in making a mark - in his first season at Ibrox he scored five times. After his successful first season at O'Hara found it somewhat harder to force his way into the first team but by the time of his arrival at Firhill he had played 32 games for Rangers and had scored seven goals. It was understandable then why Bertie Auld rated his new signing so highly. Commenting in a Thistle programme shortly after O'Hara's arrival, Auld has this to say about his new player:

"He has added a lot of skill and endeavour in the highly competitive midfield area. I feel that he will prove one of the bargain buys of the year". Certainly O'Hara wasted next to no time in making an impact at his new club.

He made his debut as a substitute against Dundee United, but the following week he was in from the start and scored the Thistle winner in a 2-1 win at Ayr United. He scored eleven goals in his debut season, a tally he would surpass just once as a Thistle player.

Of those eleven goals, three of them came in one match, a Christmas Eve fixture with Ayr United at Firhill. A whisky firm entered into a sponsorship deal whereby they donated a case of whisky to every scorer of a hat-trick. Alex's treble, only the second Premier Division hat-trick by a Thistle player (the first being Jim Melrose) made sure that there was something a little extra to celebrate at Christmas.

All in all it was a highly successful first season at Firhill for O'Hara. In addition to scoring eleven goals, and reaching the Scottish Cup semi-final, a feat he would repeat the following season, he received a call-up into the Scotland Under 21 squad for a fixture with Wales. He remained, however, uncapped.

O'Hara scored eight goals in his second season, and in 1979-80 the total dropped to five but he did have the satisfaction of scoring twice in the course of a 4-3 win against his former club Rangers.

The 1970s had been in the main a successful decade for Thistle and the 1980s too started in a positive fashion. In 1980-81 Alex topped the scoring charts for the only time during his stay at Firhill. His total of twelve goals was two more than Tony Higgins, the next player on the scoring list. Despite the departure to Hibs of manager Bertie Auld, Thistle, with Peter Cormack now at the helm, survived comfortably enough in the Premier League. That would all change the following season with Thistle relegated to the First Division on the last day of the season.

Thistle's hopes of an immediate return to the Premier Division were seriously hampered by a dreadful start the next season and they finished behind promoted St Johnstone and Hearts in addition to Clydebank.

After missing out on promotion from the First Division the first time around, Thistle looked set to make no mistake the next season. At the turn of the year they led the League by some distance and promotion looked all but secured. The second half of the season though was little less than a disaster. After the sale of Maurice Johnston to Watford it hardly helped things that O'Hara, who had scored eight goals up to then, missed the best part of three months of through injury. He only returned to the team for the final game when, typically, he scored the winner in a 2-1 win at Falkirk. By then though promotion had gone, and by the start of the next season so too had O'Hara.

After leaving Firhill O'Hara signed for Morton and he would spend the next six years at Cappielow clocking up a little short of 200 League appearances and once again taste Premier Division football. His association with Morton ended in 1990 and his last season in senior football was spent playing for Hamilton Accies. His final port of call was in the Ayrshire Juniors with Glenafton Athletic, then managed by his former Thistle team mate Alan Rough.

Appearances 289, goals 61.
Glasgow Cup winner 1981

Denis (Denny) O'Hare

1922 - 1931

Born 21 January 1900 in Renton.

There are very few players who have played for Partick Thistle and gone on to make a career for themselves playing football on the continent. Denis O'Hare was lucky enough to have a ten-year career at Firhill before emmigrating to France to become player/manager of top club Cercle Athletique de Paris.

Denis O'Hare was signed from St Anthony's at the end of the 1921-22 season with a view to replacing John Struthers at right-back, though the start of the season saw Tom Crichton covering the position. Denis did however get a regular run in the team when Crichton switched to the left to replace Willie Bulloch, who was injured, and Denis established himself as the regular right-back until injury struck in September the following season. It wasn't until the end of December 1923 that Denis returned to the team, allowing Crichton to return to left-back.

The start of 1924-25 saw Robert Paton take his right-back position, holding it for most of the season, Denis making only a handful of appearances throughout the season. Towards the end of the campaign Third Lanark, struggling in a relegation battle, asked permission to sign Denis, and Thistle agreed to a short-term transfer, but he was unable to save Thirds, and returned to Firhill at the end of April.

If Denis hoped that his run of games at Cathkin would help him regain a first team place at Firhill he was bitterly disappointed when he picked up a bad injury against Celtic in the Glasgow Cup in September 1925, and that kept him out of the team until December, when he returned as first-choice right-back.

Fully fit at the start of the 1926-27 season, O'Hare was frustrated that Paton was again in front of him as first choice, but in September, he got his chance, and was to keep his place in an almost unbroken run of League games, teaming up successfully with Stewart Calderwood to create an effective full-back partnership.

The end of the season was particularly successful as Thistle went on a run to the semi-final of the Scottish Cup, and to the final of the Charity Cup, which saw Denis pick up a winners medal for his performance against Rangers.

Denis wasn't a showy defender. Rather he was a steady full-back who read the game well, was rarely caught out of position and remained cool under pressure. Rather than kicking the ball clear as soon from his opponent as soon as he won it, he preferred

~ 142 ~

to find a team-mate with the ball, and developed good understanding with right halves such as Jamie Gibson, Harry Chatton, and laterally Alec Elliot. He was rewarded for his service to the club with a benefit match against Celtic, a 2-2 draw in September 1928.

Denis had missed out on a large number of games in his career, and he succumbed again, in March 1930, to a knee injury. It was hoped that he would return for the following season, but apart from a brief appearance in the Davie Ness benefit match against Rangers in August 1930, he didn't play again for Thistle, and was given a free transfer to help him find a new club.

O'Hare began a trend amongst British players of moving to France and in 1932 there were 20 Brits in the French League. Denis was appointed player/coach of Parisian club Club Cercle d'Athletique in 1932 and spent a successful season developing the game in France. He was selected by the French League to play in three representative games in 1933 against Brussels, Czechoslovakia and Portugal before retiring from the game and returning to Scotland.

Appearances 229, goals 0.
Glasgow Charity Cup winner 1927

DONALD PARK

1978 - 1983

Born 19 July 1953 in Inverness.

Born in Inverness, Donald Park first made his mark in senior football with Hearts, joining the Tynecastle side from the old Caledonian club from the highland capital. He made his Hearts debut during the course of the 1972-73 season, when he lined up wearing the number seven jersey in a home match against Arbroath. Hearts won 3-0 with Park marking his debut by scoring the third Hearts goal. Indeed goals would prove to be a feature of Park's early games for Hearts, no fewer than five coming his way in his first eight games. Included in that total was the clincher in a 2-0 victory over Thistle. It was hardly a surprise then considering his early impact at Tynecastle, that he kept his place in the Hearts side for the remainder of the season, something that he was able to do throughout his duration of this his first spell as a Hearts player.

Unfortunately he was unable to lay his hands on any honours while a Hearts player although he did make an appearance in the 1976 Scottish Cup Final when he replaced another future Thistle player, Willie Gibson, as his team went down 3-1 to Rangers.

In 1978, after six years with Hearts, it was time for a move with Firhill his destination. Denis McQuade and John Craig moved in the opposite direction to enable the transfer to go through. So just seven days after Park had scored Hearts' goal in a 1-1 Edinburgh derby he found himself lining up for Thistle against his old club at Firhill. Park ended up on the winning team with a 3-2 victory.

It took Park seven months to claim his first Thistle goal but when it did come it could hardly have been more important.

1978 had finished with Thistle sitting second in the League but by the time April came around a run of eight games without a win had left Thistle sitting only narrowly above Hearts, who occupied one of the two relegation spots. A midweek triumph at Tynecastle went a long way in securing Thistle's position in the Premier Division for another season with Park scoring the second Thistle goal in a 2-0 win.

Thistle's manager of the time Bertie Auld was particularly adept at maintaining Thistle's position in the Premier Division but did so with a team that constantly had to live with the label of being boring and defensive, two adjectives that could hardly be used to describe Donald Park. Standing at 5 feet 8 inches and weighing just under 12 stone he was an all action type player who combined 100% effort with the skill and talent to turn a game. He was also the kind of player that was far from popular with opposing supporters due in no small measure to his combative style of play.

Season 1982-83 proved to be Park's last as a Partick Thistle player and was easily his most productive in terms of goals scored. Admittedly Thistle, managed now by Peter Cormack, found themselves languishing in the First Division, after relegation had been confirmed, despite a Park goal on the final day of the previous season. No fewer than 15 League and cup goals came from Park, including a memorable last minute winner at Tynecastle, making him second top scorer behind Maurice Johnston who helped himself to no fewer than 32. Despite those impressive tallies, Thistle finished the season behind St Johnstone and Hearts who claimed the two promotion spots on offer.

Park, unlike Thistle, though would still have the opportunity to once again sample football in the Premier Division the following season as a summer transfer took him from an increasingly cash strapped Thistle back to Hearts. Now the wrong side of 30 his best days were perhaps behind him, but he still managed four League goals as Hearts finished in a highly satisfactory fifth position in the top league.

Park remained at Tynecastle until 1985 before winding down his playing career with, firstly Brechin City, and then Meadowbank Thistle, whom he helped to the Second Division title in 1987. While at Meadowbank, Park moved into the coaching side of things before taking over as team manager. In one of Park's first games in charge of Meadowbank Thistle he very nearly ended Thistle's promotion hopes of the 1991-92 season as he led his already relegated side to a highly damaging 2-1 win at Firhill. There was, however, a happy ending for Thistle seven days later as Thistle clinched promotion to the Premier Division.

Park spent a year as manager of Meadowbank Thistle before taking up a joint manager role at Arbroath, with another former Thistle player, George Mackie. Park left Arbroath to take up a coaching role with Hibs where he remained until he was appointed Assistant Head Coach to John Robertson at Inverness Caledonian Thistle. He would later follow Robertson to take up a similar position at Hearts.

In January 2006, Park returned to Inverness Caledonian Thistle, when he once again took up the position of Assistant Head Coach this time to Charlie Christie.

Appearances 226, goals 36.
Glasgow Cup winner 1981

Other honours
With Heart of Midlothian
First Division Championship winner 1977-78

WILLIE PAUL

1884 - 1892

Born 11 December 1869 in Partick. Died 23 October 1911

In the early days of football in Scotland things weren't properly organised. Clubs came and went and players had little loyalty – playing where and when they were asked.

There were a few exceptions, and Willie Paul was one of them, the first player to be identified as a Partick Thistle player. Willie spanned the evolution of football in Scotland, from the 1880s to the early days of the twentieth century, which saw a transfer market develop. He was in constant demand from clubs in Scotland and England but always remained true to his roots in Partick and remained with the club through good times and bad.

Willie joined Partick Thistle in 1884 from the local junior side Partick Elm and immediately began to score goals. He was a big man at a time when centre forwards had to be, both big and strong. However, it wasn't just his physique that made him such a good player.

He was known for his close control and his dribbling, and it wasn't unusual for newspapers to report that Paul had run half the length of the field, beating player after player, before scoring yet another goal.

He was club captain and a regular in the team as the club developed. Willie scored eight goals in three games when Thistle was invited to play in the English FA Cup, and was the club's first League goalscorer in 1891, against Ayr.

Willie was regularly called upon for representative matches. His crowning moment away from Thistle, was his third cap for Scotland when he turned out against Wales at Underwood Park, Paisley in 1890 and led his team to a 5-0 win, scoring four goals. He played three international matches, all against Wales, one per year from 1888. Willie also played regularly representing Thistle in games for Glasgow against teams from London, Sheffield and Edinburgh.

At a time when new players were introduced to the team nearly every week, Willie, along with goalkeeper John McCorkindale, was one of the players that the team was built around. Regularly netting a goal every two games when the team was struggling to score, his best came in 1895-96 (eleven in ten League games), and the following season. In 1896-97 Thistle won the Second Division championship and were promoted to rejoin the best clubs in Scotland.

Willie was the epitome of the Victorian gentleman footballer, he was an amateur for all his career, and his loyalty to Thistle meant that he refused many offers to make money from football and join some of the biggest clubs on either side of the border, and this devotion won him a, rare, affection from Thistle fans. Although his loyalties were to Thistle he occasionally turned out for Queen's Park and a range of other amateur selects if Thistle were not playing that day.

Willie Paul continued to play and score for another few years but his playing career gently came to an end in 1902.

His last game was playing in goal for the Thistle reserve side against Third Lanark, a few weeks after receiving a benefit match in which Thistle and Queen's Park paid tribute to him. At the end of his career he remained at the club as a member of the Board of Directors.

Shortly after attending a Glasgow Cup Final at Parkhead involving Thistle, Willie was taken ill following problems with his appendix. After a short illness, he died at home, aged 42, and was buried in Glasgow's Western Necropolis in October 1911.

Had games been properly recorded in these early days, we would recognise Willie Paul's career as even more impressive. We know he played in at least 396 games for the club, scoring at least 186 goals, but in reality almost certainly more than 200. However, whatever the statistics say, there is no doubt that Willie Paul was a superstar in the days before superstars. Without his contribution in the formative days of the club Partick Thistle probably would not exist now.

Appearances 396, goals 186.
Capped for Scotland v Wales 1888, 1889, 1890
Second Division Championship winner 1896-97

ALEX RAE

1970 - 1974

Born 23 August 1946 in Glasgow.

Alex Rae is a member of a very select group of people indeed. He has the honour of being one of only two men, in their role as captain of Partick Thistle, to lift a major trophy above their heads.

Rae's moment of glory, as if any Thistle fan needed reminding, came around 4.45pm on the evening of 23 October 1971. That was the day that Thistle defied the odds to lift the League Cup defeating Celtic in the final.

That memorable afternoon was still many years down the line when Rae's football career began in earnest when as a 16 year old outside-left he joined Renfrew Juniors in 1962. The young Rae clearly impressed while starring there and after a year with the junior side he stepped up to the senior ranks when he joined East Fife.

Rae spent five years with East Fife before, in 1968, he moved to England when he signed for Bury for a reported £10,000 fee. He spent just one season with the Lancashire side and it was at this point that his association with Partick Thistle began. Thistle were relegated at the end of the 1969-70 season and while Davie McParland had at his disposal a young talented squad of players it lacked experience. The acquisitions of Rae and Hugh Strachan were made with addressing that deficiency very much in mind.

Rae's influence on McParland's young squad was almost immediately visible. He made his debut in a League Cup-tie against Stirling Albion in August 1970. A 3-2 success that afternoon assured Rae of a winning start at his new club.

There were a few hiccups in the early portion of the season but once Thistle were off and running there was no stopping them.

Rae's contribution towards their eventual Second Division championship winning season shouldn't be underestimated. He would play in 36 League and cup matches and score six goals.

Success in season 1970-71 though was just a prelude to the season, arguably the most memorable in Thistle's long history, which was just around the corner. In Thistle's first game back in the First Division Rangers were beaten 3-2 but it was Thistle's progress in the League Cup that really got the pulse rate racing. After a memorable quarter-final win against St Johnstone, Falkirk were brushed aside in the semi-final setting up a final date with Celtic.

Celtic were as strong favourites for this game as it was possible to be, but it was Thistle's young stars that stole the show. It was one of the elder statesman, at just 25, that began the rout. A curling shot from Alex Rae ended up in the Celtic net after just ten minutes, then the afternoon just got better and better, and by half-time Thistle led 4-0. A second half Celtic goal was largely irrelevant and all that was left for Rae to do was lift the trophy.

Rae, in an internet interview some 30 years after the match, admitted that that afternoon had been a major experience for him.

"I have to say that that game has changed my life to a certain extent. I have had so many people recognise me in the most unusual places as being the man who lifted the cup for Thistle".

Although Rae's goal at Hampden in October 1971 would be his last as a Thistle player it was far from the end of his Thistle career. He missed just one game that whole season and while Thistle as a club didn't fulfil the promise that the League Cup brought, Rae played just short of 40 games the following season. Included in that total were Thistle's two against Honved during their brief European adventure.

After this, Rae though would not be a Thistle player for much longer, for following a fall out with manager McParland it became clear that his future lay away from Firhill. Kilmarnock and East Fife vied for his services and with Rae's wife hailing from Fife he returned to his first senior club, East Fife. From there he moved to Cowdenbeath and then on to Forfar Athletic.

In total Rae spent six seasons with Forfar as firstly a player then player/coach before finally taking up the reigns of manager. During his spell as manager at Forfar he came close to be part of a result every bit as memorable as Thistle's League Cup win in 1971. The venue was once again Hampden Park, but this time it was a Scottish Cup semi-final date with Rangers. Not only did Forfar hold Rangers to a 0-0 draw before narrowly losing the replay they felt they should have been awarded a late penalty.

After two seasons as manager at Forfar, Rae's career outside the game forced him to resign his position. He was out of the game for four years before taking up the role of reserve coach at Dundee. After leaving Dens Park he scouted for a variety of teams before departing the scene.

Appearances 150, goals 16.
League Cup winner 1971
Second Division Championship winner 1970-71

ALEX RAISBECK

1909 - 1914

Born 26 December 1878 in Polmont. Died 12 March 1949 in Liverpool.

"A man of Raisbeck's proportions, style and carriage would rivet attention anywhere. He is a fine and beautifully balanced figure."

There aren't many truly great legends to have played for Partick Thistle, players who were the best of the best in Scottish football. Neil Gibson and Jamie McMullan were regarded as the best right and left-halves ever to play the game, while Peter McKennan was regarded as one of the best inside-forwards, for a spell, in the late 30s. Alex Raisbeck was seen as the best centre-half ever to play for Scotland against England – *"No centre half-back ever surpassed Raisbeck in an international match against England,"* said the Daily Record.

In effect this meant he was the best player in his position at this time. Thistle were fortunate to sign Alex for £500 at a time when he was unable to guarantee a game in the Liverpool first team, after inspiring them to two League Championships in 1901 and 1906, and his transfer was regarded as the major signing made by any Scottish club in the summer of 1909. A real legend was returning to play in Scotland.

Alex's career had started in Lanarkshire with Larkhall Thistle and Royal Albert before being signed by Hibernian. After two years in Edinburgh he moved to Stoke for a short period before being signed by Liverpool boss Tom Watson in 1898. Watson was renowned for spotting Scottish talent and Alex made his debut in the First Division in the first game of the 1898-99 season, quickly becoming a regular at centre-half. He remained at the heart of the Liverpool defence for ten years, playing 341 times for the Anfield club.

Alex Raisbeck was a commanding centre-half, despite being only 5'10"; a *"broad-shouldered, flaxen-haired giant"*. His anticipation and timing meant that he was almost unbeatable in the air, even against much taller opponents, his blond hair making him instantly recognisable. On the ground he was fast and a superb tackler. At a time when centre-halves were part of the 'midfield' half-back line he was also a creative player, linking well with the forwards, and even getting forward to score the occasional goal; indeed, at Liverpool he managed 19.

His international career was almost peerless. In those early days the best players were kept for games against England, while lesser players would play against Wales or Ireland. Alex turned out for Scotland against England seven times, and was in the defeated team just once. Alex had the honour of captaining his country on four occasions, including a 2-1 win over England in 1906 in a game that writers of the time reckoned was his finest display, and the best ever from an Anglo playing for Scotland.

It was a time of uncertainty for Thistle when Alex Raisbeck signed in June 1909. Thistle had finished bottom of the First Division after a wretched season, but at last were ready to move to their new ground at Firhill, and a bright future was forecast. Big name signings were made in preparation, and Alex was just one. Welsh international Maurice Parry also joined from Liverpool, as did Tom Callaghan (Manchester City) and Robert Graham (Everton).

Alex was appointed captain of the team and immediately impressed. The Daily Record felt that Alex was the *"most finished"* player on the park, and lasted the pace well, though he had to cover for Parry as well as do his own job. However, Alex was soon to fall victim to a series of niggling injuries that kept him out of the team for a number of games, perhaps validating Liverpool's decision to transfer him. His absence was demonstrated clearly on a number of occasions – after a 1-3 defeat to Third Lanark it was suggested that the extend of the defeat would have been minimised if Raisbeck had played. After another defeat at the hands of Thirds, the Daily Record fumed:

"The Firhill forwards were lacking the physical and moral support of Raisbeck". When he did play the newspapers often ran out of superlatives. *"the outstanding personality ... a master ... outstanding player on the field ... shone in defensive work ... most reliable ... outstanding ... great judgement ... best player on park ... veritable tower of strength ... valiant leader ... very prominent ... dominated everyone and everything ... outstanding player"*.

As football tactics changed, centre-halves became more responsible for defensive duties than attacking ones, and it was defensively that Thistle relied on Alex, excelling as a clever 'breaker-up' of attacks, both in the air and on the ground. *"The Partick Thistle captain's head, in contact with the ball and otherwise, was ever in evidence."* He also had a highly sensitive awareness of tactics, and often changed players' positions during the game, depending on how they were progressing. In January 1912, with Thistle two down in a Scottish Cup-tie, Alex moved Willie Hamilton up front and dropped William Gardener back. Within minutes Hamilton had equalised to give Thistle a replay. Alex remained an attacking force too. *"He kept the forwards well on the move and distributed play to the best advantage,"* said one report.

After four years Alex returned to represent Scotland when he was chosen for the side to play England in 1911, and then again against Ireland in 1912. November 1913 saw Alex line up beside the teenage prodigy Jamie McMullan. Little did the Kilmarnock players fully realise that they were opposed by future and past Scottish international captains. It was a partnership that was not to last long. In a game earlier that month Alex had suffered a slight bump. It didn't feel serious but it was enough to convince him to avoid hard contact with opponents for a month or so.

After medical attention Alex was operated on for appendicitis, and was expected back a few weeks later. It meant he would miss playing in his own benefit match against a star-studded international select. Liverpool were late to hear about the game, and belatedly offered to send their entire first team to play, such was the esteem still felt for Alex in Liverpool. The game attracted an astonishing crowd of 10,000 and generated gate receipts of £300.

Daily reports of Alex's recuperation, from operation to discharge to resumption of training, filled the daily newspapers, though it wasn't until the end of February that he received the go-ahead to play again. However, during his convalescence Alex decided that his fitness was limiting his performances, and decided to retire from playing. Hamilton Academicals were quick to make Alex an offer, and in March it was announced that he would take up the position of secretary/manager after his playing contract ran out at the end of the season. Alex didn't play again for Thistle, and one of the most illustrious and respected playing careers ended.

Following a spell at Hamilton, Alex became manager of Bristol City for eight years, followed by a similar spell of six years at Halifax. After another managerial spell at Chester City he rejoined Liverpool in a scouting capacity. Alex remained in Liverpool until he died at the age of 70.

Appearances 138, goals 9.
Capped for Scottish League v English League 1911; v Irish League 1912.

Other honours With Hibernian
1 Scottish League international appearance
With Liverpool
8 Scotland international appearances;
English First Division Championship 1901, 1906; English Second Division Championship 1905

ALAN ROUGH

1969 - 1982

Born 25 January 1951 in Glasgow.

There are few more famous names in the history of Partick Thistle than that of Alan Rough. Alan's career though nearly never got started. An injury while still a young boy nearly resulted in the loss of an arm but thankfully for Rough and Partick Thistle the arm was saved.

Recruited from Sighthill Amateurs in 1969 Alan made his first team debut in fairly humble circumstances. Season 1969-70 was an unhappy one for Partick Thistle with the club relegated for the first time in 70 years. It was to that backdrop that Rough made the first of over 600 appearances for Thistle on 8 April 1970. Morton provided the opposition and few, if any, in the crowd of 1,100 would have envisaged that the lanky young man in the Thistle goal that evening would go on and win over 50 caps for Scotland. His debut had no happy ending either as Rough ended up on the losing side, Thistle going down to a 1-2 defeat.

Happier times though were not far away. Relegation was swiftly followed by promotion just twelve months later with Rough playing a significant part in Thistle's championship winning side, playing in each of their 36 League games, and conceding just 26 goals.

There was even more glory waiting the following season. Rough was hardly the only Thistle player that was in inspired form as they lifted the League Cup by defeating Celtic 4-1 in the Hampden final. That triumph gave Alan his first taste of European football when the team was paired with Honved in the UEFA Cup.

Ironically, despite collecting a grand total of 53 caps for Scotland, Rough would only once more taste European club football. In 1988 and then a Celtic player, Rough made one appearance in the European Cup against Thistle's opponents of 1972, Honved.

The Partick side of the early 1970's was an exciting one with a large number of extremely talented young players destined for bright futures in the game and it was no surprise when Alan Rough was given his first taste of international football, with his first of nine Under 23 caps (a record for a Thistle player at that level), against England at Kilmarnock in February 1973. Also included in the Scotland side that lost 2-1 was Jimmy Bone. Subsequent caps would follow for Alan between 1973 and 1976 against Sweden, Romania (2), Denmark, Holland (2) and Wales.

It wasn't all plain sailing for Alan in his Thistle career and he even lost his place in the Thistle side to John Arrol during the course of the 1973-74 season, However, a leg break sustained by Arrol during a Scottish Cup-tie at Motherwell gave Rough his place back in the side and he was rarely in danger of losing it again.

Once back in the Thistle side full international honours were never far away and he was duly awarded his first full international cap against Switzerland in the 1976, Willie Pettigrew scored the winner as Scotland won 1-0.

Alan had more competition for his place in the Scotland side than he did the Thistle team. He was more than capable though of dealing with the challenges from the likes of Jim Stewart, George Wood, Jim Blyth and his former Thistle understudy, Billy Thomson. In total Rough kept goal for Scotland 51 times while a Partick Thistle player - a total that makes him easily the club's most capped player. That total includes six games in the World Cup Finals of 1978 and 1982.

Prior to the 1982 World Cup Alan had enjoyed a well attended testimonial match against a Celtic side at Firhill which would have lessened a little of the pain of Thistle's relegation that season.

Rough was still a Thistle player when he returned from the Spanish World Cup in 1982 and was part of the First Division squad at the start of the season. The finances at the time though were such that it was case of when, rather than if, Rough would be on his way. The end came on 20 November 1982 against Airdrieonians at Firhill. Typically in his final appearance as a Partick Thistle player Rough kept a clean sheet as they won 1-0.

A few days later he was on the way to Hibs for the ridiculously small fee of just over £60,000. While at Easter Road Alan was part of the squad that reached the final of the League Cup in 1985, but he was unable to repeat his triumph with Thistle in the same competition 14 years earlier. Rough was also able to add a further two caps to his tally of 51 before the arrival of Andy Goram at Easter Road spelt the end of his Hibs career.

After leaving Hibs, Alan tried his luck in the USA with Orlando Lions, before returning to his native land for brief spells with Celtic, Hamilton Accies and Ayr United. He also enjoyed a successful spell as manager of Ayrshire junior outfit Glenafton Athletic and in 1993 led his side to victory in the Scottish Junior Cup Final with victory over Tayport at Firhill.

Alan returned briefly to Firhill to assist with the coaching of the goalkeepers, but later he was to be heard offering his opinions of the game on Real Radio.

Appearances 624, goals 0
League Cup winner 1971
First Division Championship winner 1975-76
Second Division Championship winner 1969-70
Capped for Scotland v Argentina 1977, 1979; v Austria 1979, 1980; v Belgium 1980 (twice); v Brazil 1977, 1982; v Chile 1977; v Czechoslovakia 1977, 1978; v England 1976, 1977, 1978, 1980, 1981,1982; v Finland 1977; Holland 1978, 1982; v Hungary 1980; v Iran 1978; v Israel 1981 (twice); v N. Ireland 1976, 1977, 1978, 1981, 1982; v Norway 1979; v New Zealand 1982; v Peru 1978, 1980; v Poland 1980; v Portugal 1979, 1980, 1981; v Spain 1982; v Sweden 1977, 1981, 1982; v Switzerland 1976; v Russia 1982; v Wales 1976, 1977 (twice), 1978, 1979, 1980, 1981, 1982

Capped for Scottish League v Irish League 1978
Other honours: With Hibernian: 2 Scotland international appearances

WILLIE (SALLY) SALISBURY

1918 - 1928

Born 23 February 1899 in Glasgow. Died 1965.

Willie Salisbury was signed from St Anthony's as a tricky wee winger, in the mould of Jacky Bowie, who had preceded him on the left wing at the Ants, just a few years earlier before taking the same path from Govan to Maryhill. And just as Sally had replaced Jacky at Moore Park, so he was to do so at Firhill.

Sally initially got his chance in the first team when he immediately took the outside-left jersey vacated by Bowie, who had moved inside to replace Neil Harris at centre-forward. Sally took his chance, and missed just two games, ending the season as Thistle's most consistent player. As a winger he was known primarily as a goal provider, his crosses from the left creating chances for Bowie and Jim Marshall in the centre. However, he did score nine goals from wide, including a wonder strike from an almost impossible angle on the goal line against Renton in a Victory up-tie, late in the game.

Renton had battled hard and almost had the game won. Sally's shot could have gone anywhere but squeezed past the 'keeper. Renton were demoralised, Sally was buoyant, and he went on to score again as Thistle won 4-3.

Sally was a willing worker, revelling in passes into space that allowed him to speed away from the right-back, and in team-mates Jamie McMullan and Jimmy McMenemy he had two of the best passers of the ball in Scottish football. He regularly took full advantage of the service and was one of the most dangerous crossers of the ball in the game. But in the traditions of tricky, mercurial, wingers he could be a little inconsistent in his final passes. However, Sally was popular with the fans at Firhill and he was always forgiven his indiscretions.

"Willie's idiosyncrasies have endeared him to the not a bit mim-mouthed Firhill faithful – they say what they think, with and without

flowers, up there. On his day – and how good he can be, and has been – 'Sally' has been cheered to the echo; when off his game he has been called not altogether pretty names. But the next minute, so to speak, when the shouters simmer down, 'Sally' is taken to their hearts again." (Daily Record)

In January 1921 Sally had contributed to lifting Thistle to third in the League, but it was for the Scottish Cup that Willie was reserving his best form. His equaliser against Motherwell kept Thistle in the competition, and in the second replay against 'Well he helped create the goals that took Thistle into their first ever Cup semi-final. There they faced Hearts, and Willie had a point-blank chance which Hearts' 'keeper Sandy Kane saved miraculously. After two drawn matches Sally helped Jimmy Kinloch score two goals to take Thistle to the final.

In the final against Rangers Sally had a number of chances to extend Thistle's lead, but with his partner McMenemy sitting back, he didn't have the support to really get shots on goal. However, he did give Rangers' international full-back Bert Manderson a most difficult game.

It took almost a year until Manderson and Sally were in opposition again, and once again Manderson struggled against Sally's speed. Indeed, the only way he could cope was to play Sally and the ball into touch – a move that delighted the Thistle support more each time it happened. This club form saw Sally selected to play for Glasgow against Edinburgh at Tynecastle in 1923, along with Harry Chatton – a 2-4 defeat for Glasgow - and this was followed up, some years later, with a return to the Glasgow team to play against Sheffield in 1927. Alex Lambie and Davie Ness also represented Thistle in the game in 1927. Glasgow won 4-1 at Hillsborough.

Sally's trademark, apart from his speed and crosses, was a curious lofted shot-cum-cross that panicked goalkeepers and allowed for hefty shoulder-charges to be applied from charging centre-forwards. Sally scored a number of goals himself from his lobs from wide, including a famous winning goal against Celtic in November 1924 at Parkhead. Sally could see the ball was going to sail over the head of Celtic's Peter Shevlin and began what was described as *"a sort of a weird jig"* in front of the shocked Celtic fans. It was a bitter blow for Celtic, who had hoped Sally would sign for them instead of Thistle in 1918.

In his time at Firhill, Sally was a player that could always be relied upon, and as such only missed a handful of games in his years at the club. However, after ten years, in 1928, he felt like a change. Before he left he was honoured with a benefit match against Rangers (a 1-1 draw) and £150 gate receipts. Just a few weeks later, in September 1928, Sally joined Liverpool for a £1,000 transfer fee, where he joined up with his ex-Thistle team-mate Jimmy McDougall. At Anfield Sally played during season 1928-29 at centre-forward, scoring three goals, before moving on again, to Wales to play with Bangor City, and then to Shelbourne in Ireland before retiring.

Appearances 354, goals 58.
Scottish Cup winner 1921
Glasgow Charity Cup winner 1927

WILLIE SHARP

1939 - 1957

Born 25 May 1922 in Glasgow

There are many reasons why Willie Sharp is considered a Partick Thistle legend. His 571 appearances showing that he has played more times for the club than all but Alan Rough, Davie McParland and Jackie Campbell. In addition, no other player has scored more goals than Willie; 229 in the 17 years that he was at Firhill. Thistle was Willie's only professional club in a remarkable career in which he reached seven cup finals. Perhaps most of all Willie is best known for a goal that might now seem unremarkable were it not for the fact that it was scored with just seven seconds from the start of the game.

On 20 December 1947, at 3pm, the referee's whistle started Thistle's game against Queen of the South. Davie Mathie kicked of to Kenny Chisholm, who flicked the ball back to Hugh Brown. The half-back sent a long ball through the middle for Mathie to chase. With the defenders watching the centre-forward the ball ran on to Sharp, and with a low shot, the ball was in the net, just a matter of seconds after the game had started.

The goal took the watching reporters by surprise. Some estimated the time taken as five seconds, some six, some seven. The general verdict was *"the quickest goal we ever saw"*, and still remains a Scottish record.

Willie signed from Shettleston Juniors in May 1939 as an inexperienced but highly thought of potential replacement for John McMenemy (son of Jimmy McMenemy) who had moved to St Mirren, and who Thistle hadn't adequately replaced.

Initially Willie struggled to make an impact too. He wasn't selected for the annual trial match for either the likely first team or the reserve team, and he struggled to get a regular game in the reserves throughout 1939. However, in due course he did impress manager Turner, and thanks to wartime demands on the regular first-teamers, made his first League appearance in March 1940, also scoring a debut goal, against Celtic. He also scored on his next two appearances, and missed just five games of the remaining fourteen, establishing himself as a young but established member of the team. He finished the season as second top scorer despite having played less than half the available matches.

Willie was a slight lad, just 5' 8" and ten stones, when he joined the club, but what he lacked in weight he made up with brains and footballing skill. The newspapers paid tribute to Willie. One described him as an *"artful ball-player and schemer"* while others paid tribute to his *"weasel like manoeuvres"* and *"bewildering dribbling"*. Although signed as an inside-left, Willie was capable of turning out at centre-forward and as an inside-right, later in his career, plus an eye for goals as his scoring statistics record. He also had an eye for a defence-splitting pass to his wingers, as Alex McSpadyen, Jimmy Walker, Johnny MacKenzie and Tommy Ewing could attest, and he collected a large number of 'assists' as a result.

By the start of the 1940-41 season Willie was well and truly established as Thistle's number ten, and he remained there until 1945, when his forward partner Willie Newall departed for Morton. Willie moved to centre-forward with great success until the arrival of Davie Mathie from Clyde at which time he moved back to inside-left. During those war years Willie led Thistle to a Charity Cup Final against Rangers in 1941 (lost 0-3), a Southern League Cup semi-final in 1942 against Morton (1-1 draw, followed by a 0-1 defeat with Willie missing) and the Summer Cup Final of 1945. Willie had missed most of the Summer Cup run, but returned for the final against Hibs, replacing the unlucky Dougie Stockdale, and helping Thistle to a 2-0 win.

Robert Reid, in The Official History of Partick Thistle, described Willie as *"... a football genius, full of artistry ..."*. In 1950 the Sunday Mail wrote, *"Sharp is a zestful player and has become the idol of Maryhill. His dazzling distribution and subtle scheming must take him close to international honours"*. Unfortunately, as Robert Reid also wrote, *"Willie must have been the finest player never to win a Scottish cap"*. He did, however, play for the Scottish League in 1952 – a 0-3 loss to the Welsh League.

The international selectors may not have valued Willie, but he was valued by top English clubs. In February 1950 Burnley offered £15,000 for his signature – a fee that would have been a world record – but were told that Willie was not for sale.

It was a bold and brave move by the Thistle directors to turn down such a sum of money, but Willie repaid their confidence in him with splendid form in 1950-51. He missed just three games out of the 48 played, winning a Glasgow Cup winners medal when Thistle beat Celtic 3-2 at Hampden.

The early 50s were a time of consistent team selections for Thistle with the likes of Tommy Ledgerwood, Jimmy McGowan, Bobby Gibb, Jimmy Davidson, Jimmy Walker, Alex Wright and Davie Mathers appearing on the teamsheet seemingly every week. Willie, of course, joined them, and in a remarkable spell between August 1950 and May 1954 missed just eight League games. Willie was described as *"the brains of the attack"*, complimenting the speed of Walker and the strength of Alex Stott. This kind of consistency – being able to regularly pick players of great ability – took Thistle to yet more cup success.

In 1952 Willie scored the semi-final goal that took the team to a Glasgow Cup Final against Rangers, and a 3-1 win. The following year Willie scored four goals in the qualifying rounds as Thistle reached the League Cup Final before a 2-3 defeat to East Fife, while another cup final defeat occurred in 1956 when Third Lanark beat Thistle in the Charity Cup Final, despite a goal from Willie.

By the time the 1956 League Cup run came round Willie's appearances were becoming limited. He did appear in the semi-final game against Dundee, but the consistent team of the early to mid 50s had begun to break up, and at 34 years of age Willie was unable to command a first team place.

Willie played his last game for Thistle against Kilmarnock on 9 February 1957, retiring from football at the end of the season.

Appearances 572, goals 229.
Summer Cup winner 1945
Glasgow Cup winner 1951, 1952
Capped for Scottish League v Welsh League 1952.

GEORGE SMITH

1954 - 1963

Born 1 June 1935 in Bathgate

In Thistle's 131 year history just ten players have scored 100 or more goals in a Thistle jersey. Of those ten, only Willie Sharp and Willie Paul have scored more than George Smith's 125 goals.

Smith arrived at Firhill from Torpichen Juveniles and made his first team debut in one of Partick's more obscure fixtures. In February 1954, Thistle were sent to Kirkcowan near Newton Stewart to play Tarff Rovers in a Scottish Cup-tie. An injury to Johnny MacKenzie provided the 18 year old Smith with the opportunity to make his first team debut for Thistle. In fairly bizarre surroundings the visitors cantered to a 9-0 win. Smith would deputise for MacKenzie on another couple of occasions that season but it would be the following season before he began to feature in the side on a regular basis.

To say that George made something of an impact in his first full season at Firhill would be a massive understatement. Although Thistle failed to qualify from their League Cup section, Smith scored his first goal in the 2-0 win against Stirling Albion in that competition. A few weeks later he managed no fewer than four goals in the 9-1 demolition of the same Stirling team at Firhill.

That pretty much set the tone for Smith's season. With 25 goals he would, by some distance, finish as Thistle's leading scorer and although not on target himself in the final win against Celtic he contributed two goals in

Partick's 5-4 Glasgow Cup semi-final win over that team.

He struggled to come anywhere near matching that total in 1955-56, scoring just twice, but that was very much a, rare, disappointing season for Smith. He again topped the Thistle scoring charts in season 1956-57 scoring 17 times. He scored 20 goals in season 1958-59, a tally bettered only by Andy Kerr who would soon be on the move to Manchester City. During that season he, for the second time, played in a losing Thistle side in the League Cup Final.

After a successful decade in the 50s, the 1960s showed a gradual decline in Thistle's fortunes and that was mirrored by George Smith's career. In the first full season of the decade Smith started the season by scoring in five successive fixtures but would end the season with just three League goals to his name. His goals-scored tally hit double figures for the last time in season 1961-62 and even as Thistle chased the Championship in the extraordinary 1962-63 season, Smith's contribution, by his own high standards, was fairly modest.

Smith remained at Firhill and there was little surprise, in the wake of Kerr's departure down south, that he finished the 1959-60 as Thistle's leading scorer with 21 goals;that tally included two hat-tricks. The first was netted in a Scottish Cup-tie against Dundee United, and the second in a 4-2 win against Celtic at Parkhead; this was Thistle's second win in the League at Celtic in three years.

Smith's goalscoring prowess though brought him little in terms of representative honours, winning just a solitary cap for the Scottish League. In September 1958 he was one of seven newcomers in the Scottish League side that ran out easy 5-0 winners against the Irish League at Windsor Park. Smith though didn't get in on the goal-scoring act.

George Smith's 124th and 125th (and final) Thistle goals were scored in the same fixture. Glentoran provided the opposition in a Fairs Cup-tie and after winning the first leg 4-1 in Belfast,Thistle won the return 3-0 with Smith netting two. His final appearance in a Thistle jersey came a couple of months later in a fixture with Falkirk at Brockville.

Upon leaving Firhill Smith had a short spell with Dundee United before taking up the role of player-manager with Ballymena United.

Appearances 343, goals 125.
Glasgow Cup Winner 1954, 1960.
Capped for Scottish League
v Irish League 1958

DOUGIE SOMNER

1974 - 1979

Born 4 July 1951 in Edinburgh.

Few players, given his length of time at Firhill, can boast of as impressive a goals to games ratio as Dougie Somner can.

Somner stepped up to the ranks of senior football when he joined Falkirk from East Kilbride Thistle in 1971, and he made his debut against Hibs on the afternoon that Thistle were busy defeating Celtic in the League Cup Final. Somner made the move from Falkirk to Ayr United in time for the start of the 1974-75 season, but his time at Somerset Park was a fairly brief one. After just a few months down at the seaside, Somner was on the move again. League Cup winner Johnny Gibson moved to Ayr United with Somner and team mate Dougie Mitchell made the opposite journey to Firhill.

The name of Dougie Somner first appeared on a Thistle team sheet on 23 November 1974 when the team travelled to face Airdrieonians. Somner didn't manage a goal in either of his first two appearances, but he soon got off the mark during the course of a 3-1 win against St Johnstone. He followed that up with a double in his next game, his first at Firhill, in a 2-2 draw with Clyde. In his first season Somner was a little upstaged in terms of goalscoring by Joe Craig, but he did still end the season with eight goals to his name from 22 appearances. Included in that total of eight goals was his first Thistle hat-trick, scored as they beat Morton 3-1.

Hat-tricks were very much a feature of Somner's first full season as a Partick Thistle player, and en route to the First Division championship, he netted hat-tricks against both East Fife and Montrose. He went one better in a Spring Cup-tie with Forfar Athletic scoring all four of Thistle's goals in a 4-2 win at Firhill. To put the feat of scoring four goals in the one match into some kind of perspective, Partick would have to wait the best part of a further eleven years before another player would score that number of goals in the one game – Billy Dodds netted against East Fife. Together with Joe Craig, Somner would form a pretty potent strike force. In all competitions that season the two players produced a combined total of 49 goals with Somner topping the scoring charts with 27.

As Thistle made the step up to the Premier Division, Somner would never again rise above the twenty-goal mark for Thistle, but he finished each of the next three seasons as leading goalscorer. In his final season at Firhill he had to share that honour with Jim Melrose.

Joe Craig was his first strike partner at Partick, but after Craig left to join Celtic he teamed up with Jim Melrose. That partnership proved to be every bit as good if not better than the one he had with Craig. In the three seasons that they spent together they scored between them a total of 88 goals.

The side, the only part-time club in the Premier Division, was arguably the most successful Thistle side, the League Cup triumph of 1971 notwithstanding, for some time.

There was though no tangible reward for their efforts. They did, however, reach the Scottish Cup semi-final in successive seasons. In 1978 Thistle went down 4-2 to Aberdeen at Hampden Park. Twelve months later Thistle and Somner came as close as possible to reaching the cup final. Once again Thistle reached the last four where this time they were paired with Rangers. Somner missed the Hampden semi that finished 0-0 but returned for the replay. It was a replay that Thistle fans to this day swear shouldn't have been necessary, Bobby Houston having a late goal disallowed in highly controversial circumstances in the first game.

While Somner didn't get to contest a Scottish Cup Final for Thistle, his talents were recognised by more than just the faithful. Twice in 1978 he represented the Scottish League, first against the Italian League, scoring in a 1-1 draw, and later versus the Irish League. In 1980 he was again capped for the Scottish League against their Irish counterparts and was once more on the score sheet, this time as the Scottish League won 4-2. By this time he was, however, a St Mirren player.

After 100 goals as a Thistle player there was naturally bitter disappointment when Somner elected to join St Mirren.

The goals didn't dry up down Paisley way either. In his first season at Love Street he topped the thirty-goal mark for the only time in his career, hitting 32 as a very talented side finished third in the Premier Division. His tally the next season was reduced to 16 but he still finished the season as St Mirren's leading goal scorer.

Somner spent a further two seasons with the club before joining Hamilton Accies for just one. As he had done so often before in his career he finished as top scorer at his club scoring ten goals, including a hat-trick against Thistle. Before he brought the curtain down on his career Somner spent two seasons with Montrose. In season 1984-85 he scored twelve goals and was inevitably Montrose's leading scorer as they won the Second Division title. He played virtually the whole of the following season before retiring at the end of it. Appropriately enough one of his final games for Montrose came against Partick Thistle.

Appearances 218, goals 101.
First Division Championship winner 1975-76
Capped for Scottish League v Irish League
1978; v Italian League 1978.

Other Honours: With Montrose:
Second Division Championship winner
1984-85

~ 160 ~

Hugh Strachan

1970 - 1974

Born 21 February 1939 in Crookedholm, Ayrshire.

When Davie McParland started to assemble a squad to take Thistle back to the top flight following relegation at the end of the 1969-70 season one commodity that he felt was lacking was that of experience. In search of that he turned to a central defender who was certainly not lacking in that respect.

By the time Hugh Strachan arrived at Firhill in the summer of 1970 he had already been a professional for a total of 13 years. He made the step up from Cumnock Juniors to Motherwell in 1957 and after leaving Motherwell he played with Morton and Kilmarnock from whom he joined Thistle in 1970.

On 8 August 1970, Strachan made the first of his 173 appearances as a Thistle player in a League Cup-tie, against Stirling Albion in a side that included Alex Rae, who also signed to add more experience to the team.

The then manager Davie McParland, in addition to nurturing some fine young talent, made a number of highly shrewd moves in the transfer market but none more so than the singing of Hugh Strachan. In his first season at Firhill he missed just four League games as Thistle won the Second Division championship conceding just 26 goals (only nine at Firhill) in a 36 game campaign.

Strachan's influence though wasn't just limited to events on the park on a matchday. His experience and knowledge on the training ground proved to be a major asset as well and by the time the 1971-72 season started Strachan had graduated to the Thistle coaching staff.

A Thistle programme of the time outlined Strachan's importance to the cause both as a player and as a coach.

> *" Strachan has proved a real stalwart in our defence in recent weeks. His work beside young Nobby Clark has been responsible for the youngsters steadily improving form. Hugh admits to being a little older than when he started in the game but he has lost none of his speed and his positional sense at times is uncanny. He still rises above most attackers in goalmouth skirmishes to clear danger. Off the park Hugh must surely be one of Scotland's most respected players. At training stints he is a real martinet as he puts the younger players through his specially devised circuits."*

On the park Strachan had a major role to play in Thistle's 1971 League Cup winning team. In a team that included two teenagers, Alan Rough and Denis McQuade, Strachan was by far the oldest member of the victorious team. Not that that showed as Strachan superbly marshalled the defence especially in the second half as Celtic frantically tried to find a way back into the game.

It was a credit too to Strachan's fitness that he missed just one game in the 1971-72 season and only two games in the next. He started the following season in the first team as well, but Thistle made a quite awful start and following a 2-1 defeat at Easter Road against Hibs at the start of September he would play just one more game for the club. That last game was on 3 February 1974 in a 4-1 defeat at Dundee. He subsequently rejoined one of his former clubs, Morton, eventually taking up a coaching role at Cappielow.

Appearances 173, goals 1.
League Cup winner 1971
Second Division Championship winner 1970-71

GEORGE SUTHERLAND

1935 - 1943

Born 5 October 1914 in Musselburgh. Died 1969.

Not many players finish their first game for a new club, and leave with a cup-winners medal in their pocket. That's exactly what happened to big George Sutherland when he made his debut for Thistle in the 1935 Charity Cup Final, and helped Thistle to a 2-1 win over Queen's Park.

George was East Fife's regular centre-half at the time, and was actually a guest player in the game, replacing Bob Donnelly who had signed for Manchester City the week before.

The final might have been his only game for the club, for he re-signed for East Fife in time for the 1935-36 Second Division season. Thistle attempted to fill the gap at centre-half by signing Alex Stevenson from Petershill, but after a handful of games they returned to Bayview to sign George, this time with a contract for the season.

He was a miner by trade, and was appropriately built for a centre-half – six feet and thirteen stone.

He had joined East Fife from East Stirlingshire after a spell with Linlithgow Rose.

George made the first team immediately, replacing Stevenson for a win over Kilmarnock in September 1935, ending a run of three defeats. *"Sutherland went after the ball without fear – and generally got it"*, reported the Daily Record. He remained in the team for the remainder of the season, never missing a game, and partnering well with Eddie McLeod and Alex Elliot beside him. Cup success re-occurred – this time the less prestigious Paisley Charity Cup - but not many Thistle players could boast of winners' medals in consecutive seasons!

A third final in three years was reached the following season but this time it ended in defeat – a whopping 1-6 score to Rangers in a replayed Glasgow Cup Final. However, in general it was another successful season for big George, playing in all but a handful of games, and reinforcing his position as a vital member of the team. George revealed one of the secret training techniques that had brought him the plaudit that he was, *"a right good stopper"* and one of the best headers of the ball in Scotland. Trainer Jimmy Kennedy had a ball suspended from the ceiling in the corridor outside the dressing room.

When the ball is headed it bounces off the ceiling and swung in an unexpected fashion. George spent hours practicing his heading after others had gone home.

The practice paid off when George was selected to represent Glasgow against Sheffield in 1937 at Doncaster, though they lost 1-2, and he continued his good form by helping Thistle through a period of 14 games in mid-season, conceding just 12 goals. Thistle finished the season in seventh place, their best position for a number of years.

Recognising his leadership qualities, manager Turner asked George to captain the team for the 1938-39 season. Modestly, George rejected the offer, preferring to be an ordinary member of the team. Ironically, a couple of months into the season he was dropped in favour of James Ewing. He must have wondered if his place would have been safer had he taken the captaincy. George asked for a transfer, though he remained at Firhill when the request was rejected, before regaining his place towards the end of the season when Ewing was rested, and then called up to the army. The following season, with war looming, George played in the 'A' team in the trial match, but lost his place to Tony Johnstone once the League games started.

When war was declared Johnstone, too, was called up, and George returned to the first team, performing solidly and consistently for most of the matches in 1945-46 and the following season.

In May 1941 George himself was called up to the army, but was released by his Commanding Officer to continue playing for Thistle at the weekends, including a Charity Cup Final defeat to Rangers. Within weeks of joining the army George found himself lining up with Thistle team-mate Alex Sharp for the Scottish Command army team's game against an SFA team which included another team-mate Peter Curran. This game was effectively a trial match for an international against England. Both George and Peter played in the corresponding fixture a year later, but neither was selected for either game.

George continued playing for Thistle during most of 1941-42, and also turned out for the Scottish Command team, reaching the final of, and losing, the Army in Scotland Cup.

In his army absence Thistle arranged for Manchester City's Leslie McDowall to play in George's place, and McDowall looked good – George would struggle to get his place back. Donald Turner agreed to allow George to play with Hearts, but when McDowall reneged on his agreement to play for Thistle, George was recalled and played as well as he ever had. However, his war duties dictated that his game against Albion Rovers in February 1943 would be his last for Partick Thistle. A week later he met up with former colleague Peter McKennan to play for Scotland against England in an army international.

After the war George found himself in England, and played for spells with Leyton Orient, Hereford United, Guilford City and Dartford before retiring from football.

Appearances 251, goals 2.
Glasgow Charity Cup winner 1935

JOHN TORBET

1924 - 1933

Born 26 September 1904 in Benwhat, Dalmellington. Died 1957.

John Torbet was a young outside-left full of potential when he signed for Partick Thistle from New Cumnock United in the summer of 1924 as cover for regular winger Willie Salisbury. Such was 'Sally's' consistent form for the next four years, though, that John had to content himself with learning about senior football whilst in the reserve team, making occasional first team appearances substituting when Sally was injured.

1926 saw John's first opportunity for an extended series of games while Salisbury was injured. John took the opportunity and played a stretch of over thirty until the senior player returned towards the end of the season. John combined well with Sandy Hair and between them they scored 62 goals in the season. Although ostensibly a winger, John loved nothing more than cutting inside and his powerful shot gave many goalkeepers problems.

The prolific Thistle forwards helped the team to a Scottish Cup semi-final, although defeat to East Fife ended that interest.

The following season saw John again relegated to the reserves, but in August 1928, following Salisbury's transfer to Liverpool, John was given the left-winger's jersey. He had learned from his spell in 1926, and was soon regarded as *"one of the most improved and most promising extreme forwards in the country"*. Certainly his wing play had developed – strong passes to Davie Ness on the opposite wing opened up Thistle's forward play. *"Torbet never hesitates to leave the touchline, and he can shoot"* said the Daily Record, and John's scoring record of 19 goals in 1928-29 confirms that review. He ended the season as top scorer, and his goal in the Daily Record Dental Cup Final against Rangers gave him a winners' medal too.

The following season merely emphasised that the previous one was no fluke. *"He can take along a ball, he can centre it or shoot it."* Again he ended the season as top scorer, and again he supplied his centre-forward well – Johnny Simpson scored 22 in a 20 League game run before Simpson was hit by injury. The Daily Record explained what they liked about John, and just how he could improve.

"This Torbet boy is already a good one, and – he'll come on a lot yet. I like his low down and body high crosses, but an occasional high one, one that would go farther Ness-wards, would come amiss."

Ironically, Torbet and Ness did combine to great effect in the Scottish Cup Final Replay against Rangers, though it was John who was the goalscorer from a Ness pass. The goal equalised the opener, but Rangers went on to win the game 2-1.

John had already been capped when he played for Glasgow against Sheffield in September 1929, and he was further recognised when he was chosen as a reserve for Scotland's games against France in Paris and Wales in Glasgow. This was the closest John was to come to full international honours, although the Daily Record suggested that the Scottish League team to play England in 1930 should include a Thistle left wing of John, Johnny Ballantyne and Eddie McLeod, but none played. John played again for Glasgow against Sheffield in 1932.

The next few seasons saw John continue to turn out regularly, and score goals as Thistle regularly finished well up the League table. 1931 saw them finish fourth, while in 1932 they went on a twelve game winning run. John scored nine goals in that historic event. He thrived in his partnership with Ballantyne, who would regularly send him in on goal with a disguised pass from midfield.

In 1933 money was tight at Firhill, and John, along with Ness, Alec Elliot, Stewart Calderwood and Bob Donnelly, were unhappy at the terms offered. Eventually all signed, with the exception of John, and he was frozen out of football until Preston approached Thistle for his transfer.

The move to Preston wasn't a huge success, for John left at the end of his first season, then playing, in short spells, with non-League Burton Albion, and Stockport County before returning to Ayrshire in 1936 to play for Ayr United, Alloa and Leith Athletic.

Appearances 269, goals 116.

Jimmy Walker

1947 - 1956

Born in 1925 in Detroit, USA. Died 25 September 2000 in Milwaukee, USA.

Born in Detroit, USA in 1925, the family moved back to Kirkcaldy, Scotland when Jimmy was just six years of age. His football education followed a traditional route and in October 1944 he joined Hearts from Renfrew Juniors while aged 19. While at Tynecastle, he helped Hearts to lift the Southern League Cup (a wartime forerunner of the League Cup), in season 1945-46.

A bright future at Tynecastle looked to be assured, Walker being described by a contemporary source of the time as being *"destined to scale the heights of international soccer"*. Indeed international honours did come his way when he played in the international matches against Belgium, alongside Jimmy McGowan, and Switzerland, alongside Jackie Husband, to celebrate the Allies victory in the Second World War. These matches though would be classed as 'unofficial' and Walker would remain uncapped at full international level, though playing in those games would be vital in Jimmy's later career.

Walker's Hearts career though was to come to a fairly abrupt end. In March 1947 he was suspended by the Tynecastle club after failing to appear for a Scottish Cup-tie at Arbroath.

A few short weeks later he was off to Firhill in a transfer that saw Bobby Parker move in the opposite direction.

Jimmy's Thistle debut came in the third last fixture of the 1946-47 season and was, to say the least, a somewhat inauspicious one. Thistle were sitting in fourth spot in the League at the time but still contrived to lose 1-6 to a Falkirk side that were just four spots off the bottom. The Evening Times' assessment of Thistle's new player though was fairly positive if a little less than unequivocal. *"Walker, lately transferred from Hearts was making his debut as a Thistle player and appeared a little uncomfortable at first in the strange company. But he showed a versatility and nippiness which once he is more at home ought to fit in well with the Firhill scheme of things"*.

To say that things would get better for Walker at Firhill in subsequent seasons would be something of an understatement. Walker scored his first Thistle goal just a week after the hammering at the hands of Falkirk and the following season began the with a real bang, when he scored a hat-trick as Thistle just edged out Falkirk in a thrilling League Cup-tie by the incredible score of 6-5.

All in Walker would score 121 goals for Partick Thistle - a total only bettered by three Thistle players either before or since; Willie Paul, Willie Sharp and George Smith being the only players to hit the back of the opposition net more times for Thistle than Jimmy Walker. Many of those 121 goals were from his famous left-foot thunderbolts. There were also four hat-tricks or better including a treble in a League Cup Quarter-Final against Kilmarnock in September 1953 and a four goal haul against Hibs the previous December.

Arguably the best of Walker's Thistle goals came against Motherwell at Fir Park in January 1950. Collecting the ball on the halfway line his pace took him clear of the Motherwell defence before drilling a shot into the back of the net. Walker was very much a man for the big occasion and three times he was a cup final goalscorer for Thistle. In May 1949 he was on target as Thistle defeated Celtic 2-1 in the final of the Glasgow Charity Cup.

Almost two years later he was on target against the same opposition, this time though he scored twice as Partick lifted the Glasgow Cup, beating Celtic 3-2 in a replay. Walker's third cup final goal though was scored in bitterly disappointing circumstances. In October 1953, Thistle and East Fife battled it out at Hampden Park in the League Cup Final. Thistle quickly found themselves trailing 0-2 but a Walker goal two minutes after half-time hauled Thistle right back into the game. When Johnny MacKenzie fired home an equaliser with little more than 15 minutes remaining Thistle looked set to go on and lift the trophy.

Johnny MacKenzie on the right and Jimmy Walker on the left tore East Fife to shreds but Thistle couldn't quite find a winning goal. With seconds remaining hearts were broken when Frank Christie sent one flying into the back of the Thistle net from fully 30 yards out.

Described once as *"the king of the outside left profession"*, Walker, those two unofficial internationals during his Hearts days aside, was denied the opportunity to play international football. He had looked set to be selected to play for Scotland against Ireland in 1949 until attention was drawn to the fact that he had been born in the USA. Cruelly he was also denied the chance to play for the USA in the 1950 World Cup Finals. The USA FA approached their Scottish counterparts asking for approval to play Walker in the World Cup. It seemed though that in playing against Belgium and Switzerland, unofficial as those internationals were, debarred Walker from representing the USA on the world's biggest footballing stage.

After playing just a handful of games in the previous two seasons Walker left Firhill in November 1956 to join Third Lanark.

Appearances 248, goals 121.
Glasgow Cup winner 1950, 1952.
Glasgow Charity Cup winner 1949
Capped for Scotland in Unofficial Internationals v Belgium 1946,
v Switzerland 1946.

Other Honours: With Hearts:
Southern League Cup winner 1945

KENNY WATSON

1980 - 1989

Born 5 January 1956 in Aberdeen.

The 1980s were a largely forgettable period for Partick Thistle. Premier Division status was lost at the end of 1981-82 and by the time the decade ended Thistle had not, nor for some years looked remotely like, regaining their position in Scotland's top division. In what was an otherwise black time for one bright spot was the contribution made by Kenny Watson.

Kenny started his career in the north east of Scotland with Montrose in 1973 and remained at Links Park for two years, signing for Rangers in 1975. Watson spent the best part of five years at Ibrox and although he was by no means a regular in the first team he still came to Firhill with an impressive pedigree. He was capped twice for the Scotland Under 21 side,0 against England and Sweden while at Rangers, and included amongst his 62 first team appearances were a number of European fixtures. Highlights of those were probably starring in a win against PSV Eindhoven and marking Argentinean World Cup winner Mario Kempes in a tie against Valencia.

It was something of a coup therefore when Bertie Auld managed to land the services of Watson in time for the start of the 1980-81 season, Thistle paid a reported fee of £50,000 to bring him across the Clyde to Maryhill. Watson was initially signed as a midfielder although as the years rolled by he tended to occupy a position either at left back or in the centre of the Thistle defence. He made his Thistle debut in a home game with Hearts in August 1980, a game that Thistle won 3-2, and his first goal followed a few weeks later in a League Cup-tie with Queen's Park at Hampden Park.

It took Watson a little time to win the Thistle fans over but once he had done so he became a firm favourite with the fans. In his first season at Firhill he played in all but a handful of fixtures and was part of the side that finished the season by defeating Celtic to lift the Glasgow Cup.

Thistle were by now under the tutelage of Peter Cormack and that Glasgow Cup triumph was supposed to herald a new exciting era for the club. It didn't quite work out that way. In Cormack's first full season as manager at Thistle were relegated. Watson though made as positive contribution as any other player, and again he missed only a few games; his tally of five goals was bettered only by a youthful Maurice Johnston.

There was to be no immediate return to the top flight either. Twice Thistle came close to promotion with Watson scoring twelve goals in 1982-83, the only season when his tally would reach double figures. After missing out on promotion back to the Premier League in two successive seasons, it then became more and more of a struggle with relegation fights rather than promotion battles becoming the norm. That Thistle didn't drop to Scotland's basement League during this era wasn't singlehandedly down to Kenny Watson, but his contribution shouldn't be underestimated. A beautifully placed free kick with time running out at former club Montrose that gave

Thistle a 1-0 win was one such crucial intervention.

As the quality of the players around him began to deteriorate, Thistle started to rely on Watson more and more. Sadly though, his career became increasingly blighted by a series of injuries that denied the team of his services for significant periods. In season 1987-88, his last at Firhill, for example, Kenny played just 18 games. His presence was much missed. Injury finally ended Kenny's Thistle career early on in season 1988-89.

He appeared as a substitute in the opening game against Dunfermline Athletic but that would be the last time that the fans would see Kenny wear the Club's red and yellow kit. With the arrival of John Lambie just round the corner and with him better times, it was cruel in the extreme that Kenny didn't get to play in a better Thistle side than he did for the majority of his time at Firhill. At the age of just 32 there was little doubt that a fit Watson still had a major role to play.

Appearances 315, goals 54.
Glasgow Cup winner 1981

Other Honours: With Rangers:
Capped for Scotland Under 21s v England 1977; v Switzerland 1978.

BRIAN WHITTAKER

1974 - 1975 & 1983 - 1984

Born 23 September 1958 in Glasgow. Died 7 September 1997.

Brian Whittaker arrived from Firhill from Sighthill Amateurs, a rich source of talent for Thistle over the years, at the start of the 1974-75 season. The classy left sided full-back would spend his first season at Firhill in the reserves but did enjoy success at that level. In April 1975 with an otherwise disappointing season drawing to a close, Thistle would fail to secure a place in the first Premier Division.

However the reserve side carried off the Scottish Reserve Cup defeating Dundee 2-1 in the Firhill final. The victorious side included a number of first team stalwarts of seasons to come was as follows: Billy Thomson, Jim Holmes, Brian Whittaker, John Kennedy, Bobby Clark, Ian Gibson, Tommy Rae, Frank Coulston, John Marr, Steve Chalmers and Archie Lochrie. Subs Jim Kelly and Danny McCluskey.

The following season Thistle made light work of winning the first ever First Division title in Scotland's new three division format. At home the team lost just one League game all season. That game, against Airdrieonians on a foggy afternoon in October, just happened to also be Whittaker's first team debut. That was Whittaker's solitary appearance in the League that season - his first team appearances otherwise being a League Cup-tie with Clydebank and to the inaugural and only Spring Cup competition. Whittaker played in seven of Thistle's eight games in that competition and once established in the first team he was rarely out of it. In season 1976-77, Thistle's centenary season and first in the Premier Division, he played in every League game - a feat he would repeat two years later. In 1977-78 and 1979-80 he missed just one League game each season, and the following campaign he missed two. Not until season 1981-82, when Thistle were relegated from the Premier Division was Whittaker missing from the first team for any significant period of time.

Although a near permanent feature in the Thistle squad Brian was anything but a prolific goalscorer, but as a defender that was perhaps no great surprise. On only five occasions did Whittaker find the net for the club, with the pleasant habit of chipping in with the occasional goal against Rangers.

The first of his quintet of goals was the winner in a 2-1 win against Rangers at Firhill in October 1976 and he also scored in a 1-1 draw against the same opponents in April 1981.

The kind of consistency that Whittaker demonstrated naturally brought him to the attention of others. Although called up into the Scotland Under 21 squad he wasn't capped at that level. He did, however, twice line-up for the Scottish League, appearing against the Irish League in 1978 and against the Italian League in 1980. In addition he was included in the Scotland Select team that faced Rangers in John Greig's testimonial match.

Back at Firhill the introduction of the Freedom of Contract severely hampered Thistle's chances of holding on to their top players. In the summer of 1979 they lost Colin McAdam, Jim Melrose and Ian Gibson and for a while it looked as if Whittaker would join them. Whittaker had trial periods in Germany with Hertha Berlin and Borrusia Dortmund and in general made little secret of his desire to play his football at a higher level. As it turned out Whittaker would have to wait a few years before getting his move but in the meantime his reputation with the Thistle supporters had been damaged.

The last of Whittaker's 358 appearances for Thistle came on 9 August 1983 when he played against Celtic in a Glasgow Cup-tie at Firhill.

A few days later he, ironically enough, became a Celtic player with John Buckley coming in the reverse direction as part of the deal.

Whittaker lasted just one season with Celtic making ten first team appearances. He enjoyed altogether more success with his next club, Hearts. He made over 150 appearances in his six years at Tynecastle and was part of the squad that came so close to winning the League and Cup double in season 1986.

His playing career was rounded off with a spell with Falkirk before he returned to Tynecastle to take up a position on the Hearts coaching staff. In September 1997 Brian was tragically killed in a car crash. He was just 40 years of age.

Appearances 358, goals 5
First Division Championship winner 1975-76
Glasgow Cup winner 1981
Capped Scottish League v Irish League 1978; v Italian League 1980.

ANDREW WILSON

1898 - 1905

Born in Strathclyde

Andrew Wilson played his football in an altogether less 'sophisticated' and tactical time than today. A time when the two full-backs in a team were the only defenders, often faced with a rampaging line of five forwards and with little option but to kick the ball as far as they could as there simply wasn't the time to do anything else. On a good day the ball would return to the other end of the field to allow the full-back's team-mates to take their turn to rampage towards the other goal, giving some respite to those defenders, but putting the other full-backs under pressure. Full-backs had to be robust, stubborn and unyielding, and able to take the physical challenge and give it back with interest.

This was the world of football that Andrew Wilson joined when he signed for Sunderland in 1896 from his local junior team in the east end of Glasgow, Strathclyde.

Andrew didn't make the grade at Sunderland but it was a tough level - Sunderland had been English champions a year earlier. Instead he returned to Glasgow, and returned to Strathclyde, where he played for a couple of years until Partick Thistle signed him in the summer of 1898.

Andrew was immediately selected for the Thistle team, partnering Jamie Auchencloss at full-back for much of the season. Alas, it wasn't a successful campaign for Thistle, although relegation wasn't automatic. However, Thistle's name was drawn out of a hat, and Second Division football was the order for the next season.

Towards the end of the previous season Thistle had welcomed back an old favourite, and one that also played at full-back, Robert Campbell, who had returned after a spell with Airdrieonians.

Season 1899-1900 was to be one which saw a much higher standard of football from Thistle, inspired in no small way by the back play of Andrew, particularly evident in the lower league. His kicking had been refined, for no longer was he content to launch the ball as far forward as possible. Now he preferred to try to pick out one of his teammates directly. However, Andrew was noted for his powerful kicks, and many opposition players were taken by surprise at the change in the game's direction from one of Andrew's clearances.

The promotion in 1900 was followed by relegation the following year, and then promotion again in 1902, and Andrew was a constant for most of this period. Alongside Campbell they became known as *"the old reliables"*, and Andrew was often picked out as being the most influential player on the field.

When Campbell retired in 1903, Andrew continued with his forceful and thoughtful defensive play, linking well with namesake Harry Wilson who played just in front of him at left-half. Their lniking gave Thistle another dimension, and Andrew another option to the long clearance upfield.

Andrew lost his place in the team when Thistle signed George Gilchrist from Rangers at the start of the 1904-05 season, and his appearances were few and far between. He signed for Alloa at the end of the season.

Appearances 201, goals 0.
Second Division Championship winner 1899-1900

MATT WILSON

1920 - 1924

Born Glasgow

Matty Wilson was an unexpected Scottish Cup hero for Partick Thistle in 1921. He was signed as cover for the half-back positions from Queen's Park in 1920 and appeared in the last three games of the season, covering while Jamie McMullan and Willie Hamilton rested after a long period. The following season Matt had only played three times by the time Thistle began their Scottish Cup campaign, again as replacement for the injured Hamilton.

Thistle had an eye on the Cup Final, and Matt deputised regularly for the struggling-for-fitness Hamilton at centre-half in League games, stepping out again as Hamilton was selected for the glamorous cup-ties. The young stand-in began to catch the eye for his untiring energy and effort. The plan to rest Hamilton when possible seemed to be working as the veteran pivot inspired Thistle through the cup while Matt's performances kept Thistle in the top five of the league.

Matt's first appearance in the Cup came in the semi final replay against Hearts, this time replacing McMullan at left-half and his hard work gained Thistle a second replay. McMullan returned and Matt again stood down from the excitement of the Cup. Thistle won the replay and qualified for the final of the competition. Matt was no doubt delighted for his team mates.

When Hamilton was injured three days before the Final, manager George Easton appeared unconcerned. Matt would be an ideal substitute for his regular centre-half despite having played fewer than ten games in that position. The manager was happy that his policy of giving the Firhill youngsters experience appeared to have paid off.

Rangers' supporters must have fancied their team's chances – Thistle's half-back line was inexperienced, with Walter Borthwick playing at left-half for only the third time in his career. In the biggest game to then, it took Matt a little time to settle to the occasion, and Rangers might have taken an early lead. However, once Matt settled down he gave Rangers' international inside-left Tommy Cairns no rest, and contributed to the spirited defence that clinched the trophy for Partick.

The untimely death of Willie Hamilton meant that Matt kept his place in the team for the following season, and his combination with Jamie Gibson and Joe Harris lifted Thistle to third in the League at the New Year. Injury ruled him out of the team for some months, and when he returned he discovered that Alex Lambie had replaced him at centre-half. Matt showed his versatility again by filling in across the line. His attempts to hep take Thistle to a second Cup Final failed through a defeat in the semi against Rangers.

While his more famed colleagues Gibson, Lambie and Harris, struggled with consistency throughout the 1922-23 season, Matt was a rock, missing only four games as he covered right and left-half and the centre-half positions. The following season he again was a vital part of the squad, this season covering mainly at left-back while Tom Crichton moved to the right of the defence. Matt was even asked to play at centre-forward once, taking the place of Sandy Hair against Raith Rovers. Matt scored Thistle's only goal but the experiment was not a success - he had been missed from the defence.

For a player who played over a hundred times for the club, Matt had been unable to make any of the positions his own, and he was frustrated for he wanted to play regularly. Manager Easton realised this, and as a symbol of Thistle's respect for Matt's part in the club's success, offered him a free transfer in lieu of a benefit match. Matt accepted gratefully, and a week later accepted terms offered by East Fife.

Matt played for a number of seasons with the Methil club, and latterly with Clyde, before he immigrated to New York. He played for a season in the American Soccer League with the New York Nationals before retiring from football.

Appearances 117, goals 7.
Scottish Cup winner 1921

ALEX WRIGHT

1949 - 1962

Born circa 1930. Died January 12th 2000.

Alex Wright was drawn to the attention of Partick Thistle by his PE teacher at Lambhill Secondary School in Glasgow. Thistle manager David Meiklejohn clearly spotted potential in the young Wright and farmed him out quickly to Ayrshire Junior outfit Dalry Thistle to toughen him up.

In many respects David Meiklejohn was ahead of his time in terms of nurturing young talent. A policy of his was, from time to time, to give young promising players a taste of first team football. It was under those circumstances that Alex and Bobby Gibb made their Thistle debuts on 29 January 1949. This was no gentle baptism into first team football either. The opposition was Rangers and the venue Ibrox. A crowd of 50,000 assembled to watch Thistle record a more than creditable 2-2 draw. And so for Alex, a Thistle career that would span three decades was born. In his 351 appearances he played in a Partick jersey he would fill the roles, with equal distinction, of wing-half, inside-forward or as centre-forward.

Although Wright would maintain a place in the Thistle side for much of the remainder of the 1948-49 season he had to wait several years before he would truly cement a place in the Thistle first team. He played just twice in the first half of the 1949-50 season, scoring the first of his 85 goals for Thistle in a fixture against Dundee, although he would finish the season by playing in each of the last eight matches.

You need really to look to season 1953-54 before you find the name of Alex Wright appearing on the team sheet more often than it didn't. That season he missed just two games and finished the season with 26 goals to his name - a total bettered only by Willie Sharp. Included in that number was a hat-trick, his first as a Thistle player, against non-League Tarff Rovers in the Scottish Cup. Arguably his most important goal was the one that helped Thistle to a 2-0 League Cup semi-final win against Rangers. The final, though, ended in heartbreaking defeat at the hands of East Fife; a club that Wright would later become associated with.

For the remainder of the 1950s Wright's name would become strongly associated with arguably Thistle's best ever team; he was top goalscorer again in seasons 1954-55 and 1955-56.

In the following season Wright was again on target in a League Cup semi-final, this time Thistle defeating Dundee 3-2 in a replayed tie at Ibrox. History would repeat itself again though with Thistle losing, to Celtic this time, in the final.

Thistle and Wright would be back at Hampden for another League Cup Final in 1958 where they chalked up a hat-trick of final defeats when they lost heavily to Hearts. A Glasgow Cup Final victory over Celtic in September 1960 was little consolation to either Thistle or Wright.

Despite being a feature of the Firhill side for 14 years and clocking up over 350 appearances for the club, Alex was sadly largely overlooked when it came to representative honours. Only once was he honoured in such a way when he was picked for a Glasgow Select side to play their Sheffield counterparts. Typically Wright was the man of the match as the Scots ran out 5-1 winners.

Wright played his last match in the Thistle first team in January 1962 in a Scottish Cup-tie at Stirling Albion. After leaving Firhill he had a spell as a player with East Fife for whom he played over 30 times and scored five goals.

A move into coaching was a logical progression for Wright. He coached the reserve teams at East Fife, Clyde and back at Firhill before he was appointed manager of St Mirren in October 1966. He spent just under four years at Love Street and a further two years would follow as manager of Dunfermline Athletic at the start of the 1970s.

After leaving Dunfermline he was assistant to Jackie Stewart at Dumbarton before stepping up to the role of manager upon Stewart's departure during the course of the 1972-73 season. It was while Wright was manager at Boghead that future internationals Murdo MacLeod, Graham Sharp and Ian Wallace were introduced to the Dumbarton first team.

Wright eventually moved upstairs to the boardroom at Dumbarton, taking up the role of full-time executive director, a position he held until 1990. In addition he did, briefly, return to the role of manager when he took up a caretaker role in season 1985-86.

Following his retirement from full time employment he scouted for Bolton Wanderers and Kilmarnock. Alex sadly passed away early in 2000.

Appearances 351, goals 85.
Glasgow Cup winner 1952, 1960.

Yore Publications

(Established 1991 by Dave Twydell)

We specialise in football books (only), normally with an historic theme.

Especially: Comprehensive Football League club histories, over 30 to date (notably: 'Partick Thistle - The Official History' (2002) now out of print), Reading, Bolton Wanderers, Partick Thistle, Rochdale, Hull City, etc.

Other 'Who's Who' books, recent clubs include:
Oldham Athletic, Brentford, Queens Park Rangers, Notts. County etc.

Some titles of a more unusual nature include:
'The Ultimate Directory of English and Scottish Football League Grounds"
(An encyclopaedia detailing every ground on which a League match has been played)
'Through The Turnstiles Again' (A history of football related to attendances)
'Rejected F.C.' (A series of books providing the histories of former Football League clubs

Plus non-League - The 'Gone But Not Forgotten' series
(histories of defunct non-League clubs and former grounds)

Yore Publications, 12 The Furrows, Harefield, Middx. UB9 6AT
~ See our Website: www.yore.demon.co.uk which includes all our current titles ~

Or: Send a s.a.e. for a copy of our latest Newsletter